MR BARRY'S WAR

Caroline Shenton was Director of the Parliamentary Archives at Westminster from 2008 to 2014. Her first book, *The Day Parliament Burned Down*, won the inaugural Political Book of the Year Award in 2013. It was also shortlisted for a number of other prizes, including the Longman-History Today Prize, and was a Book of the Year for the *Daily Telegraph*, *New Statesman*, *Daily Mail*, and *Herald Scotland*. This is its sequel.

Praise for *Mr Barry's War*

'A real jewel, finely wrought and beautiful, just like the Palace of Westminster it describes.'

Lucy Worsley, Books of the Year 2016,
BBC History Magazine

'a great book'

Chris Bryant MP, co-chair of the Joint Committee on the Palace of Westminster, *Hansard*

'If Shenton's first book was like a grotesque Gothic novel, this is an epic, with a hero at its heart.'

William Whyte, *Literary Review*

'not only a fascinating read but a timely one, too'

Tony Rennell, *Daily Mail*

'vividly written . . . an authoritative and lively account of the political and artistic machinations involved in the creation of one of the capital's most familiar landmarks.'

Ian Critchley, *The Sunday Times*

'This beautifully-crafted book walks us through a tumultuous fragment of our history, deftly illuminating every extraordinary step—the rivalries, the soaring ambitions, the barely-hid betrayals, the spectacular personal suffering. As the new Palace of Westminster rose from the ruins of the old, it was at times dwarfed by the personal battles that lay behind its creation. This is politics laid on with a mason's trowel.'

Lord Michael Dobbs, author of *House of Cards*

'This is a wonderful tale, brilliantly told. I shan't ever look at the Houses of Parliament quite the same again and can't wait to visit soon with new knowledge from this exceptional book.'

Mike Paterson, *London Historians*

'Shenton brilliantly outlines how from conception to completion, the design and construction of the new Palace of Westminster were a fearsome battleground . . . [Parliamentary] colleagues who want to consider the current options and challenges should read Caroline Shenton's *Mr Barry's War*.'

Keith Simpson, *Total Politics*

'Shenton seeks [. . .] to correct the historical record and succeeds definitively'

Rosemary Hill, *Times Literary Supplement*

'A very worthwhile addition to the bookshelves of aficionados of Victorian design and architecture.'

Chris Pond, *Context*

Mr Barry's War

Rebuilding the Houses of Parliament
After the Great Fire of 1834

CAROLINE SHENTON

OXFORD
UNIVERSITY PRESS

Great Clarendon Street, Oxford, OX2 6DP,
United Kingdom

Oxford University Press is a department of the University of Oxford.
It furthers the University's objective of excellence in research, scholarship,
and education by publishing worldwide. Oxford is a registered trade mark of
Oxford University Press in the UK and in certain other countries

First published 2016
First published in paperback 2018
Impression: 2

Published in the United States of America by Oxford University Press
198 Madison Avenue, New York, NY 10016, United States of America

British Library Cataloguing in Publication Data
Data available

Library of Congress Cataloging in Publication Data
Data available

ISBN 978-0-19-870719-6 (Hbk.)
ISBN 978-0-19-870720-2 (Pbk.)

Printed and bound by CPI Group (UK) Ltd, Croydon, CR0 4YY

For my husband
Mark Purcell

CONTENTS

Contents

IV EARTH (1852–1860)

ACKNOWLEDGEMENTS

Anyone who attempts to tell the story of the rebuilding of Parliament must recognize that they stand on the shoulders of the giants who have made this and related topics their lifetime's work. I could not possibly have written this book without the scholarship of Margaret Belcher, Rosemary Hill, Michael Port, Phoebe Stanton, and Alexandra Wedgwood having laid the foundations and much of the superstructure, to which I have added a few of my own decorative details. I must also thank a number of people who have helped me in its construction. They are Bill Hamilton, my agent; Matthew Cotton and all the team at OUP; many colleagues across Parliament—in the Parliamentary Archives, the Libraries, the Curator's Office, and the Parliamentary Estates Directorate; Elizabeth Hallam Smith; Kathryn Rix; Simon Wellings; David Adshead; Rebekah Moore; Deborah Dooley and Bob Cooper; and my parents, Peter and Jill Shenton. Mark Collins, Ayla Lepine, Francis O'Gorman, and Mari Takayanagi generously undertook the reading of the draft and made many valuable comments and corrections, but of course any errors remain my own. Last but not least, my gratitude to Mark Purcell to whom this book is dedicated and without whom it would never have been completed.

Note to the reader

Pugin's typically eccentric spelling and capitalization has been reproduced faithfully in this book. As a result, the author particularly wishes to thank her copy-editor and proofreader for their forbearance.

Key to the 1844 Plan of the New Palace of Westminster, Principal Floor

1. Sovereign's Entrance with Victoria Tower above (originally the King's Tower)
2. Queen's Robing Room
3. Royal Gallery (originally the Victoria Gallery)
4. Prince's Chamber
5. House of Lords Chamber, with throne
6. Central Lobby (originally the Octagonal or Central Hall)
7. House of Commons Chamber
8. Clock Tower
9. House of Lords Library rooms (committee rooms above)
10. House of Commons Library rooms (committee rooms above)
11. Speaker's House
12. St Stephen's Hall (site of the former House of Commons), undercroft chapel below
13. St Stephen's Cloister
14. Westminster Hall
15. Lawcourts

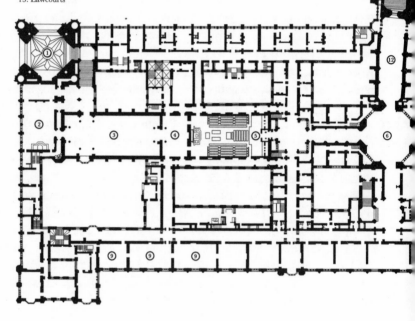

0   200 feet

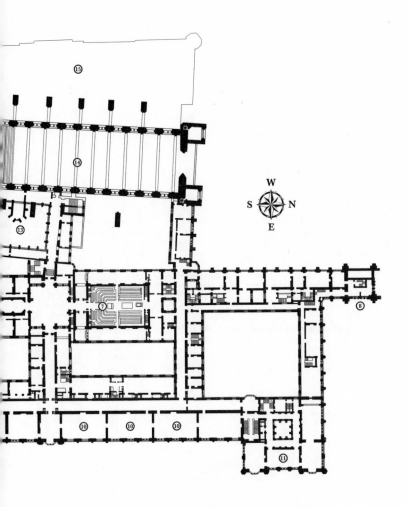

Prologue

T HE NIGHT OF 10 May 1941 was the worst of the Blitz. Almost
one thousand five hundred civilians lost their lives. The British
Museum and Waterloo Station and many other London landmarks
were hit. Westminster Abbey suffered awfully: its central lantern gave
way and crashed to the ground, and the medieval Deanery was destroyed.[1]
At the Houses of Parliament, the scaffolding around its massive keep,
the Victoria Tower, left there from pre-war stonework repairs, caught
fire as the incendiaries dropped. Two policemen keeping watch were
blown out of one of the turrets and killed. A bomb plunged right
through the gilded roof of the House of Lords and buried itself in the
floor, unexploded. The resident Staff Superintendent perished in the
attack. Westminster Hall was saved only at the expense of the House of
Commons chamber, though the glass and stonework of its south window had already been shattered the previous September. Outside in
Old Palace Yard, through the smoke, stood the statue of Richard Coeur
de Lion: still bearing signs of the damage it had incurred when lifted
bodily from its plinth during a previous raid, and now brandishing a
bent but defiant sword towards the skies. An earlier assault had also
smashed to pieces half the medieval cloister of St Stephen's Chapel
deep inside the building. That night another bomb struck the Clock
Tower too, stoving in part of the belfry, and broke the glass on its south
dial, but the Great Bell—Big Ben—and the clock mechanism miraculously

The Palace of Westminster during the Second World War

kept going and the chimes of the most famous timekeeper in the world continued to be broadcast as usual on the BBC Home Service, on the hour, as a symbol of national resistance.[2] Clambering over the fallen stonework and twisted metal the day after this, the worst of the 14 bombings of the Palace of Westminster, Churchill wept in the ruins of the House of Commons.

Two and a half years later MPs discussed the question of rebuilding their home.[3] They were now rehoused in the Lords chamber, while Peers themselves were debating in Church House, adjacent to the Abbey. Introducing the debate, Churchill asked the House to consider whether it should build the chamber up again, and how, and when. 'We shape our buildings and afterwards our buildings shape us', he told the modest number in attendance. He had his own firm views on a replacement at Westminster, which would 'sound odd to foreign ears'. The first was that its shape should be oblong and not semi-circular. 'Here is a very potent factor in our political life.' The Continental hemicycle, he believed, enabled 'every individual or every group to move round the centre, adopting

2

various shades of pink according as the weather changes', but the UK party system, he went on, 'is much favoured by the oblong form of Chamber. It is easy for an individual to move through those insensible gradations from Left to Right but the act of crossing the Floor is one which requires serious consideration.'[4] Churchill remained firmly wedded to the design of the House of Commons, its layout a distant echo of that time long, long, ago when MPs had begun meeting in the royal chapel of the old Palace of Westminster with its two rows of prayer stalls set opposite each other.[5] Secondly, he felt that the Commons chamber should not be big enough to seat all its members at once and there should be no question of every member having a separate seat reserved for him or her.[6] The very survival of parliamentary democracy was at stake in the war, for

> the vitality and authority of the House of Commons and its hold upon an electorate, based upon universal suffrage, depends to no small extent upon its episodes and great moments, even upon its scenes and rows, which, as everyone will agree, are better conducted at close quarters. It is the citadel of British liberty; it is the foundation of our laws; its traditions and its privileges are as lively to-day as when it broke the arbitrary power of the Crown and substituted that Constitutional Monarchy under which we have enjoyed so many blessings.[7]

All of this the building embodied, and

> I am, therefore, proposing in the name of His Majesty's Government that we decide to rebuild the House of Commons on its old foundations, which are intact, and in principle within its old dimensions, and that we utilise so far as possible its shattered walls. That is also the most cheap and expeditious method we could pursue to provide ourselves with a habitation.[8]

The debate which followed was almost unanimous—the motion passed by 127 ayes to 3 noes. Rebuilding and restoring on the same site would improve the inconveniences of the old House with its troublesome ventilation and acoustics, and cramped public and press galleries; it offered the opportunity to provide offices for members, which would be better equipped with modern conveniences such as telephones and typewriters, and places in which to greet constituents. There were only a few dissenting

3

voices. Jimmy Maxton, MP for Glasgow Bridgeton, one of the Commons' most colourful characters (that colour being a very vibrant shade of red), wanted a spanking new building beyond London suburbia, with a railway station, aerodrome, and a 'fine car park' attached to it. His suggestion was drowned out by those scoffing at a 'Potter's Bar Canberra'. Nancy Astor, MP for Plymouth Sutton and the first woman member to take a seat in the Commons, thought it might be better if Ministers and ex-Ministers did not have to face each other on opposing benches, 'almost like dogs on a leash', and debates would become less violent and would therefore appeal more to the general public.

But most did not agree and, above all, what characterized the debate was the strong conviction that the building itself embodied the values of Britain and its political freedoms; that the nineteenth-century Houses of Parliament somehow *was* the ultimate architectural manifestation of representative democracy. 'It is true', said one MP at the time, that the destroyed chamber, 'was only about one hundred years old but it is also true that it came into use shortly after the Reform Act and saw very many changes, and it died in the battle which the democracy which that Reform Act had largely helped to shape is fighting against tyranny'.[9]

Yet this was not the first time a replacement House of Commons had been discussed after a wholesale obliteration. The same issues had been debated following the disastrous and epoch-making fire of October 1834 at the old Houses of Parliament. And similar thoughts had passed through the mind of its architect, Charles Barry, in 1835 when designing a new Palace of Westminster—not just a new Commons as Giles Gilbert Scott did after the Second World War. Today, that new Houses of Parliament is one of the most recognizable buildings in the world, ranked alongside the distinctive silhouettes of the Eiffel Tower, the Taj Mahal, and the Empire State Building, with which it shares all the characteristics of landmark, temple, and skyscraper, and visible (until recently) across large parts of the city. Rising serenely from a site which has been the centre of power and government in England from the earliest times, it is a masterpiece of Victorian architecture and design, a spectacular feat of civil engineering, a building of immense beauty and seemingly invincible confidence, admired even by those who may loathe the politicians within.

Prologue

It would therefore surprise many to discover that from conception to completion, its design and construction were a fearsome battleground. Old-fashioned even before it was completed, today its confident façade seems quintessentially Anglo-Saxon, yet in fact Greek, Roman, Egyptian, Italian, German, and Flemish influences can all be seen in its design. The practical challenges, even by the standards of Victorian invention, were enormous. The new building was required to cover 8 acres of unstable gravel beds. Its river frontage, a quarter of a mile long, had to be constructed in the treacherous currents of the Thames. Its towers were so gigantic they required feats of engineering and building technology never seen before, in order to construct them on a cramped site. And the interior design demanded a revival of ancient styles and craft techniques not used since the Middle Ages, alongside the invention of new ones.

There was a disastrous strike, plans for ventilation which would have blown the Palace sky-high, and the Great Bell cracked not once, but twice. Fighting back the elements and built on quicksand, the architect, Charles Barry, developed the strategy and led the armies that overcame those obstacles. But the political and personal conflicts were just as overwhelming. Battling the interference of 658 MPs, plus Peers, press, and royalty; coaxing and soothing his collaborator, Pugin; fending off the mad schemes of a host of crackpot inventors and assaults from the egos of countless busybodies intent on destroying his reputation; and coming in three times over budget and 16 years behind schedule, its architect eventually won through—after countless setbacks and rows. Constructed during the age of the Chartists, the anti-Corn Law League, the Irish potato famine, the railways, the Great Exhibition, and the Crimean war, Mr Barry masterminded it all—and his war is the tale of the greatest building programme in Britain since the Middle Ages.

I

FIRE

1834–1837

The bellows are burned, the lead is consumed of the fire; the founder melteth in vain: for the wicked are not plucked away.

Jeremiah 6:29

1

A New Tooth

October 1834 to June 1835

O N 16 OCTOBER 1834 the old Palace of Westminster burned down. The story of that terrible fire need not detain us any longer here, for the problem of what to do about the ramshackle, patched-up, and wholly unfit-for-purpose collection of ancient parliamentary buildings on the banks of the Thames was at last resolved. Even before its ruins had cooled, the press was speculating about how the Palace should be replaced.[1] In the words of one magazine:

> The aching tooth that interrupted all enjoyment, is extracted by a sudden wrench, in spite of the fears of him who suffered most from its vested interest in his mouth...And now he must have a new tooth, which shall perform its proper function of mastication, and prepare his food for the process of digestion. Already he begins to rejoice that his boring friend is gone, to trouble him no more; and that its place will be supplied by one which will save him from pain and trouble, and give him health, ease and happiness.[2]

It took five days for the embers to be finally extinguished and, once out, the immediate concern was how to provide temporary accommodation for the sittings of the Commons and Lords and new homes for the officials and servants who had previously lived on site. So it was that, on the same day that the last fire engine left the site, the Office of Woods—the curiously named department in charge of maintaining royal palaces at the time, sometimes known as the Office of Works—received a report from their in-house architect, Sir Robert Smirke. In it he described how he had 'examined the state of the Walls of the House of Lords and Painted Chamber, and I find that when partially repaired, they will be in a condition to receive a Roof and the fittings necessary for their temporary use with perfect safety'. Three days later the Treasury agreed to Smirke's plan and granted £30,000 to build a pop-up Houses of Parliament amid the ruins of the old one, heedless of the offers (including one from the King to take over Buckingham Palace) to move elsewhere.[3] Just over a week after the terrible disaster, which had changed the face of Parliament forever, the decision to stay on site until a permanent solution had been found was made without anyone considering the consequences for the future, thus laying the foundation for years of strife.

The shell of the former House of Lords chamber, where the disastrous blaze had originated, was still standing, and Smirke believed that its medieval walls were sturdy enough to be reroofed to become the temporary House of Commons. It was certainly larger and potentially more comfortable than their previous home. Nearby, the former Painted Chamber, one of the forgotten treasures of the old Palace, was in a similar state, and Smirke recommended that it be transformed into a temporary House of Lords chamber for the duration. All could be completed by February 1835 and, in the meantime, Parliament was prorogued several times.[4] The suggestion that Westminster Hall could be fitted up for the use of both Houses in session found little favour with Smirke, who pointed out that the work of the adjacent Lawcourts (based at Westminster until the 1880s) would have to be stopped and activities moved out, and that it would pose a severe fire risk to a portion of the building—its most magnificent and ancient portion—which had only just been saved from total incineration the week before. He also remarked that his proposal

> would leave the whole area between Westminster Hall and the River, a
> space exceeding four hundred feet in length and more than 250 feet in
> width, clear for the arrangement and erection of any Buildings that may

be required for the permanent reception of the Houses of Parliament or other purposes.[5]

The government took the hint. Smirke wanted the contract for any rebuilding, and the new Prime Minister, Peel, was already inclined to give it to him.[6] This was a mistake. Only nine days after the fire, the *Spectator* had warned, 'The cost is not an object. Money is not to be wasted, but it is not to be spared. There are also evils to be shunned— jobbing, secresy and precipitancy.'[7] Just as the fire had swept away the old Palace, now there was a chance to throw the old way of doing things onto the bonfire as well, including 'jobbery': in other words, the fixing of public commissions for political favourites.

With Smirke's ambition well known and the ugly building schemes of the Office of Woods so spectacularly expensive, Sir Edward Cust took up the cudgels beyond Westminster. Cust was a discontented man. A former Tory MP, he had lost his rotten borough seat of Lostwithiel in Cornwall with its 24 voters due to the Great Reform Act, and had not sat in Parliament since 1833. In an open letter to Peel at the end of January he declared that he hoped the rumour of jobbery was untrue, and doubted that the 'poverty of [Smirke's] taste is counterbalanced even by his other professional accomplishments and by the unimpeachable respectability of his character'.[8] This was just the first of hundreds of letters in which the matter of the rebuilding of the Houses of Parliament was played out in front of a public audience over the next three decades. Cust's own suggestion was for a Royal Commission comprising five gentlemen of an artistic bent which would devise a competition to select an architect from a shortlist of prominent professionals, and direct the design and rebuilding, while the Office of Woods should be in charge of the budget. He, of course, would be more than happy to serve as its Chief Commissioner, (naturally 'without fee or reward') in order, 'to try the experiment of a better method of selection and control over the architect' than had been the case with the Office of Woods' notoriously maladministered works.[9]

Parliament reopened in its makeshift accommodation on 19 February 1835. The King, William IV, lamented, 'the destruction, by accidental fire, of that part of the ancient Palace of Westminster, which has been

Robert Smirke's temporary House of Commons (left) and House of Lords (right)

long appropriated to the use of the two Houses of Parliament' and went on to express his 'wish to adopt such plans for your permanent accommodation as shall be deemed, on your joint consideration, to be the most fitting and convenient'.[10] Peel, stung by Cust's intervention, then proposed a select committee to consider 'the best means of remedying the mischief which had been done'. He had drawn up a list of its members himself for the approval of the House, to make things easier and quicker. Yes, the government had 'called in the advice of a Government architect, that Gentleman had drawn out a plan, which had met with the full approbation of his Majesty's present advisers, and this plan would be submitted to the proposed Committee'. But should the committee dislike it, 'nothing had passed with the architect which rendered it incumbent on the Government to adopt the plan in question'. Peel scored a temporary victory in this early skirmish, for in deciding that Parliament itself should specify the design requirements for the building of the century rather than an independent commission, he made sure that its members did not include the irritating Cust. Joseph Hume MP, the Radical who had pressed so hard for a relocation of the Commons to the West End or Marylebone in the years leading up to the fire, immediately responded to Peel's statement by asking whether the committee would be considering a completely new site.[11] He was not alone. *The Westminster Review* had already expressed surprise that half of the public appeared to think 'that it would be a ravishment of the constitution to put the legislature anywhere but Westminster'.[12] Other papers, of all political persuasions, then piled in to make the point that public competition alone was the only way forward.[13]

This set the pattern for decades of argument over the location of Parliament, arguments which did not cease even as the building rose up around the debaters. The Tories wished it to stay on its ancient site, cheek-by-jowl with Westminster Hall—so redolent of former glories and national pride—thereby imbuing the new Houses with legitimacy and gravitas. The Whigs similarly clung to Westminster, but wanted a modern approach to appointing the architect, through an open competition, rather than the Tories' favoured option of sticking with tried and trusted methods which had served well for years; while the Radicals never ceased to yearn for a new parliamentary building elsewhere, far away from the pestilential quarter around the Abbey: modern, utilitarian, and shed of its associations with the corrupt politics, religion, and class-ridden traditions of the past. Peel knew he was beaten and following this firestorm of press lobbying and political pressure, at the beginning of March he appointed a large select committee of 23 members to decide the matter. Among them were a number who had helped fight the fire, and they now turned their thoughts to what might go in the old Palace's place. They met several times in the first weeks of the month, hearing evidence from clerks, the Commons' Librarian, Mr Vardon, and from Mr Bellamy the caterer (whose entire business had burned down in the fire), as to the space required for various operations beyond the chamber. Members already had decided views.[14]

Almost as soon as the politicians had moved into Smirke's papier maché, deal-boarded, interim chambers early in 1835, they began to complain about them, continuing the squabbles of the pre-fire Parliament. The diarist, Greville, a regular at Holland House, expressed the view that the temporary House of Commons was very spacious and convenient, but that the 'present Lords is a wretched dog-hole'.[15] The Duke of Newcastle felt lost in it: 'it is so small and mean looking [and] So like a private theatre, that one feels the more the degradation of taking our own room for the Commons & giving us a little hole that will not hold more than 250 people'.[16] The new public gallery in the House of Commons, reserved for reporters, caused quite a stir: Greville thought it 'quite inconsistent with their standing orders, and the prohibition which still exists against publishing their debates. It is a sort of public and avowed homage to opinion, and a recognition of the right of the people to know through the medium of the press all that passes within those walls.'[17] Some months later, the Duke of Newcastle was still moaning about the chamber:

> our present room is so degradingly bad that it has called for universal complaint & the result is that this Evening a report was made, that the architect could construct a good and commodious room Equal to the old House of Lords for about £4000 & it was the opinion of the Lords that it was advisable to provide this temporary room for our better accommodation whilst the permanent buildings for the future Houses of Parliament are being builded.[18]

Additions and changes were being suggested to the temporary arrangements throughout the first half of the year, the Lords wanting 'more convenient' spaces and the Commons asking for additions to the library provision and also a second division lobby.[19] Yet when the total outlay on the remedial work was announced, Herbert Curteis, MP for Sussex East, considered £44,000 'for building this and the other miserable House of Parliament most enormous; and he strongly protested against it'. In response he was told that £15,000 of this sum was for furniture, and that 'the very short time allowed for restoring the buildings, unavoidably increased the expense; and, under all the circumstances...the country had no reason to quarrel with the charge'. Curteis huffed that he considered the charge for furniture 'to be most scandalously extravagant. The country was called upon to pay upwards of £10,000 for nothing but a parcel of deal tables and a few rusty old chairs'.[20] It was already proving impossible to find a consensus among politicians on the issue of their accommodation.

Artists were also circling the rotting corpse of the old Palace. In March the Duke of Wellington had to tell Benjamin Haydon—who had watched the fire with glee six months before—that his petition about creating paintings for the new Houses of Parliament would be considered by a Lords committee, but that the scheme for the whole building would need to be under the control of a single painter.[21] Another was George Scharf. He had emigrated to England in 1816 from Bavaria, but never sold a single painting and instead had made his living from producing fashionable engravings and illustrations for scientific books. His lifetime bestseller was an exotic lithograph of the giraffes at London Zoo 'with the Arabs who brought them over to this country' which, when it was published in 1836, sold some five hundred copies in just two weeks. Like dozens of other artists in the days immediately after the fire he had wandered the ruins of the Palace and made drawings on the ground, but then, when the walls began to totter, and the salvage teams had moved in, and it became too dangerous to sketch, he had climbed up a stair and got out onto the roof of Westminster Hall. Taking two large pieces of paper, he began working in oils on a panoramic view across the Palace. To his right was the dismal scene of the Painted Chamber and the ruined House of Lords where the fire had been kindled. To the left from his vantage point, on a level with the chimneys, he could see the cloisters with a fire crew still checking for embers with their fire engine. Behind him were the Lawcourts and the Abbey, while ahead of him was the roofless House of Commons now revealed to be the medieval chapel it originally was. Residents of the Palace peered out of their windows at the destruction, and the debris left behind from the firefighting. Beyond was the river, then the houses of Lambeth and Southwark, and in the far distance, round the bend in the river, he could see Ludgate Hill and St Paul's Cathedral.

Panorama of the ruins of the Old Palace of Westminster by George Scharf, 1834

But George had become so engrossed in painting this scene that when darkness fell and he tried to leave, he found that the door through which he reached his crow's nest had been locked. He was stuck. Stranded. *Völlig festsitzen*, as they said back home. Shouts for help and prolonged banging on doors finally resulted in his rescue over the rooftops, down a ladder, and through the house of the Yeoman Usher of the Exchequer, William Godwin. Mrs Godwin was highly amused with the adventure and told him he was welcome to use their house as a thoroughfare at any time. Accordingly, almost every day for the next three weeks Scharf did just that, and on at least one occasion he took his wife Elizabeth, his two sons, and a party of friends with him to see the view. His seemingly respectable rescuers were the very same William Godwin who had in his younger days been the philosopher-anarchist and husband of Mary Wollstonecraft, and Mrs Godwin was thus the stepmother of Mary Shelley, author of *Frankenstein*. The old firebrand, Godwin, was in fact spending his twilight years mouldering at the heart of the Establishment, and must have viewed the fire with a degree of ambiguity—for it had originated in the worn-out procedures of the corrupt Exchequer of Receipt itself.[22]

On 30 March 1835 Scharf exhibited his completed panorama of the ruins of the Palace of Westminster at the New Water Colour Society's annual exhibition at Exeter Hall in the Strand. His diptych—half of which is now in the Parliamentary Art Collection, the other half lost long ago—was so favourably received that Scharf decided to extend its commercial appeal by seeking subscribers for a giant printed version of the same, at the cost of £2 if hand-coloured. Only one person signed up for his printed version at Exeter Hall, but when Scharf arranged for it to be put on display in a committee room in the House of Lords, it was seen by many more people, including not just politicians but also visitors to the temporary buildings and ruins. Scharf's project never attracted enough interest to go ahead, nor, true to form, did he ever manage to sell his original painting, but he did persuade ten more people to sign up—including the Duke of Wellington, and a 39-year-old architect called Charles Barry.[23]

Mr Barry had been observing developments at Westminster closely since the fire. On the night of the disaster he had been travelling back to the city from business in Brighton. His son Alfred takes up the story:

> A red glare on the London side of the horizon showed that a great fire had begun. Eager questions elicited the news, that the Houses of Parliament had caught fire, and that all attempts to stop the conflagration were unavailing. No sooner had the coach reached the office, than he hurried to the spot, and remained there all night. All London was out, absorbed in the grandeur and terror of the sight.
>
> The destruction was so far complete, that preservation or restoration was out of the question; the erection of a new building was inevitable, on a scale and with an opportunity for the exercise of architectural genius, hitherto unexampled in England. The thought of this great opportunity, and the conception of designs for the future, mingled in Mr Barry's mind, as in the minds of many other spectators, with those more obviously suggested by the spectacle itself.[24]

Charles had more reason than many to wonder about the future of the Palace, for he had grown up in its shadow: he was the ninth of 11 children of Walter Barry, a government Stationery Office supplier who lived at 2 Bridge Street, which ran along the northern side of New Palace Yard. Some 50 years after his birth on 23 May 1795, the Clock Tower of the New Palace of Westminster—its most well-known feature—was constructed opposite his birthplace, which stood there until 1867. He was christened at St Margaret's, Westminster, the parish church of Parliament, just a few steps from home. When Charles was 3, his mother Frances died in childbirth, but she was soon replaced by a devoted and rather extraordinary stepmother, Sarah, who took over care of the whole family when Walter himself died in 1805, as well as her husband's business concerns. The family's modest position meant that Charles emerged from school in 1810 with only 'a superficial knowledge of English, a good proficiency in arithmetic, and a remarkably beautiful handwriting'. He regretted his lack of formal education for the rest of his life, and may have embroidered details of the location of his schooling when he later became a prominent public figure.[25]

The warm-hearted, spirited, and mischievous boy, who drew caricatures of his incompetent drawing master, turned into an amusing, impulsive, and inquisitive 15-year-old articled to Middleton & Bailey, surveyors of Paradise Row, Lambeth. For the next six years they trained and mentored him, giving him the technical education and business skills which he needed to set up in practice on his own.[26] For the first 21 years of his life then, Charles Barry lived and worked in the immediate neighbourhood of the Houses of Parliament, very different to the one which is familiar to us today. The Palace was ever-present. His commute over Westminster Bridge to Lambeth provided fine views of its eastern flank. From the top of the Barry home it would have been possible to see the north door of Westminster Hall, still with the Lawcourts held inside them, as they had been ever since Magna Carta, as well as the roof of St Stephen's chapel and the Georgian 'Gothick' turrets and crenellations added to the buildings by the Surveyor General of the Office of Woods, the architect James Wyatt, the year before Charles became an orphan aged 10. Growing up beyond its walls and then walking to and from work each day would have imprinted on Charles's vivid imagination the muddled shapes and textures of the riverside Palace, which had been home to the House of Lords since the thirteenth century, and to the House of Commons since the Reformation.[27]

At Middleton & Bailey's Charles finally started to obtain the education so long denied him. His employers took a 'strong and affectionate' interest in him and he filled notebook after notebook learning his craft: surveying and architectural geometry, quantity surveying and financial estimates, and a sound technical understanding of building materials, techniques and workmanship. In later life he deplored the increasing separation of architectural design from construction engineering, regarding it as 'a serious evil, both in theory and in practice'. All of this, in addition to the family business run by Sarah Barry, made him in later life an exceptionally gifted manager of both people and his own firm.

One thing he couldn't be taught at Paradise Row though was creativity. This he had innately. From the time he left school he drew and painted in his spare time and constantly decorated and remodelled his attic bedroom. He built grotto-like structures in it and painted murals on its walls to turn it into a 'hermitage' with a rocky interior but 'with openings looking out onto a sunny landscape'. Once it was finished he used it as a painting studio and drew large-scale figures of all kinds on its walls. Sarah, whom he called mother, and his brothers and sisters looked on indulgently and with amusement as his ambitions grew. In 1812, at the age of 17, he successfully entered a drawing for exhibition at the Royal Academy for the first time. Tellingly, its subject was the interior of Westminster Hall. Over the next three years his designs for 'a church', 'a museum and library, with an observatory', and 'a group of buildings for a nobleman's park' all won a place on its walls.[28]

In May 1816 Charles attained his majority and thus a share of his father's inheritance, which had been put in trust for him until he reached 21. It comprised just a few hundred pounds and a freehold property in Northamptonshire. By then Charles had been working as Middleton & Bailey's business manager for a few years but he decided to quit his job and see the world to complete his education as a gentleman would. With funds in his pocketbook and encouraged by his formidable step-mother, at the end of June 1817 he set off to spend 12 months in Europe, with all the advantages of 'a handsome person, great fascination of manner, high spirits and a sanguine temperament'.[29]

Following victory at Waterloo two years before, the Continent had opened up once again to the English. A Grand Tour of this kind was starting to become as *de rigueur* for aspiring architects in this period as a postgraduate training is today. For the self-taught stationer's son it also became the university in which he was exposed to wholly new ideas and influences, made lifelong friends and contacts, and began to polish his London commercial manners so he could move comfortably into wider social circles. He also visited, sketched, and measured many of the architectural masterpieces of Europe and the Ottoman Empire, which were to prove an inspiration to him when designing Britain's most iconic building, nearly 30 years later. Charles first spent three months in Paris, where he considerably improved his basic French through tutoring, and then by lodging with a French family. He spent days in the Louvre studying and drawing old masters, and began to teach himself Italian. He then travelled to the sunny shores of Lake Geneva and through the Simplon Pass, Napoleon's scheme of 1805 connecting Brig in Switzerland to Domodossola in Italy through the Alps. It meant that the mountains and the sublime scenery were navigable by stagecoach for the first time: a wonder. 'It is difficult to say who deserves the greatest admiration', wrote Charles in his travel diary, muffled into his woollen greatcoat:

> the mind that conceived it or the mind that executed it . . . in some places tunnels are cut through the solid rock, with long icicles hanging from the roof. Near the top, the road was covered with 8"–10" of snow, and there were fine romantic views . . . It must be the finest route in Europe and will ever reflect much honour on Buonaparte. Though he has been the author of much evil, he has also done an infinite deal of good.[30]

Forever after, grand civil engineering schemes fired his imagination and he strove to emulate them.

At the time Charles was travelling, Italy was not a nation, but still a collection of many individual kingdoms, dukedoms, city-states, and papal territories, despite Napoleonic reforms. Bribing border officials to ensure swift passage, armed with a couple of pistols in case of roadside brigands, and fighting off regular incursions from carriage fleas and bedbugs, he continued on his way via Milan, Piacenza, Parma, Bologna, Florence, and Siena: a familiar route for backpacking art students today. Everywhere he went he studied paintings and sculpture in galleries and visited cathedrals, palazzi, and classical antiquities. In November he entered Rome, where he had letters of introduction from Benjamin West, the President of the Royal Academy, to give to Canova. On his first full day in the city Barry went to visit the famous neoclassical sculptor and found him in his studio 'engaged upon a fine figure of Venus, intended for the Prince Regent'. He stayed in Rome until the following Easter, sketching buildings everywhere, often visiting the Vatican galleries to draw with the help of Canova's permit, circulating among the *bel mondo* in parks, at churches and the opera, dancing, and perfecting his Italian. The Swiss Guards he thought similar to Beefeaters ('their dress a patchwork of red and yellow, with cocked hats and each carrying an old-fashioned pike').[31] In Rome he fell in with a group of London artists and scholars, including Francis Johnson, an oriental linguist teaching at Haileybury, the East India Company college, and William Kinnard, an architect with a strong interest in ancient Greek buildings. Through them he was introduced to an English artist based in Rome who was to become a lifelong friend and collaborator at the Palace of Westminster, Charles Eastlake (1793–1865). Eastlake's first encounter with Charles was, however, not promising, whom he recorded in his diary as 'an Irishman called Barry, more an amateur than an artist'.[32] Eastlake clearly found Barry's accent difficult to place, and his views on architecture were enthusiastic but untutored and naïve, so it was clear there was a considerable social and intellectual gulf to bridge if he were ever to make a favourable impression on the wealthy upper classes.

The quartet left Rome at the end of March 1818 for Greece, via Pompeii and Naples, crossing from Bari to Corfu in a felucca called *Le Anime di Purgatorio*. The boat lived up to its name and Charles was horribly seasick, but, fortified by Greek sausage, cod roe, white cheese, bread, and oranges once on dry land, they visited Mount Parnassus and Delphi by mule in the scorching sun, explored the bazaars of Corinth, and— braving rumours of a plague outbreak in Athens—finally rowed their way by moonlight to Piraeus and the Parthenon ('the truest model of grandeur, beauty and symmetry', he thought). At the end of June they parted ways with Eastlake, who wanted to stay in Greece to study the antiquities there, but he would come back into Charles's professional life in 1841, alongside much more august company. The others went on to Constantinople via Smyrna, which had their own artistic and architectural wonders to discover.[33]

In Athens they had made the acquaintance of a Mr David Baillie, and now he met up with them again on the crossing to Smyrna, arriving in the city during Ramadan in mid-July. Charles had now been away from home for a year, and his original intention had been to return to Westminster after 12 months, but when moving on to Constantinople with his new friend, Baillie proposed that Charles should continue to travel and study with him, at a salary of £200 a year—all expenses paid—in return for his producing sketches and plans of the buildings and antiquities they visited, with the chance to make his own copies at the same time, so long as they were not published. Charles rightly judged this as too good an opportunity to miss, and so he agreed.[34] It was the making of him. This bold decision would keep him away from London for another two years, but was to provide him with an unrivalled experience of near- and middle-Eastern culture among his contemporaries.

In later life Charles regularly declared the ancient city of Constantinople 'the most glorious view in the world'.[35] The capital of the Byzantine and Ottoman empires, its massive fortress walls and projecting square towers, was an inspiration: one which found its way into the elevations and planning of the Palace of Westminster many years later, as anyone viewing the river front of the Houses of Parliament today may see. Yet while Constantinople had become the must-visit destination for his fellow architects, his next travels to Egypt, Palestine, and Syria were virtually unheard of as a professional excursion: 'Egypt is a country which so far as I know, has never yet been explored by an English architect', he said.[36] It also gives an early sense of the combination of boldness, imagination, and opportunism which later characterized his work on the new Palace of Westminster. He and Baillie sailed on to Cairo with some new companions: Thomas Wyse (who also came back into Charles's life in 1841 as a member of the Fine Arts Commission) and a Mr Godfrey.

Through November and December they travelled up the Nile and here Charles discovered a string of astonishing sites: the temple at Dendera, which he measured and sketched ('no object I have ever seen made such a forcible impression on me'), Luxor, Karnak ('stupendous'),

Philae, Abu Simbel, and the Great Pyramid and Sphinx at Giza.[37] Charles now chose to dress in an Arab costume of 'loose trousers tied round the waist and a long gown of coarse linen, and a silk handkerchief on the head'. Travelling by camel across land, camping in tents in the desert, and suffering from food poisoning and the heat, Charles and his companions continued their travels to Gaza and Jaffa in the middle of March 1819, and reached Jerusalem shortly before Easter, where they stayed in the Latin Quarter. He washed in the River Jordan and floated in the Dead Sea. He met the Pasha of Damascus and went to Bethlehem. Days were spent surveying and sketching the Church of the Holy Sepulchre, until finally they were ready to move off once again at the end of April. Things were getting wilder for the travellers. The food was more erratic in both quality and quantity. Their Christian guide was incompetent and came to blows with their Muslim hosts. Their servants amused themselves by firing guns as entertainment. At Jerash, 'much annoyed by mosquitoes', Baillie and Barry travelled on, touring Nazareth, Beirut, and Baalbek where they stopped three days to study, and finally arrived in Damascus where, with their beards and tanned faces, 'we were universally taken for Turks': unrecognizable to polite London society.

On the way to Homs they were mistaken for a party of Bedouin raiders and shot at, and worse was to come when, on the road to Palmyra, they were kidnapped by Bedouins who hoped to ransom them and were forced to ride their camels at a gallop across the desert. Shots were fired and some of the party were wounded in the fight to get free. This was too much for Mr Baillie, who, once the group had recovered and made their way to Tripoli in Lebanon under the protection of the local governor, decided to end his employment of Barry and scurry back to the safety of Naples. Charles had made 500 sketches for Baillie over the previous ten months and had copied most of them for his own reference too.[38] It was now the end of June and he, Godfrey, and Wyse left Palestine for Cyprus, Rhodes, and finally reached Smyrna again, 'with heartfelt satisfaction. Our mameluke costume caused some curiosity.' There they shaved off their beards and changed back into clean European clothes, and were recognizable once more as the young men who had left the same city on their adventures a year previously. After recuperating for a while, they cast off again across the Mediterranean,

Charles Barry's sketch of the ruins of Jerash, 1819

this time in the direction of Malta—a British possession—where they were quarantined, and then they spent two weeks exploring the island. In the autumn and winter of 1819 the adventurous trio discovered Sicily, but Charles's precious portfolio of sketch copies from his travel, so carefully kept through all his journey was stolen. He was devastated. Once back in Naples the group was reunited with Baillie, and they explored the sights nearby together including the Palace at Caserta and Mount Vesuvius, climbing up to the active craters, getting stifled by the gases, and watching closely as the lava flowed past them at the rate of a foot a minute, and whose luminous streams at night were 'very grand'.[39]

By February 1820 Charles was back in Rome, but had met up with the man who was to become another lifelong friend, John Lewis Wolfe. He had studied under Joseph Gwilt in London, but was much more an academic than practical architect. He quickly became his new friend's informal tutor and mentor. Although three years his junior, he now put Charles through a short but tremendously intensive period of critical architectural analysis, as they travelled through Florence, Pisa, Bologna, Venice, and the Palladian villas of the Veneto. They parted company in July at Verona, but the two men stayed in touch, and forever after Charles would discuss all his designs with Wolfe.[40] Finally, Charles returned home by way of the glories of Turin, Nîmes, Avignon, Lyon, Autun, and Paris. He arrived back in England on 1 September 1820 ready to take on the world.

From modest beginnings, Charles attempted to launch his professional practice. He rented a small house in a Georgian Terrace at Ely Place, Holborn, as his home and office, directly opposite one of the finest surviving medieval churches in London—St Etheldreda's, a Gothic masterpiece. However, without rich patrons or the backing of a wealthy family, his first year working was difficult, and his early income came from modest alterations to urban churches. However, by 1822 two new Commissioners' churches at Prestwich and Campfield, Manchester, were being built to his designs, creating new places of worship in industrial areas where the population now outstripped the availability of spiritual nourishment. A growing string of church and hospital commissions in wealthy Manchester and fashionable Brighton followed, aided by recommendations from John Soane (who at that time was redeveloping parts of the chaotic Palace of Westminster, including knocking down the old House of Lords building which Guy Fawkes had tried to blow up in 1605). A widening circle of satisfied clients brought Charles to the attention of the Duke and Duchess of Sutherland who commissioned him to work on Trentham House in Staffordshire. He was then awarded first prize in the competition to build the Manchester Institution in 1825—now Manchester Art Gallery—in a neo-Grecian style. This was followed by his breakthrough London win in 1829 with the Traveller's Club in Pall Mall. It won wide critical acclaim not just for its daring introduction of the Florentine Renaissance palazzo style to London—that he had so admired with Wolfe on their final months of travel in Italy—but also for its elegant adeptness in planning and interior circulation, one of the later hallmarks of Charles's genius.[41]

Then in 1833, when he entered a design for the new Birmingham Grammar School competition, he took the decision to employ a Perpendicular Gothic style, as he had done in a number of previous church commissions, starting with his much-admired church of St Peter on the Steine in Brighton (1824), which launched his career when still under 30.

St Peter's Church, Brighton

Architectural historians generally now agree that in the grammar school, with its long street façade, which required repeated verticals to break it up, its brilliant management of the interplay between corridors and staircases to aid the movement of hundreds of boys around the building, and 'the stone panelling, the rich roof with bosses, the lighting from windows which open onto an interior court' were a testing ground for Westminster and would have been thoroughly familiar to anyone who wanders the corridors of power there daily.[42] The grammar school building is long since demolished, but Barry's central corridor with his fan vaulting still survives today as the chapel of the relocated school, now King Edward's, Edgbaston.

Charles wasn't just turning into an architect of some fame. The early death of his parents; his youthful capacity for hard work; his society experiences in Europe; his hair-raising adventures in the Levant; and a string of competition disappointments, as well as successes, had begun to form in him quite some resilience to adversity. Dealing with aristo-cratic patrons, competition judges, and rich industrialists in the 1820s had made him more practised at handling the tricky and demanding. From 1833 he was starting to move in the highest Whig circles, dining a few times a year with the Holland House set (including the Prime Minister, Melbourne) at their fashionable town house political and literary salon in Kensington.[43] This was exposing him to the ways of politicians and that in turn increased his ability to suppress his naturally outgoing, curious, and sociable personality into a smoother, more flattering one in order to achieve his artistic and professional ends. He was to need every ounce of those attributes in the decades that followed—when creating the new Houses of Parliament became both the greatest architectural achievement of Victorian Britain and, simultaneously, the biggest professional headache imaginable.

2

A Clump of Thistles

June 1835 to January 1836

W HEN BARRY HAD arrived back in England on 1 September 1820, the greatest royal scandal of the age was engulfing the country and, in particular, Westminster. The coronation of the new King, originally scheduled for August, had been postponed.[1] Parliament had instead been the scene of the trial of Queen Caroline, which continued into the autumn. Caroline of Brunswick had married George, Prince of Wales, in 1795. The groom collapsed drunk in the fireplace on their wedding night at the thought of bedding his bumptious and grubby bride and claimed only to have slept with her three times, twice on the wedding night and once the night after. Exactly nine months later she had given birth to their only child, Charlotte Augusta. Very shortly afterwards the Prince and Princess of Wales separated. She had gone to live in Blackheath with her own household. He had returned to a life of excess: drinking, gambling, and circulating between his mistresses and the woman he had married illegally in 1785, Mrs Fitzherbert.[2]

By 1820 both husband and wife were in a sorry state. George was by now grossly obese and a laudanum addict, both of which accounted for his orange skin by the time of his death, which he failed to conceal with heavy layers of makeup. And for some years Caroline had been travelling around the Mediterranean with a small retinue and her luxuriantly mustachioed Italian manservant, Bartolomeo Pergami. Scandalous stories of their antics on the Continent regularly made their way back to England. The heiress presumptive, Princess Charlotte, had died in childbirth in 1817, leaving behind her devastated widower, Prince Leopold of Saxe-Coburg-Saalfeld. The young couple's full-term son was still-born after a protracted labour. The physician and *accoucheur* (male mid-wife) responsible later committed suicide.[3]

So when the old King George III died in January 1820, and Caroline announced her intention to return home, there was no way that the new George IV, now aged 57 and Regent since 1810 on account of his father's madness, was going to allow his detested wife near a crown. A method had to be found to de-queen her, but the options open to the King were limited. As Caroline's alleged adultery had been committed abroad she could not be charged with treason. And since his own sexual past was also extremely colourful he could not seek an ecclesiastical divorce. Instead, the King presented two sealed 'green bags' of evidence of her misconduct to both Houses of Parliament and expected them to act on it. Both Houses voted, after consideration in secret committees, to con-duct an investigation by means of a 'Bill of Pains and Penalties', a pro-cess used only once in the previous 200 years. In short, Caroline's fitness to be Queen was to be tried by act of Parliament.[4]

The House of Lords chamber was the trial venue. In the space of just two weeks, the architect Sir John Soane designed and installed two elegant temporary galleries and ventilation improvements costing over £1,500.[5] The trial opened on 17 August and barriers were erected in Old Palace Yard to keep back the crowds who were firmly and noisily on the Queen's side when she rode to the House each day in her carriage. Over the next 11 weeks the Lords heard all the servants' gossip about boatdeck frolics, naked bathtime romps, and soiled bedlinen. In this, Caroline was supported and defended by the ambitious Whig lawyer and MP for the rotten borough of Winchelsea, Henry Brougham, inside Parliament; and by William Cobbett, the radical journalist, outside it. Although finally the evidence showed that Caroline undoubtedly had been having an affair with Pergami, the unrest outside Parliament and the unpopularity of the King was such that, on 7 November, Brougham brought the Queen the news that following a very close vote in the Lords she was 'Regina still, in spite of them!'[6]

As George's rescheduled coronation approached on 19 July 1821, preparations were underway to fit out the buildings to a suitable level of splendour as befitted the King's extravagant taste. Inside Westminster Hall, the Lawcourts were removed, two tiers of galleries supported on iron pillars were erected along either side, and a Gothick ogee archway was built at the north end. A covered walkway wound its way 1,500 feet from the Abbey to Westminster Hall for spectators; while 23 temporary kitchens were set up in Cotton Garden on the river side of the Palace to feed the coronation banquet guests. The King's Champion entered the Hall on his charger, riding in splendour up to the royal daïs clad in cloth of gold. The heat from the chandeliers and the wax dripping onto the spectators in the galleries was mightily inconvenient for guests, but they were compensated for their six-hour wait by the chance to eat up all the leftover food, falling on it with some alacrity once the King had departed. The total cost of all the decorations, feasting, and clothing (including George's 27-foot crimson velvet train peppered with gold stars) amounted to £243,000.[7]

Caroline made one last attempt to assert her role as Queen on coronation day. Despite having been advised by the Prime Minister that it was the King's 'Royal Pleasure that the Queen shall not attend' (George having refused to read or write any letter to her for 20 years), Caroline arrived in a yellow carriage in a violent silver and purple outfit. But George was damned if he would see her crowned. Having been blocked from entering the Abbey at three separate entrances, she then marched over to Westminster Hall, banged on the door, and demanded admittance. The sentries crossed their bayonets as the pages opened it, blocking her way. There was a short scene—'let me pass, I am your Queen, I am Queen of Britain!'—and the Deputy Lord High Chamberlain ordered the great north door slammed in her face. The crowd's attitude was very different to what it had been the year before. Shortly after her trial, Caroline had accepted a payoff of £50,000 from the King and in doing so had relinquished her position as the darling of the people. She had sold out. Now the crowds booed and whistled and hissed: 'Go away! Go back to Pergami!' Maybe Barry was in the crowd himself, watching the spectacle unfold outside the buildings he knew so well. Returning to the Abbey she tried to get in once again, then gave up, and

The Coronation banquet of George IV in Westminster Hall

tramped across Bridge Street to pick up her carriage and return home humiliated.[8] Three weeks later, unexpectedly and abruptly, the Queen died of stomach cancer.

And so ended one of the most unfortunate royal marriages of all time. All was not lost, however, for Prince Leopold, George IV's son-in-law, and his dynastic ambitions. In the scramble to father a legitimate heir following Princess Charlotte's death (for which Parliament offered a financial incentive) Leopold's attractive sister managed to snare George's 51-year-old brother, the Duke of Kent. A year later, in 1819, she gave birth to a daughter. And the wife of Leopold's elder brother Duke Ernst gave birth to a second son a few months after that using the services of the same midwife as the Kents. The first cousins married in 1841 and are better known to history as Victoria and Albert. Both were to play a significant role in the development of their new Palace at Westminster, a royal building which the monarch had for centuries graciously allowed the Houses of Parliament to occupy.

On 3 June 1835 the Commons select committee produced the long-awaited report on its future home. It wanted a debating chamber nearly as wide as it was long (unlike the temporary one they were in), with accommodation for up to four-fifths of MPs. The debating chamber had to be connected to voting lobbies, and there should be a room for meeting 'strangers' (that is, non-MPs) nearby. Thirty committee rooms were required—small, medium, and large—and a library comprising three rooms with accommodation for the librarian and shelving space in other areas for when the book collection expanded. The Speaker was to have his own official residence within the Palace. The Commons administrators, known as clerks, were allocated office space, but the most senior of them—the Clerk of the House—did not get an official residence within the Palace as he had in previous times. Also on the list were two prison-rooms, a kitchen, wine cellars, a Members' dining room, and a strangers' dining room where MPs could entertain visitors.[9]

The House of Lords, a completely separate entity, but sharing the same charred and blackened site, followed with its own similar report, including in its specification a robing room for the King; six committee rooms and four waiting rooms for witnesses; a coffee room and dining suite; an official residence for Black Rod, the monarch's representative in the House of Lords; a dressing room for its doorkeepers; a five-room apartment for their librarian; two huge fireproof repositories for paper and documents, measuring not less than 8,000 square feet; and enough private rooms to house its own clerks, the Lord Chancellor, three archbishops (Canterbury, York, and Dublin), 24 bishops, and many others besides. Having now had several months of occupation in the heavily repaired Painted Chamber, their Lordships were very insistent on the measurements of any new debating chamber. It would have to hold 300 peers, have plenty of space between and behind the benches and around the royal throne, and a large lobby where members of the Commons 'and other persons waiting to be called in' could stand.[10]

But there was a shock in store for both Peel and Sir Edward Cust. Neither got his way on how a suitable design would be chosen. Instead of a shortlist of architects being approached to offer up plans, 'it is expedient', declared the Commons committee, 'that the designs for the rebuilding of the Houses of Parliament be left open to general competition', and, 'that the style of the buildings be either Gothic or Elizabethan'. The shell of St Stephen's Chapel, the erstwhile House of Commons, its ruined walls now revealed in all their beauty, had astonished more than antiquarians in the months after the fire. The politicians had, outside their very doors in the Palace, a reminder of the ancient glories of medieval architecture, and this—along with the intense debates in the press about what constituted an appropriate national style—played a part in their most famous competition rule. The Lords concurred. Five hundred pounds was to be given to the best submissions, with the outright winner promised an additional £1,000 as a consolation prize if for some reason the work did not go ahead. Anyone could enter and receive the entry pack on payment of £1 to the Office of Woods in Whitehall Place: drawings to be submitted at a scale of 20 feet to 1 inch, uncoloured, on or before 1 November 1835.[11] Robert Smirke was paid £300 for his time; an attempt to soothe the sting that, as he put it, 'in consequence of a subsequent resolution of the Committee of the House of Commons to procure designs by general Competition and for buildings of a much more extensive and costly nature, my drawings have been useless'.[12]

As soon as he read the competition rules in the select committee report, Barry sought to get ahead of his competitors. He set out across the Channel with his best friend Wolfe, the architectural critic. While the groundplans were still awaited from which he could begin to make detailed drawings, in seeking to comply with the known stipulation for 'Gothic or Elizabethan' there was no reason why he could not start to gain inspiration from original buildings.[13] A Gothic palace was needed, and the nearest thing Barry could think of were the town halls of late medieval Flanders, in northern Belgium.[14] At the time, Belgium was a brand new country; an independent nation only since the revolution of 1830, and its first King had been invited in by its new government in 1831. The man they had chosen as their head of state was none other than George IV's luckless son-in-law and uncle of Queen Victoria, who thus became King Leopold I of the Belgians. The civic buildings of Brussels and Leuven particularly struck Barry, with their high hipped roofs, precipitous clock towers, and repeating decorative facades, and following intense discussions with Wolfe, he sketched out his first ground-plan on the back of a letter during a visit to his old friend, Godfrey.[15]

Back in Britain the country was abuzz with this novel open competition and the newspapers were busy dissecting its rules. The acrimonious debate about modern architecture sparked by the fire continued to inflame the public. 'In as much as Grecian is repudiated, we are glad,' said *The Spectator*, 'for the style is not adapted to an irregular and complicated mass of building: nor is it suited to our cloudy climate, where porticoes and colonnades are not wanted to screen us from the sun.'

The Gothic style, it thought, 'will perhaps more generally please', as 'being in accordance with the Hall and Abbey'. But it declared that the aristocratic mansions at Hatfield and Wollaton containing 'such monstrous incongruities and puerile extravagancies as constitute the style called Elizabethan, are utterly unfit for the national edifice'.[16]

Meanwhile, some in the Commons wanted women to be able to watch their debates, officially, for the first time (in the old Commons they had illicitly viewed them through a ventilation shaft in the attic of St Stephen's). Somewhat unexpectedly, Grantley Berkeley (MP for West Gloucestershire, son of an earl and a butcher's daughter, dandy, sportsman, and inclined to beat up those who wrote poor reviews of his books), put down a motion in early August 1835 for ladies to be allocated places in the Stranger's Gallery. Yes, said 83 MPs; No, said 86.[17] In the other House Henry Brougham (ennobled since the trial of Queen Caroline and now Lord Chancellor) declared 'that the Ladies would be infinitely better employed in almost any other way than in attending the Debates of that House...he wished also always to see them in their proper places'.[18] Brougham had also expressed concern about the potential expense as soon as the competition was launched. For himself, he 'would rather have a plain building, but substantial and good, than one that would look fine and cost but little'. To execute public works on this latter plan 'was the greatest blunder that could be committed; and he hoped that the system of competition which was to be adopted on the present occasion would not lead to such a result'. He saw, according to the specification,

> that there would be in and about the House between 100 and 120 rooms, besides two or three residences; and the other House of Parliament, he supposed, would be furnished in the same proportion. If this were so, it would be most expensive, and would besides take a very long time before the buildings could be completed.[19]

He was prescient about how long it was going to take to build, but not about the rooms. The final Palace had over a thousand.

The entry pack for the competition was supposed to include a lithographic plan of the site. Along with this, competitors would receive a specification indicating the size of the principal offices and apartments to be included, the number of members and officials to be accommodated, and so on. The instructions were formally advertised on 21 July in the *London Gazette* and the site plans for competitors to use were expected on 27 July. But when released they were incomplete, there were delays reissuing them, and it was only a month later, on 25 August 1835, that the final coloured site plans were at last released by the Office of Woods, some three months after the competition was first announced in Parliament. These showed the layout of the long thin wedge of land by the Thames which the new Palace would need to occupy, and the vantage points from which prospective architects were expected to supply elevations of the exteriors. Colour washes indicated which buildings of the old Palace complex were to be demolished (such as the Painted Chamber), which were definitely to remain (such as Westminster Hall), and which the competitors could keep or destroy at their discretion (such as St Stephen's Chapel). There were also details of land occupied by residential buildings to the south of the ruins and nearby temporary ones which could be acquired if necessary for development.

Because of the delays, the 1 November deadline was now horribly short. All over the country and beyond, architects were frantically devising their schemes. The stress killed at least one competitor. Francis Goodwin's doctor told his inquest that the 51-year-old architect had suffered a stroke on 30 August, 'so intense had been his studies...that...he was unable to obtain any rest at nights—so completely engrossed were his thoughts upon the plans he was engaged in drawing out'.[20] Barry simply could not complete alone all the work required in the ten weeks available. He had known failure as well as success in his career so far, and was still smarting from the Birmingham Town Hall disappointment when he won the Birmingham Grammar School competition in 1833.

From that early sketch on the back of a letter, Barry swiftly worked out the overall plan in his mind and transferred it to paper quite rapidly in pencil. He then moved on to producing a larger and more detailed set but time was beginning to press.[21] While unequalled in his planning capability, and able to turn his hand to most styles, he now desperately needed help with the decorative detailing of the elevations which would convince the amateur judges; and which he had decided would match the east end of Westminster Abbey and the surviving cloisters of the old Palace. And so he turned to a then-unknown 22-year-old who was already working for him on the furnishings for the grammar school. His name was Augustus Welby Northmore Pugin. From this point onwards the two men's fates become inextricably linked. Starting to emerge as a brilliant designer and medieval fanatic, just as importantly, Pugin was also an incredibly speedy draughtsman in ink, as required by the government competition. Barry's forte was pencil. It is not certain how they originally met. It might have been through an introduction by Cust, with whom Pugin dined at the end of March 1835, or it could have been through the furniture dealer Edward Hull.[22] At any rate the two men first dined together on 18 April,[23] a momentous occasion both for their lifetime partnership and for their reputations: not that they realized it at the time.

Pugin was the only child of a French émigré. Auguste Charles Pugin settled in London in 1792 where he entered the Royal Academy Schools and subsequently became a draughtsman for John Nash, favourite architect of the future George IV. Romantic stories of the reasons for Auguste's departure from Paris swirled about him for the rest of his life—involving tales of derring-do during the French Revolution and drawing on a lineage which could allegedly be traced back to medieval Switzerland. Auguste was responsible, with the publisher Rudolph Ackermann and figure-painter Thomas Rowlandson, for one of the early nineteenth century's most *de luxe* publications, *The Microcosm of London*, which appeared in parts between 1808 and 1810, and contained 104 hand-coloured plates showing entertaining scenes from late Georgian city life, including some interiors of the old Palace. In 1802 he married Catherine Welby, clever daughter of an Islington banker, and their only child was born ten years later.[24] From the start their son was indulged and doted on, the apple of his mature parents' eye, and surrounded by Auguste's numerous drawing pupils in their house in Bloomsbury— quite a contrast to the more business-like upbringing which the orphaned Barry had experienced in a home full of brothers and sisters. Enormously precocious, at 15 Pugin designed a set of rosewood and gilt furniture for George IV at Windsor Castle as part of a commission which had been passed on to him by his father. Though the great sideboard was destroyed in the devastating Windsor fire of 1992, the rest of the set survives, including two smaller sideboards, the dining table, and chairs (not very practical, as it takes two footmen to move each one).[25] He also designed the so-called Coronation Cup for George IV, a silver-gilt goblet set with diamonds and precious stones and manufactured by Rundell, Bridge & Rundell, the Royal Goldsmiths, who specialized in plate heavily influenced by the tales of Walter Scott, the King's favourite author.[26]

After this initial burst of adolescent spark around 1827, Pugin spent the next few years in a more rackety existence, as a set designer and stagehand for William Grieve at Covent Garden, undertaking freelance carving and designing joinery, punctuated with regular trips to France with his parents. Barry had converted his attic into an Italian *grotto*: Pugin turned his into a model theatre. In May 1831 he bought a small boat and learned to sail by undertaking a five-day trip from Westminster Bridge, travelling up and down the Thames and Medway, making landfall only once. Boats became a lifelong passion.[27] From this point Pugin rushed at life and life rushed at Pugin. In January 1832 he married. Already pregnant with his first child, Anne died four months later giving birth to a healthy girl. Within a year both his parents were also dead, and he married again in June 1833. He moved to Ramsgate with his small family to be near the sea, but was often away touring English cathedral towns and travelling on the Continent, in France, Germany, and the Netherlands, forming his own architectural and religious imagination. 'I have seen the house of albert Durer, I have sketched his tomb. I have ascended the spires of Strasbourg chartres Antwerp & the Great tower of Malines. I have got precise information on many points which the cursed reformation has precluded the possibility of discovery in England', he wrote in his characteristically awful handwriting with its eccentric orthography, a lifelong testament to his random education.[28]

In October 1834 he was in London, dealing with the administration of his aunt's estate, so on the night of the fire at Parliament, he was there in the crowd almost from its outbreak, and watched the House of Commons go up like a Roman Candle.[29] Elsewhere in the same monstrous crowd was Barry but, even before the two men met six months later, Pugin had decided views on the rebuilding of the Palace. Only a few weeks after the fire he had dashed off a typically impetuous letter to a friend setting out his worries about how a replacement would be handled:

> I am afraid the rebuilding will be made a compleat job—as the execrable designer smirke has already been *giving* his opinions which May be reasonably supposed to be a prelude to his *Selling* his diabolical plans & detestable details. if so I can contain myself no Longer but boldly to the attack ill write a few remarks on his past works—& if he do not writhe under the Lash his feelings must be hard than his cement as if I spare him I hope I may sink myself. his career has gone on too Long & this will be a capital opportunity to shew up some of his infamous performances.[30]

To another friend he complained in December 1834 that Smirke 'seems to attend burnt buildings Like a fireman—and has not yet been killed by any of the falling ruins at St Stephen's'.[31] Pugin despised the Gothick fantasies of James Wyatt at Fonthill and Ashridge, preferring to study real-life medieval examples to develop his own ideas. He was *Ivanhoe* to Wyatt's *Mysteries of Udolpho*. It was Pugin who designed many of the brilliant decorative details to the new Palace: the carved woodwork, the coloured tiles and vibrant carpets, the stained glass, the extraordinary wallpaper, the leather chairs with their Portcullis symbol, the beyond-vulgar explosion of gold and scarlet which is the interior of the House of Lords, the icon that is the Clock Tower, and the gilded vanes on the finials of the exterior which glitter against the London skyline whatever the weather. Pugin gave birth to Victorian Gothic as we know it today. Passionate, impulsive, and always falling in and out of love, he eventually married three times and had a number of agonizing *affaires*. A largely self-taught workaholic, he was full of artistic temperament, crippled by mystery illnesses, and often driven to distraction by business difficulties, finding it hard to manage his business relationships and his accounts.

By April 1835 Pugin had a number of other jobs on the go as well as working for Barry on designs for the grammar school, and this continued through to the end of August.[32] At the same time he was providing drawings for the Edinburgh architect, Gillespie Graham, for Heriot's School, and this income provided him with the wherewithal to carry on with the project occupying most of his time: the decoration of his new home in Salisbury, St Marie's Grange, on which he had spent much of his inheritance. The medieval-style, three-storey, red-brick house with turrets and chapel, designed by himself, was both scandalizing and amusing his neighbours: a little piece of Picturesque on the main road to Southampton.[33] In June that year—three days after the competition was announced in the Commons—he was received into the Catholic church: equally startling to the neighbourhood.

Thus when Arthur Hakewill, an architectural theorist, issued a pamphlet during the heated summer debates about a new Westminster decrying the Abbey and Hall as 'a clump of thistles', Pugin felt compelled to reply.[34] In his very first published work, a short pamphlet of 20 August 1835, he defended not only Gothic against Hakewill's classical longings but, especially, that vast and magnificent structure, the Regal Hall of Westminster, the sumptuous shrine and chapel of Henry VII., and the towering and venerable pile of the Abbey Church, which have ever been regarded as chef-d'oeuvres of the styles in which they were erected, and looked upon by those who have souls to feel their extraordinary beauties, as an inexhaustible source of study and improvement—these buildings you term weeds, impeding the planting of the Greek Flower, which you wish to establish. Yes, Sir, they do impede it, for while such wondrous proof of the consummate skill of the builders of the ages (termed by you barbarous) remain, you will have some difficulty in persuading the country that their vicinity should be disgraced by another of those half-English, half-Pagan erections which have so wofully [*sic*] disfigured the architecture of the last century.[35]

From all of this public controversy Barry stood apart. He was certainly disinterested, and perhaps even uninterested. Despite the new Palace of Westminster making the most decisive intervention into the argument for Gothic revivalism during the entire nineteenth century, his aim was always to work to the brief he had been given by his client, regardless of his own artistic preferences. For him, unlike for Pugin, architecture was never a religion or a moral statement but always a profession—and one at which he intended to excel.

At some point in September 1835 Pugin began work on the elevation details for Barry. It is hard to establish exactly when his work on the grammar school ended and Westminster began, but by 24 September things were sufficiently advanced that Barry travelled to Salisbury to see Pugin in his new house (he had only moved in ten days before) to discuss the drawings he required. Pugin continued on them in the first part of October and then travelled to London where he 'drew at Mr. B' for eight or nine days from the eleventh.[36] Fortunately, the competition deadline was extended to December—the first of many slippages in the timetable which beset the creation of the Palace. Unknown to Barry, at the same time Pugin was also providing Westminster designs for Gillespie Graham which he had begun in August. But Pugin was also in for a surprise. Barry had equally strong views about what he wanted. He took each of Pugin's worked-up sketches, considered them, and treated them as an architectural model, testing what worked and rejecting what didn't within his overall scheme as his own ideas developed. It was during this week of work that Pugin realized that Barry was not swallowing his ideas wholesale, as Gillespie Graham did, but analysing and transforming them to refine his own vision of the Palace. This Pugin had not expected. He had not previously encountered a man with a genius different but equal to his own. Around this time, Pugin told his friend Talbot Bury, who was helping Pugin to juggle his work for two masters, that Mr Barry's was 'a very remarkable design, the plan being most ingenious and comprehensive, and the elevations treated in a very original and effective manner'. He saw that the older man had sought to give an Italian outline to Gothic details, and, though *he* should not have treated the composition in that manner, the general effect would make a noble work and he—somewhat wistfully, recognizing Barry had improved his ideas—anticipated a decision in Mr Barry's favour.[37]

Returning again to Salisbury Pugin spent several days on Graham's elevations and then, on 2 November, Barry came down to St Marie's Grange once again and stayed for nearly a week. During this time Pugin suffered a day-long inflammation of his eyes, disastrous for a fine draughtsman. This must have worried Barry considerably given the closing date was less than a month away, and his own enormous challenge working on other aspects of the submission. The day Barry left, Pugin made a temperish comment in his diary: 'The present condition of architecture is deplorable. Truth reduced to the position of an interesting but rare and curious relic.' Whether this arose from a reflection on his influence with the more experienced and determined Barry is unknown; it might equally well apply to his opinion of his neighbours or comments on the labourers still working on St Marie's Grange (the following day he notes 'Men left').[38] Barry continued to work in London on the overall plan, forging a mature design. During those three months Barry survived on just four or five hours' sleep a night.[39] In a final desperate push, Pugin joined Barry again in London on 20 November, both working intensely together for another nine days, leaving just 24 hours to get the drawings mounted ready for submission.[40] Pugin was still revising the Graham entry at the picture-framers on the evening of 1 December, and Barry submitted his with only a few minutes to go before the deadline.[41]

Pugin was paid 300 guineas by Graham for his assistance. Barry paid him 400 guineas. Pugin confided his amusement about this lucrative situation to his Covent Garden friend Grieve: 'Is this not a regular joke? Here are these two rivals competing for one prize and I am making the designs for both!'[42] Although subsequently hotly contested, Barry's overall grip of the plan was to ensure that (in the words of his son Alfred) his 'principles of symmetry, regularity, and unity, so dear to his artistic taste' drove the design.[43] Pugin's contribution was to help Barry visualize the decorative scheme, provide the fabulous ornamental detail and execute drawings which would delight the judges. This was syncretism made manifest on the banks of the Thames—that is, the collision of the taste of one man with the belief system of another to form a startling but harmonious third way. Barry's classicism, and his delight in the monumentalism of the ruins such as those he had seen at Palmyra and on the Nile, merged with Pugin's Christian principles and instinct for theatrical design. Their respective roles seem to be borne out by Pugin's famous comment that the Palace was 'all Grecian, sir; Tudor details on a classic body'.[44] As Rosemary Hill, Pugin's biographer, points out: 'while Barry might not have won the competition without Pugin, Pugin could certainly not have won on his own'.[45] More than that, as would become clear, Pugin lacked the mental and physical robustness to cope with the arduous political, technical, and financial battles in the years to come. Even so, Barry himself collapsed with exhaustion and stress shortly after the entry went in and was confined to bed for days.[46]

Ninety-seven entries to design a new Houses of Parliament were received by the Office of Woods on 1 December 1835. The rules ensured that submissions were anonymized. Each architect had been asked to mark his drawings not with their name, but with a *rebus*—a small symbol in the upper right-hand corner. Each entry was accompanied by a sealed envelope containing the competitor's *rebus*, and their name and address, which would only be opened once the winner had been chosen.[47] The sixty-fourth entry to be numbered by the Office of Woods used as its *rebus* a portcullis. This was Barry's. The little heraldic iron gate was carved all over the Henry VII chapel at the east end of Westminster Abbey, so close to his boyhood home. It had long been a subtle part of the visual appeal of Westminster, and was the badge of one of the most brilliant women of the fifteenth century, Lady Margaret Beaufort (1443–1509). She was the mother of Henry VII, whom she conceived aged 13, and gave birth to him three months after his father—a half-brother of the unstable Henry VI—had died of plague. She had no more children, but the political protection of two further husbands enabled her to survive the War of the Roses to become a consummate politician and powerbroker. She lived not only to see her son but also her grandson, Henry VIII, ascend the throne as the first Tudor monarchs. From her ancestors, the illegitimate line of nobles descended from John of Gaunt (1340–99), Duke of Lancaster, she inherited the sign of the Beauforts, a heavy iron grating at the entrance to a castle gateway: a portcullis. When she endowed Christ's College Cambridge in 1505, three crowned portcullises were incorporated into the design over the great gate on St Andrew's Street. Her son's endowment at King's College chapel followed suit the next year, as did St John's College by her posthumous endowment in 1511. So when Henry VII planned a new Lady chapel at the east end of Westminster Abbey to be a mausoleum to his family, the exterior decoration naturally included the badge of his mother's power. It was an inspired choice in 1835 by Barry, the Westminster boy born and bred, and when Pugin integrated it so cleverly into the decoration of the new Palace of Westminster it subsequently became the universal badge for Parliament.

The judges, or Competition Commissioners as they were properly known, comprised four men of taste and experience. Charles Hanbury Tracy MP was their chairman. He had designed his own house at Toddington in Gloucestershire with only a draughtsman to assist. Cust was another: he had finally got his wish to shape the future of the new Houses of Parliament. The other two judges were the Hon. Thomas

One of Thomas Hopper's designs for the new Palace

Liddell and George Vivian of Bath. All of them were enthusiasts for Gothic, but of a rather conservative kind, and with no professional expertise other than taste and opinion. Meeting in the undamaged portions of the charred Speaker's House in the Palace they sat through December and January and had to ask for an extension of time to examine the 1,400 drawings which had flooded in.[48] Entrants had responded to the demanding brief in a range of ways, some more successful than others. The open competition had attracted not only fine designs from well-known architects, but also a number of pedestrian, rule-breaking, and idiotic ones.

In his gigantic scheme, Thomas Hopper, a favourite architect of George IV, had decided to restore St Stephen's Chapel for the Commons and then duplicate it for the House of Lords as well. He also incorporated a second Westminster Hall into New Palace Yard, and added two Fonthill-style towers for good measure.[49] John Tertius Fairbank proposed a great circular corridor 800 feet long to provide the requisite access to offices, based around 'a colossal circular tower...a vast and ornamental object'. Some competitors had embanked the eastern side of the Palace by the river and ran a road along it to provide access to the building. Other designs were too monotonous, proposing a single block; or conversely, too disjointed, with individual buildings making up a varied complex; or simply too ecclesiastical.[50] Some competitors had ignored the rules altogether. C. R. Cockerell, architect of the Ashmolean Museum in Oxford, defiantly entered a neoclassical design based on Greenwich including two large domes, loftily claiming, 'Elizabethan cannot be defined, the Examples all differing.'[51] Some architects of the Grecian persuasion did not even attempt to enter, including J. M. Gandy, an assistant of John Soane, famed for his working-up of plans into full scale architectural fantasies. A painting now at the Royal Institute of British Architects, co-founded by Charles Barry, shows his favoured solution for Parliament: a new 'Senate House' for the Lords in St James's Park comprising a giant classical rotunda with huge marble portico, citizens lining the approaches all in white, while floating in the blue sky above is a misty rendition of Westminster Hall and St Stephen's ablaze in the corner. The judging dragged on.

After his nervous collapse Barry soon recovered his energy and 'his mind most characteristically threw off its anxiety until rumours began to ooze out' that number 64 was the favourite to win. Excitement and anticipation in the Barry household grew.[52] The result was published on 29 February 1836. In coming to their decision, the judges had confined themselves to consideration of the 'beauty and grandeur of the general design; to its practicability; to the skill shown in the various arrangements of the building, and the accommodation afforded; to the attention paid to the Instructions delivered, as well as to the equal distribution of light and air through every part of the Structure'. They had not considered any aspects of acoustics or ventilation—or the cost. 'We are all unanimous', they told the King,

> that the one delivered to us, marked 64, with the emblem of a Portcullis, bears throughout such evident marks of genius and superiority of talent, as fully to entitle it to the preference we have given it in our classification; and we have no hesitation in giving it as our opinion, that the Elevations are of an order so superior, and display so much taste and knowledge of Gothic Architecture, as to leave no doubt whatever in our minds of the Author's ability to carry into effect Your Majesty's Commands, should you be pleased to honour him with your confidence.[53]

It was a sensational, life-changing win. His reaction is not recorded. But on that clear October night in 1834 when all London was out watching Parliament burn down, Barry had exclaimed even then: 'What a chance for an architect!'[54]

3

A Beautiful and Appropriate Design

February 1836 to July 1837

AN IMMEDIATE AND furious row broke out among both politicians and the disappointed competitors. It was a dangerous moment. Barry might have won the competition prize, but the rules had stated that the government was not obliged to carry the winning design into execution. What was more, a number of disgruntled MPs were now trying to alter the location of the rebuilding altogether. Joseph Hume decided to reprise his favourite theme. When the judges were finalizing their report, he had stood up in the Commons to complain about continuing to use the ancient site at Westminster, whose 'situation was low, and was attended with many inconveniences', and loomed over by the towers of the Abbey where the sun disappeared early and they lost 'an hour or an hour and a half of daylight'. Move the Lawcourts to Lincoln's Inn Fields and the Commons to St James's Palace, where it would be quieter, lighter, and airier, he suggested. Even the site of the barracks at the back of the half-built National Gallery would be better than their current situation. Once again, he lost the vote, but not before he had exasperated Peel (his long-term opponent on the subject) and had been accused—in a most unparliamentary fashion—of 'humbug'.[1]

Joseph Hume

There never having been a public competition before on such a scale with such a prize at stake, the disgruntled losers did not know how to behave graciously in the face of defeat. Lacking a common agreement of what professional behaviour should be expected of architects in such a situation, an all-out slanging match now took place in private and burst out in the press. Barry was accused of improperly influencing the judges and of having cheated by including ornamental details, against the rules. The judges were accused of corruption and having been in favour of Barry from the start, some already said to be well acquainted with him. For the next few months controversy raged between battalions of losing architects, opinionated politicians, and the embattled government.

Barry's design drew on everything that had impressed and astonished him architecturally up to that point, and by doing so he created something wholly new, still within the competition rules, but daring and innovative. The massing of the building he had taken from the antiquities of Egypt and Syria. The impression of impregnable walls and turrets came from

Jerusalem and Constantinople. For its outline and the classical planning of its interlocking courtyards he had drawn on the great buildings of ancient Greece and Rome. From Renaissance villas he had taken the ranks of endless repeating bays and from the Georgian Picturesque, two asymmetrical towers, to the south-west and north-east of the building: one with a spire, the other with a vaulted ceremonial entrance at its base and an archive repository above. The roofs and surface decoration (what he called a 'diapering of the whole') came from Flanders, Westminster Abbey, and Pugin's archaeological approach to Gothic detail inspired by cathedrals across England. Inside, the four-storey building was equally as stunning. Above the ground floor was a principal floor, where the main elements of the Palace were situated in an elongated cross—the Lords and Commons chambers and lobbies would face each other down a lengthy north–south axis, and intersected at a central hall by another main axis which stretched east towards the river and west towards the Abbey. Westminster Hall, St Stephen's, and the cloisters were brilliantly preserved within the overall groundplan, which was shaped like a wedge, to fit onto the limited site available. On the land side, the floors of the Palace were mainly offices, while along the riverside stretched ranks of committee rooms, the libraries and the dining rooms, and luxurious residences for the Speaker and others.

On 10 March a select committee hearing by the Commons opened in one of the temporary committee rooms to ponder the outcome. First, the four judges were themselves judged on how they had come to their decisions. Did they know that number 64 was Barry's entry all along? Cust defended himself by saying that, as the only one of the selection panel who knew the winner beforehand, he had

> signified to Mr Barry my desire that we might have no communication with each other pending the inquiry, and that whenever we might meet, the subject of the plans of the Houses of Parliament should never be brought into conversation between us, which he so strictly fulfilled, that until I saw his plan in the due course of examination, I never had the slightest glimpse of a sketch, nor the slightest hint of any kind from him or from any common friend, which could lead me to infer that No. 64 was the design of Mr Barry.[2]

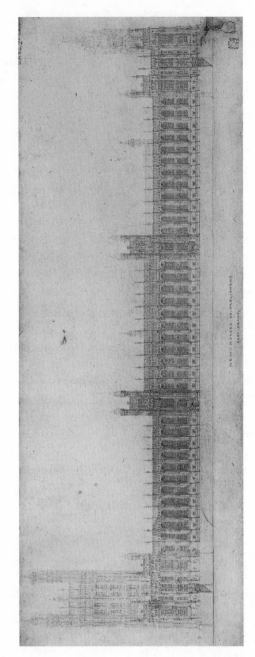

Barry's east front design

And Hanbury-Tracy protested,

> I never had the pleasure of seeing but one design of Mr Barry's in my life; I knew nothing of his style, and was not even personally acquainted with him; but I had heard so much of the merits of his plan, when No. 64 passed in review, which was not till I had seen the greater number of those which were submitted to us, I certainly had a strong suspicion from the beauty of it that it could be no other than Mr Barry's; but I had nothing in the world to lead me to this belief excepting the superiority of the design.[3]

Accordingly, five days later the Chancellor of the Exchequer assured the House that none of the Commissioners had known number 64's identity until the seals had been broken on the envelopes. Yet the Commissioners seemed curiously unable to articulate just why Barry's design had been chosen over all the others. They had considered around 1,400 individual plans, but their decision rested on gut instinct or, as Hanbury-Tracy put it: 'it is a point of feeling and taste'.[4] As was recognized much later by architectural historians, the gentlemen judges were more influenced by Pugin's gorgeous elevations and less by Barry's masterly planning. But had the competition been judged by professionals, Barry's ground plan would most likely still have beaten all the other entrants. Either way, number 64 would have won. This did little to quash the rumblings from the losers that Barry had won by underhand, though mysterious, means.

Peel reminded MPs that the Commons, 'naturally distrusting its own judgment on a matter of this kind', had told the government to select the Commissioners in the first place when he had been Prime Minister. Then, the select committee which reviewed the results felt it could not recommend Barry's scheme be taken forward 'without first taking some steps to ascertain the expense'; and this was a job which should fall to the Office of Woods. If it should appear, Peel added, that Mr Barry's plan, 'beautiful in its exterior, and convenient in its arrangement as it was—could only be carried into effect under an enormous and unjustifiable outlay, which would require too great a sacrifice of economy', there was no obligation on the House to proceed with it.[5] Nevertheless, in early March the Duke of Newcastle 'saw the new plan for the Houses of Parliament, designed by Barry, which certainly is a beautiful & appropriate design & he himself told me it would not cost above half a million'.[6] Yet wild rumours were already circulating about the likely cost. The competition had specifically excluded the need for architects to produce any estimates for the construction. Now reports were spreading abroad that Barry's plan might cost between one and a half, or even two, million pounds. Hanbury-Tracy, as chair of the judges, thought it would not be more than half a million and,

> considering the magnitude of the building, it is impossible to conceive a design equally magnificent, and at the same time less expensive than that proposed by Mr Barry. The part which will be the most expensive is the great [Victoria] tower...But it is an extremely beautiful feature of the composition, and I should regret that its effect should be injured by any mistaken notion of economy.[7]

Benjamin Hall MP thought that all the plans should be publicly exhibited before a final decision was formed, but that Mr Barry's plan would not be practicable on account of the expense. Little did he know that he would become closely involved in its construction later in life, and that he would in due course be immortalized in the nickname of the Great Bell of the new Palace. Sir John Hobhouse soothed the MPs by reminding them, 'the Report pledged the House to nothing, and merely declared that the recommendation of the Royal Commissioners had been adopted by the Committee'.[8]

Meanwhile, despite all the misgivings of Parliament, the Office of Woods was quietly starting to work out how the design would be put into effect. In the final week of March Barry informed them that he wanted to alter the line of the river embankment on the eastern façade of the new Palace. Instead of having a corner cut off beside the bridge, he now wanted it to run straight up to it to provide more space for the gigantic building he envisaged. The Office of Woods accordingly wrote to the Navigation Committee of the City of London to tell them of the proposed deviation from the line originally agreed upon.[9] A public exhibition of the competition designs had also now opened at the new National Gallery, though the first, second, third, and fourth prize winners' drawings were held back by the Office of Woods for government use. On the exhibition's opening, with the also-ran designs arranged by architect on the walls of five of the new rooms on the upper storey of the Gallery, a letter to *The Times* from 'An Observer' declared them, 'Like to Jeremiah's figs/The good are very good, the bad not fit to give the pigs.'[10]

Two smarting competitors then made their grievances very public. In the first week of April Lewis Cottingham and Thomas Hopper were turned away from the Office of Woods when they arrived on the doorstep demanding to see the four 'premiated' sets of competition drawings. The next day this caused 'An Architect' to complain to *The Morning Post*: 'What has the profession done to deserve such treatment? Or have the *amateur* commissioners done anything which might suggest the prudence of depriving the public of the opinion of profession?'[11] This incident then found its way to the Commons. Peel, Hume, and others asked the government why architects had been turned away from the Office of Woods when they wanted to see the unsuccessful designs, and why were the four prizewinning designs not going to be included in the public display at the new National Gallery.[12]

In his very first appearance before a joint parliamentary committee, on 22 April, Barry was assailed with questions, a number of them decidedly sceptical. If he was congratulated on his win and praised for his design, then no record of it survives in the proceedings. He had his supporters on committee—Peel, Hobhouse, and Hanbury-Tracy—but Joseph Hume was also there. Barry was questioned about the alterations he had made to the plan since it was submitted, and why the stone he proposed was the most expensive available. The quantity surveyors—Thomas Chawner from the Office of Woods and the leading independent quantity surveyor whom Barry used, Henry Hunt—were pressed hard on how they had come to their calculations. Chawner had estimated the cost of the building at £724,984 based on a figure of 9½d. per cubic foot, excluding the foundations, but with a contingency of 2d. per cubic foot. Hunt, who had been involved in the estimates for the Carlton, and Oxford and Cambridge Clubs, the Westminster Hospital, and Westminster Prison, based his calculations on Barry's costs for the Birmingham Grammar School and concluded that it was impossible to provide an accurate figure which would satisfy the committee 'without a detailed specification and working drawings, which would occupy twelve months in preparing, and it would then require me to devote four months to the estimate'.[13]

The design continued to change. Hanbury-Tracy considered, 'there is no such thing as perfection in architecture; Mr Barry may go on improving this plan, and I do trust that if it is adopted it be will be improved from time to time ... until the building is completed' (words he conveniently forgot he had uttered when he disagreed with the architect some eight years later).[14] Barry had indeed already altered it to address some of the complaints which Hume had put to the competition judges at the earlier hearing. The groundplan was now virtually rectangular rather than wedge-shaped, the internal courtyards squarer, and the overall length increased by extending it south towards Millbank and also by building closer to Westminster Bridge. The King's Tower at the southern end, which had been so admired, was now taller, and the slimmer tower proposed at the northern end by the bridge Barry had now decided should have a clock.

When Barry's designs, and those of the other winners, finally did go on display at the National Gallery on 28 April, Hopper and Cottingham were furious. Their complaints found expression in a letter to *The Times* penned by someone called 'Anti-Selim'.[15] It is hard not to imagine that these bitter accusations came from this pair themselves, who roped in another loser, William Wilkins (1778–1839), the architect of the almost-completed National Gallery itself. Wilkins already had form in complaining in acrimonious pamphlets when he lost competitions, as the Senate of Cambridge University had discovered when it failed to award him a series of commissions in the 1820s. Now Hopper claimed that Barry had plagiarized Cottingham's plans in his redesign which, 'although pronounced surpassingly beautiful and greatly superior to all the rest was discovered upon examination to be merely a drawing for the sake of effect'.[16] When Pugin, author of those controversial details, went to London to look at the exhibition himself, he (and all other visitors) was accosted at the door of the Gallery and given Wilkins's pamphlet, *An Apology for the Designs of the Houses of Parliament Marked Phil-Archiamedes*. Gallingly for Wilkins, the building in which his latest defeat was being displayed was one which itself had been roundly criticized. The novelist

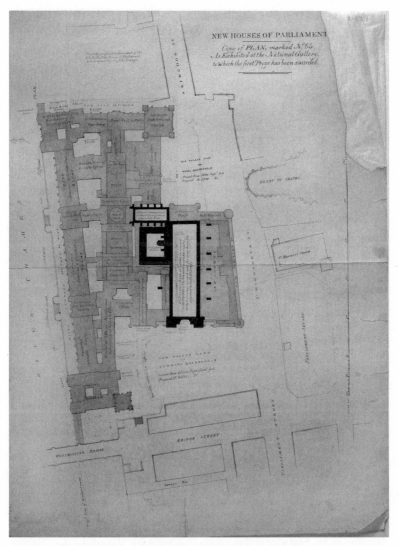

Rough copy of Barry's original 1835 groundplan

William Thackeray had even gone so far as to describe his Grecian Pinacoteca as 'a little gin shop'.[17]

Yet the press was of a very different view in relation to Barry's design. 'The majority are captivated with his beautiful drawings', wrote *The Times*:

> With great appearance of simplicity and beauty, they combine the most graceful elegance of decoration: all seems perfect harmony, although glittering like a glass chandelier. There is a chastity and purity that delights and fascinates, so well has Mr Barry understood pictorial effect...the ornament, which in Mr G. Graham's drawing being used in a truly Tudor design, looks rich and overcharged, when applied to Mr Barry's Grecian form, appears to be simple.[18]

Unwittingly perhaps, this perceptive reporter exactly described what made Barry and Pugin's artistic collaboration so outstandingly successful.

At the beginning of May the select committee declared itself 'not satisfied' with the proposed budget forecasts and, before any money could be granted towards the monster building project, 'the most minute and accurate Estimate that can be formed' was needed. Barry was entrusted with drawing this up, and his calculations would be checked by the Office of Woods, 'on the understanding that the Committee do not thereby commit the Public in the slightest degree to the ultimate adoption of the Plan'. All this was reasonable and prudent. However, the committee then continued, provided the original budget 'be not exceeded in any material degree', it saw 'every probability that that Plan will be adopted'. If Barry wanted the work then the Commons was indirectly saying he would have to dissemble about the extent and scale of the building he wanted to achieve. It was virtually encouraging Barry to fudge the design in order to keep the contract. When asked about what sum he thought appropriate for producing the working drawings, specification, and estimate, Barry went along with this for the time being: 'On the subject of remuneration...I am willing to place myself in the hands of the Government.'[19]

By now, 34 of the most disappointed competitors had ganged together to form their own militia and presented a petition to the Commons, via Hume, demanding a commission of inquiry into how the competition had been run, attacking the judges, the lack of professional input, and the alleged inferiority of Barry's plan (including a minute lithograph of where he had supposedly gone wrong). Leading the charge was the magisterial figure of C. R. Cockerell (he of the Ashmolean Museum in Oxford and later a good friend of Barry) who declared himself weary of the 'barbaric carvings and disgusting monstrosities of Gothic architecture'.[20]

As a result, on 21 July a lengthy debate took place in the Commons. Joseph Hume said he

> felt bound to stand up and arraign the conduct of that Committee, which had most negligently, and for want of due consideration, led the House and the Government into a very disagreeable predicament, there being no hope whatever, that the projected new buildings would be ready for two or three years to come, unless some different arrangement were immediately adopted...He thought it quite possible that an architect might draw a very pretty picture to gratify the eyes, without attending to the more essential particulars of good accommodation and convenience in the interior arrangements...No doubt Mr. Barry's plan was a fine picture, well calculated to deceive one young and inexperienced in architecture, but it ought not to have imposed upon such old, tried, and practised artists as the Commissioners.[21]

Would the country believe, he went on,

> that, by this plan of Mr. Barry's, three arches of the bridge, all but twelve feet, would be blocked up, and that in fact the building was to rise out of the water like the buildings of Amsterdam, and that those who were obliged to pay for its erection would have the satisfaction of being enabled to see it only from the opposite side of the water?[22]

After some minutes of further invective against Barry and his design, Sir John Hobhouse for the government got to his feet to protest

> that if Mr. Barry should succeed...in securing the admiration of his country and of future ages—if he should succeed in producing the most magnificent building of modern times—he would have paid a penalty, and the Commissioners would have paid a penalty, too great to be counterbalanced by the personal gratification; for never since the principle

of competition was first established had such unfair, such unjust, such violent, such incessant attacks been made as had been made by the unsuccessful competitors in the present case against Mr. Barry, and against the Commission.[23]

Peel for the opposition, and Barry's continued champion, also rose to defend the judges. There was one point on which he had firmly made up his mind, namely,

> never again to act as a Commissioner upon any subject of this kind, where a preference was to be given to the skill of one man as compared with that of others who had entered into competition upon the same work. Because, if Gentlemen who acted as Commissioners gratuitously, and at the expense of a great deal of personal convenience, were afterwards to be assailed in a manner that the Commissioners in this instance had been, and, moreover, were to see the whole of their labours quashed in a way so unceremonious as that proposed by the hon. Member for Middlesex, he knew not where for the future any gentleman would be found hardy enough to undertake the office.

But, he continued, he would rather be a commissioner than a successful competitor, 'to be hunted and pursued with every species of invective in the way that Mr. Barry had been. If the consequence of successful competition were to be exposed to such a series of attacks as those which had been directed against that gentleman, he would infinitely rather remain in privacy and oblivion.' Peel's original view had been that an open competition was not desirable and now 'the circumstances which had since transpired had not much tended to induce him to alter it'. But if the House agreed to Hume's motion and the competition was annulled,

> they would strike a fatal blow at the principle of competition. They would postpone the execution of a great national work for an indefinite period, and they would teach the most eminent of living architects to rue the day when in compliance with their invitation, they sent in plans which had the misfortune to be entitled to the preference.[24]

By the end of this fractious debate, Hume once again found the opinion of the House against him and huffily withdrew his motion. Subsequently, the bruised competitors attempted a petition to Parliament, but were fatally split between themselves—some simply objecting to the process of the competition in general, others making it personal against Barry—and thus they failed to make any headway.[25] So Peel and Hobhouse had seen off the critics and Barry was now free to draw up and refine the plans on which the financial estimates would be based. But these early skirmishes indicated the shape of battles to come.

What Barry privately thought of the criticism following the competition is unknown, though it is not hard to guess. Not much of his correspondence survives to tell us any of his thoughts about the Palace, and virtually nothing of a personal nature. Impressions of him come mainly through the eyes of others and, as the new Palace grew, from the evidence he gave to select committees (never a very accurate representation of anyone's real personality), and the letters he had published in the papers at times of crisis in the construction. Barry was a man who wasted few words in public; he was a practical man, not a talker. He has to be judged by his actions, but without understanding his own particular point of view, that can be misleading. The architect as celebrity or hero was alien to the Georgians and early Victorians, and Barry maintained a taciturn professionalism in most of his doings. As a result we know far more about Pugin and his feelings, for he was as voluble and tactless in public as Barry was reserved and politic.

In August 1836 the two men met in London in order that Barry could commission Pugin to work up the interior sketches which would form the basis for the estimates. To each other, they seem to have been charming and friendly at this stage; the only other man each one knew whose talent they respected and appreciated. They settled into a happy routine whereby Barry would send his traced plans to Pugin in Ramsgate for further work on the fine detail—firstly the two chambers, the Royal Gallery and staircase, the Robing Room and the other most important rooms on the Principal Floor—the *piano nobile* of the Palace. In no time at all, Pugin had produced a first set of drawings for Barry to use. Designs for model fireplaces, archways, doors, and wall framings poured out of him and Barry was both astonished and delighted: they 'will answer the purpose exceedingly well', he wrote to his friend and collaborator, 'many of them are excellent'. Barry considered each one from Pugin, altered it, and advised on further modifications to fit with the whole scheme he wanted. 'Perhaps it would be as well to do one or two more *rather* richer for the Speaker's House, but remember the motto "simplex etc".' On sending through the plans by post for St Stephen's Porch and Hall, the Central Hall, committee rooms, and the staircase to the Upper Waiting Hall, Barry realized that, 'I think you now have enough to do for some little time to come, notwithstanding your *50 horsepower of creation.* Let me hear from you on receipt of the parcel, and believe me ever, Yours very faithfully etc Charles Barry.' In October Barry once again wrote to Pugin after a second group of drawings arrived from him: 'Being from home yesterday I could not acknowledge, by return of post, the receipt for the drawing of the House of Lords, King's Stairs etc., which came safely to hand last night, and afforded me a rich treat. They will in all respects answer the purpose most admirably.'[26]

Pugin's second wife, Louisa, had just given birth to his daughter, Agnes, and he was also reeling from the negative reaction in some quarters to *Contrasts*, his revolutionary manifesto for a return to Gothic architecture; long planned, but which was published just as the parliamentary rows of the summer came to an end. Barry was aware of this and wrote kindly of the returned designs:

> I can easily imagine the great labour they must have cost you, and, knowing all the difficulties, I cannot but wonder that you have been able to accomplish so much in the time. I am not much surprised to hear your health suffers from excess of application. Do not, however, I beseech you, carry too great a press of sail, but take in a reef or two if you find it necessary in *due time.* I send by this morning's mail a packet containing tracings of the grand public entrance and approach to the Houses and Committee rooms. They are most wretchedly dull and destitute of feeling as the board on which he draws. They will, nevertheless, I have no doubt, afford you all the data you require. I am much flattered by your hearty commendation of the plan, and shall know where to look for a champion if I should hereafter require one. Truly it has cost me many an anxious thought and an extraordinary degree of perseverance. With

many thanks for your glorious efforts in this cause, believe me my dear Sir Yours most truly etc.[27]

And when another parcel of designs reached Barry in November 1836, as soon as he received them, he let Pugin know his views in almost brotherly terms:

> I am sorry you have had to endure a moment's suspense concerning the safe arrival of the box containing the last set of exquisite details, which on my arrival from the country where I have been for the last three days, I have just received. I can only say. "Go as you have begun and prosper," for nothing can be more satisfactory than the result of your labours hitherto. Ever yours, most truly, etc.[28]

These amiable exchanges give a clue to how these two very different self-made geniuses managed to get on with one another so successfully for so long. The reality is that the relationship between the two men was a true partnership, so much so that in many parts of the building it is now impossible to tell who designed what. The answer is both, together. Each respected the other's ability, and their initial collaboration was harmonious and good-humoured, affectionate even, until the cracks caused by the intolerable pressures of the building programme as it wore on began to show. Barry had the vision, Pugin filled in the details, but Barry had the final say on what would eventually be built, constantly refining and changing ideas until he achieved the result he wanted. Both were workaholics, perfectionist, and driven, but yet complete opposites. Pugin was many wonderful things, but a savvy political operator was not one of them. His heart ruled his head, whereas with Barry it was the other way round. The architecture of one was driven by idealistic passion; the other by a steely determination to achieve his ends. Neither could have done it without the other. Together these two men made the most famous building in Britain, but at huge personal cost to themselves and to their respective reputations. Pugin found it difficult to compromise to meet a client's needs, whereas Barry was well practised in doing so (or at least, appearing to do so).

For who exactly was Barry's client for the rebuilding of the Palace? The arguments of 1836 indicated that Barry was going to have work for, and satisfy more, than one master. But who should be given the upper hand? The government, in the form of the Office of Woods, funded by the Treasury? Parliament as an institution made up of two legislatures occupying a single building, with competing practical and procedural needs? Or—most difficult of all—over a thousand MPs and Peers, fractious, opinionated, vocal, partisan, and above all with as many individual views on how the work should progress as there were members? Deciding who was the real client at any particular moment would prove to be a mind-bending task for Barry over the next four and twenty years.

From the start public opinion was behind him. During most of the skirmishes and full-on assaults, it was the politicians and the so-called experts foisted on him—and the resulting rise in costs—which became the butt of public jokes and anger. There was something about Barry— affable, charming, a consummate professional, and above all a highly skilled architect and business manager—which enabled him to see off all these annoyances over the years. But it was not without its price. By devoting himself to the Houses of Parliament project he lost about two-thirds of the income he could expect from a private practice, and it certainly shortened his life.

Some of Barry's resilience was a result of his domestic contentment. He had become engaged to Sarah Rowsell just before he set out on his Grand Tour in 1817. Barry's younger brother, Fred, had married Sarah's sister, Betsey, while Charles was abroad and the families must have first met through their fathers since Samuel Rowsell was also a stationer, with a shop at 31 Cheapside, in the City; he became Master of the Skinners' Company in 1826.[29] Due to his modest circumstances, on returning home in 1820, Charles and Sarah delayed their marriage until December 1822 when he was in a better position to support her. Children quickly arrived in the shape of Charles junior (1823), Alfred (1826), and Emily (1828). As Barry's practice flourished in Brighton and he became better known in fashionable London circles he moved his growing family in 1827 from the edge of Hatton Garden to Foley Place (now Langham Street) in the West End. Edward Middleton Barry (1830), took his second name from his father's first employers, while Godfrey (1832), and John Wolfe (1836), were named after his father's closest friends from his Grand Tour days.

Barry kept to a regular and balanced routine throughout his career. He rose before dawn, and worked for four hours, before breakfast at eight. Occupied with business in his office during the day, he liked nothing better than to return to the society of his family, with whom he dined at six or seven. He then had a quick refreshing snooze, chatted with his wife and children, or played the flute, or read until eight, drank tea, and then carried on with work until midnight. This highly effective regimen sustained him in the first ten years of his involvement with the Palace. Pugin's style, on the other hand, which only became more extreme as the years worn on, was to work in frenzied bouts of activity at home until exhaustion and other physical ailments prostrated him.

While the arguments about whether or not to go ahead with Barry's scheme were occupying MPs, both Houses were starting to chafe against their temporary accommodation inside the Palace. Members felt too hot, too cramped, and too generally inconvenienced. Ever since they had moved in, additions and changes had constantly been being made and on 29 July 1835 the Lords expressed the opinion that they needed more convenient accommodation than they currently had. Moreover, the Commons needed even more library rooms, committee rooms, and an additional division lobby.[30] Those pressed into use for committees included the nearby Westminster Sessions House, the deserted and smoke-stained apartments of the burnt-out Speaker's House, and even rooms rented by the week at King's Arms Tavern in Palace Yard.[31] Finally in May 1836 ladies were permitted to sit in the public gallery in a special area, just as they were in France, America, and some German states. Though a few MPs still scoffed at such an 'idle and ridiculous proposition', they were outnumbered by those who felt that women ought to know what was being discussed in Parliament, both for their own and their families' education, and for the salutary effect it would have in 'bridling of the manly passions' in the chambers.[32] Once victory was declared for the Competition Commissioners and Barry's design, Hanbury-Tracy then overreached himself in proposing his own alterations to the temporary House directly to the

Speaker, in order to improve the division lobbies in Smirke's Commons. The Office of Woods wrote to the Speaker informing him that 'this Department having received no official instructions upon the subject of this alteration, no orders have been given relating to them'.[33]

Early in 1837 the Commons Library needed to be enlarged (again), and Black Rod demanded a new stove to keep the Peers warm near their makeshift, drafty, entrance. Some of these works Barry took over to ensure that they were coordinated with his own plans and by the autumn of 1837 he was having to find space for more Commons committees as well as coping with the Home Office's requisitions of existing committee rooms for the Royal Commissions on unemployed handloom weavers and municipal corporations.[34] Pressure on the building site was intense and looked set only to become worse once construction was underway. No one seems to have considered that moving the members out would make it easier and faster to construct the new Palace rather than adding complexity to an already monumentally difficult project by having to work round them.

From the earliest conception of a replacement building, its ventilation had exercised the Office of Woods and members. Recalling how stuffy and noxious the old chambers had been without a reliable supply of fresh air passing through, the temporary chambers had to include a satisfactory system. From their opening, the hot air blowing through the floor was causing problems with noise during debates. It was therefore of quite some interest to the MPs to hear about the plan of Dr David Boswell Reid of Edinburgh in the summer of 1836 to apply his ventilation and acoustic system to Smirke's temporary House of Commons. Reid was originally a medical doctor, but also a chemist and President of the Scottish Philosophical Society. Although both Smirke and the scientist, Michael Faraday, expressed caution about Reid's theories, both MPs and the Office of Woods were impressed by the work carried out in his experimental shed in Edinburgh, and were keen to take up his ideas. Thus the Treasury gave approval for Reid's machines to be installed without delay, without prejudice to any solution which might be adopted for the new building.[35] Work went on through the autumn and Reid was ordered to be in London on 30 January 1837, without fail, in order to superintend the operation of the ventilation at the State

Opening, when the temporary House would be packed.[36] His arrival ultimately led to 15 years of bitter dispute and terrible delay.

Winter that year was bitterly cold and snowbound, and there was an epidemic of flu in London.[37] Throughout this time Barry worked with Pugin and his office draughtsmen to finalize the plans and costs. On 1 February 1837 Thomas Chawner, the surveyor from the Office of Woods, and his boss, Benjamin Stephenson, met Barry to examine the final estimates.[38] Once again, the financial forecasts had been prepared single-handedly by Henry Hunt, whose attention to detail marked him out as the founder of modern quantity surveying.[39] This meeting marked the end of the beginning and six weeks later, on 18 March 1837, Barry paid a visit to Kensington Palace to introduce his future monarch to her new Palace which had at last received the go-ahead. The 17-year-old Princess Victoria wrote in her diary that night: 'At 2, we saw Mr Barry, who brought his model & drawings for the new Houses of Lords & Commons, which are very beautiful.' Victoria at this time was still living under the overprotective regime of her mother's private secretary, Sir John Conroy, and she obviously enjoyed Barry's visit for the variety of company it provided her, for she added: 'He is a young, & very clever man.'[40] The King, William IV, who had succeeded his brother in 1830, had vowed to remain alive until his niece Victoria had attained her majority on 24 May 1837, in order that her mother and the detested Conroy should not become Regent. This he duly did, and Victoria was woken early in the morning of 20 June, to be told the news of her uncle's death aged almost 72, which she received steadily from the Archbishop of Canterbury and the Lord Chamberlain: 'I got out of bed and went into my sitting-room (only in my dressing-gown) and *alone*', and vowed to do her duty.

On 17 July the new Queen attended her first State Opening of Parliament. She entered the old Palace through the Royal Entrance and up the *Scala Regia* designed by John Soane in the 1820s, which had survived the fire. She processed through Soane's repaired Royal Gallery to the temporary House of Lords to make her speech. 'The house was very

Queen Victoria processing through the unburnt Royal Gallery, at the State Opening of Parliament in 1837

full and I felt somewhat (but very little) nervous before I read my speech, but it did very well, and I was happy to hear people were satisfied.'[41] Disrobing in the Lords Library, it would be another 14 years before she could use the Sovereign's Entrance and Royal Gallery Barry had shown her in his model that spring.

By the summer of 1837 the plans were finally signed off by the Office of Woods and the estimates completed. Barry's charge for this eventually came to £1,607.[42] It was time to turn his attention to the site itself, where the new Palace had been waiting for three years to rise phoenix-like from the ashes of the old. 'Had all been forseen', wrote his son Alfred many years later, 'it cannot be doubted that Mr Barry would gladly have faced it all in the service of his art. But he would hardly have entered on his work with so much buoyancy and hopefulness of spirit, with so much self-reliance, and so much confidence in the future.'[43]

II

WATER

1837–1843

There go the ships: there is that Leviathan,
whom thou hast made to play therein.

Psalm 104:26

4

A Clear
Understanding

July 1837 to December 1838

T HE CHALLENGE FACING Barry was immense. It was one thing
to produce a magnificent design on paper, but now he had to make
his plans reality. No one had ever built such a huge building, covering 8
acres, along a riverfront nearly a quarter of a mile long. The new Palace
would project right into the Thames and, with the site extended at both
ends, its footprint was set to be at least four times that of the old Houses
of Parliament. The mud and gravel of Thorney Island which under-
pinned the ruins of the old Palace was treacherous and unstable, and the
work of Parliament had to continue in both Houses, uninterrupted. The
only option was to begin by building from the river inwards, reclaiming
land from the water as the work spread westwards: gradually replacing
and overtaking the old Palace buildings as, one by one, they became
obsolete, while at the same time swallowing up residential and business
premises to the south to solve the want of space on the cramped site.

In July Barry submitted to the Office of Woods the names of building
contractors he felt would be suitable to construct a giant hoarding in

New Palace Yard and, more significantly, he was put in touch with James Walker.[1] Walker was an eminent civil engineer, President of his profession's institute, and inheritor of much of Thomas Telford's practice. Walker, a Glaswegian, 'prompt and decided... prudent and cautious', had been responsible for an array of high-profile construction projects throughout the British Isles: docks, harbours, some of the earliest railways, the first iron bridge over the Thames at Vauxhall, and any number of lighthouses for Trinity House, including his masterpiece at Bishop Rock on the Scillies. Here was a man who knew how to manage and control water where it met land. And he was also familiar with the dangerous and capricious character of the vast flow of the Thames, having been responsible for the East India and Commercial Docks down river, and the maintenance of Westminster and Blackfriars bridges nearby.[2]

Caissons—sealed box-like constructions enabling bridge footings, harbour walls, and other foundations to be dug by labourers under water—incorporating pressurized breathing systems, were only invented in the middle of the nineteenth century. Without this knowledge, but armed with the *sangfroid* that characterized their generation, Walker and Barry instead devised a scheme for a 'cofferdam' in the Thames at Westminster. First of all, a trench would be dredged 27 feet out parallel to the former gardens on the shore of the old Palace.[3] It was to stretch 920 feet along the western side of the river and, at either end of the site, it would run at ninety degrees to join up to the wharf walls by Westminster Bridge to the north and Millbank to the south. This would form a rectangular ditch 8 foot deep. Then two parallel rows of iron-shod wooden piles, 36 feet deep, were to be driven into the river bed along the line of the ditch, through layers of mud, sand, yellow gravel, and then finally London clay. These principal piles were intended to support a wall of close-jointed wooden sheet piles 10 feet apart. The riverbed between the walls would then be dug out and the whole filled with puddle clay, creating a double-skinned waterproof seal that would prevent the brackish river, with its populations of roach, dace, flounder, mullet, seabass, salmon, and eels, from breaching the sealed walls. This was in the days before the invention of the steam-driven pile driver, so the shafts would have to be driven in by manual means, pulleys and weights.

The east front in progress in 1842 showing the cofferdam and navvies huts on the east front

Once the walls were sealed, the water in the interior of the dam was to be pumped out to create a dry dock, and here Barry and Walker did at least have the advantage of a 10-horsepower steam engine to aid the process. When the interior of the walled dam was dried out in this way, it would then enable the building of the river wall and foundations, and become the location for contractors' huts.

An invitation to tender first for building the river wall and then to create the embankment foundation was sent to ten contractors selected by Barry on 5 August 1837. Throughout August the specification and drawing was available to view between ten and four at the Office of Woods. Barry and Walker opened the tenders at one in the afternoon on 29 August and selected the firm Lee's of Lambeth to undertake the work.[4] The contract for £24,195 (excluding machinery) was signed on 11 September, but Walker's firm had already been making test borings in the river and the first pile of the undertaking was driven into the Thames mud on 1 September 1837.[5] On the day the contract was signed, the Lord Mayor ordered that the three navigable arches of Westminster Bridge closest to the Palace would be stopped up for the purpose of building the new Palace.[6] The cofferdam took 16 months to construct and, once operational, would remain in place for the next 12 years, kept dry by two 18-inch steam pumps beating at a relentless 14 strokes a minute, day and night.

At just about this time, Benjamin Stephenson, of the slippery Office of Woods, warned Barry in relation to the building:

> that the Lords of the Treasury have not yet fixed that amount of the professional remuneration to be paid for building the New Houses of Parliament; and it will therefore be necessary that the Works about to be undertaken by yourself and Messrs Walker & Co should be executed with a clear understanding on your parts, that your remuneration for the same, must depend upon the future decision of their Lordships upon this subject.[7]

But it was too late for Barry to back out. Even at this point, others were coming up with their own solutions and additional requirements for the building. Among other requests, Robert Peel (now leader of the opposition) queried whether the King's Tower at the southern end of the Palace could not be used to store the public records of the kingdom as well as the parliamentary ones. This was in support of the bill to keep the government archive more safely following the 1834 fire; storage was badly needed since some of the official papers had been filling up two wards at the nearby Westminster Hospital ever since the disaster.[8] With another kind of safety in mind, the Home Office wanted dedicated accommodation to be found for the police in the Palace. Then the Law Society declared it also needed room for its use.[9] Parliamentary business continued in and around the disrupted spaces while the site and its immediate vicinity was cleared. Carts travelling to and fro with all manner of materials ran alongside carriages containing politicians, government officials, and the architect and his assistants visiting the site and making plans. Queen Victoria visited for a second State Opening in November and to give royal assent to a series of bills including the Slave Compensation Bill in December, reimbursing plantation owners for the economic consequences of having abolishing slavery in the colonies in 1833. On both occasions she once again made use of the Lords Library as an ad-hoc robing room.[10] As Christmas approached, Barry, along with the runners-up John Chessell Buckler, William Railton, and Robert Hamilton, were informed that they could finally pick up their prize money of £500 at any time from the Office of Woods 'on application to the Cashier of this office any day between the hours of 11 and 2'. It was, after all, a mere two years since they had entered their designs.[11]

In the Commons, members were now in rebellion about the outbreak of sore throats, asthmatic coughs, and 'feverish heat' they were suffering due, they thought, to the overly dry air in Smirke's chamber. Furthermore, the winter mud on their boots soon dried into an irritating dust which covered their clothes or settled on the floor of the House, making them splutter even harder.[12] In the first week in January the Edinburgh chemist Dr Reid, of whom there were high hopes, began to experiment with gas lighting in the chamber to try to solve the problem. The temperature at ceiling level rose from 56°F to 106°F, and the Office of Woods hastily put an end to the experiment 'on the ground of probable danger and increased expence'. However, it did consider that 'the principle of Dr Reid's may eventually be adopted with advantage in the new Houses of Parliament, under other circumstances, and in Rooms constructed for

Smirke's temporary chambers after Reid's alterations, 1839. House of Commons (top) and House of Lords (bottom)

76

the purpose, and made fire proof'.[13] Scottish science was, after all, the essence of modernity. The failure of the experiment led to a debate in which members put forward—at length—their own ideas about how to remedy the air quality in their home. The Hansard reporter became so fed up with it that, on the second occasion, he failed to take down any notes and reported with exasperation: 'The hon. Member then proceeded to describe minutely the alteration which he proposed.' On that occasion, the MP concerned, Sir Frederick Trench, a Tory sitting for Scarborough, even suggested that Barry's design was wholly unfit for the techniques he was proposing, and the Office of Woods would need to think again.[14] Again, this was a pattern which would be repeated many times over before the Palace was completed, of MPs and Peers proposing their own solutions to the mind-boggling architectural and engineering challenges of the new building and seeking to implement them in defiance of the professionals to whom they themselves had given the task. The building was, after all, home to their Houses, so some members took the view that as occupiers sent there by their voters (or by their title), they knew best. At no point does it seem to have occurred to any of them that the dust and grit in the air of the Chambers was due to their being in the middle of the biggest building site in London.

Finally, at the end of February 1838, the Treasury came up with details of the sum it intended to pay Barry for work on the Palace. It declared that £25,000 would be 'a fair and liberal remuneration' for the superintendence, direction, and completion of the intended edifice over the timescale proposed. Yet the government also added that, 'although cases of the magnitude involved in the proceedings of Mr Barry are likely very seldom to occur', it had rethought how it would pay architects in future. Based on the fact that it was offering Barry a fixed sum, rather than a percentage of the overall costs, which was usual at the time, the percentage system 'will advantageously admit of some modification' and the fixed sum method should be used in future.[15] With the estimates drawings paid for by him, the cofferdam underway, and any number of other engagements already entered into,

Barry was in no position to walk away from the offer. But he no doubt realized that though fixed-sum payments might initially appear attractive over a percentage, their appeal would soon tarnish if projects ran over budget or were delayed, and they locked the architect into completing a never-ending work long after the original payment had been spent.

It was clearly Barry's practice to make use of the very best expertise on any aspect of the new Palace's construction and design. He had already contracted the services of Pugin and Walker. In April he was in contact with the celebrated scientist and Director of the Royal Institution, Michael Faraday, who among other things had discovered electromagnetic rotation and induction (essentially inventing the first electric motor, first transformer, and first dynamo). Barry was keen to discuss the new Palace's ventilation.[16] Heating and cooling was certainly occupying the minds of many at Westminster. Barry was now in charge of works to the temporary buildings as well as the new ones. There were ongoing difficulties warming the replacement committee rooms set up in the old Speaker's House. And in the first half of 1838 Barry had created temporary dining rooms for the MPs at a cost of over £600 by appropriating the razed area over the lower crypt of St Stephen's, where the former Commons chamber had stood before the fire. By the following winter, the members eating their suppers were complaining of the cold, so Barry had to install swing doors to keep the draughts out, the Treasury having turned down his proposal for fireplaces.[17] Barry had in fact fudged what he intended to do with the ruin of St Stephen's Chapel. Most competitors had tried to incorporate it into their proposals, and Barry was no different, indicating that he intended to restore it as a grand space leading from the main entrance by Westminster Hall into the heart of his new Palace. But 'restoration' in the 1830s was a loose concept indeed and in the middle of 1837 Barry had decided that the walls of the upper chapel would need to come down and in their place would go new ones, though with the same dimensions as the old. He told the Office of Woods his intentions at the end of July and by the early autumn the upper chapel had disappeared forever.[18] This was perhaps with considerable regret and his son, John Wolfe Barry, later donated some watercolours of the ruins, today in the Parliamentary Art Collection, which his father may have purchased as mementoes of that decision.

St Stephen's Chapel ruins after the fire. This watercolour was once in the possession of John Wolfe Barry, Charles Barry's youngest son

Outside, work on building the cofferdam was dangerous, and health and safety legislation on construction sites non-existent. Early in January 1838 the Royal Humane Society deposited 'Drages and Apparatus to be in readiness in case of accidents to the workmen employed upon the coffer-dam'. The society had been founded in 1774 in order to promote the new and controversial technique of resuscitation for victims of drowning, and it subsequently awarded medals for lifesaving bravery. That very year, 1838, its gold medal went to 22-year-old Grace Darling, and her light-housekeeper father, for their celebrated rescue of nine survivors of the *Forfarshire*, wrecked on the Outer Farne islands on its way from Hull to Dundee. The Office of Woods made a donation of £10 to the society.[19] Fatalities among the navvies went largely unreported, but in May that year came the first reported site death when 'an immense block of stone' fell from a crane behind the old Speaker's House and one man was crushed to death (his 'every bone appeared to be broken'), while another sustained a smashed femur and was 'otherwise severely injured'.[20] A year later the widow of a workman killed at the site, who had become destitute and desperate, tried to slash her throat on the steps of the East London Work-house following yet another refusal of poor relief for her and her three children. She and her family were finally taken in and cared for.[21]

By the early summer of 1838, the gestation of the monstrous new Palace was also putting pressure on its immediate neighbourhood. The growing number of workmen on site led the Serjeant at Arms in the Commons to take control of their chaotic refreshment requirements, which had been overwhelming for local hostelries.[22] Pope Brothers & Co, coal merchants of Abbey Wharf, introduced a test case into the courts to sue the government as a result of their eviction from their riverside premises. Thesiger, Bodkin, and Channell, their Dickensian-sounding solicitors, won them an extra £2,704 more compensation from the Office of Woods: over a third more than they had been originally offered. Other claimants watched with intense interest.[23]

80

As for Charles Dickens himself, he had had a career change since the fire. His first novel, *The Pickwick Papers*, had been received well, and he had been able to throw in his work as a parliamentary reporter to concentrate full time on writing novels. In 1838 he was hard at work on a serialization of his third, *Nicholas Nickleby*, drawing on his own experiences of the Houses of Parliament. His years haunting the public galleries and the lobbies of the Palace had left him with little sympathy for politicians. Sir Matthew Pupker MP's attempts to pass a bill on behalf of the United Metropolitan Improved Hot Muffin and Crumpet Baking and Punctual Delivery Company, of which he was Chair, intended to improve the moral lot and working conditions of muffin boys and supply the deserving poor with 'muffins of first quality at reduced prices' is an initial stab of satire in the novel. Later on in the story, among a number of other political episodes, there is the failed attempt by Nicholas, impoverished but chivalrous, to obtain a job as a personal secretary to Mr Gregsbury MP, of Manchester Buildings, Westminster, who expects Nicholas to cram him with all the information he requires and see to all his affairs for the paltry sum of 15*s.* a week. Nicholas refuses.

In May £12,000 was spent on compulsorily buying up houses in Abingdon Street to make space for the building site to the south. By midsummer Barry was asking for another £30,000 for more purchases. The headmaster of Westminster School requested an alternative way for his boys to get safely to their boats, 'which they had heretofore been enabled to do from Parliament stairs and cause-way now removed for the works for the new Houses of Parliament'. And at the opposite end of the social scale, the Thames watermen plying the stairs of Westminster Bridge petitioned the Office of Woods about the disruption to their customary landing place by the creation of the cofferdam.[24]

Mud from the river, stirred up by the swirling currents being redirected round the piles, was pushed downriver and began to accumulate in quantity at Whitehall Stairs, provoking complaints. The man put in charge of sorting out the silty mess was none other than Richard Weobley, still Clerk of Works at Westminster despite being one of the principal culprits behind the fire of 1834.[25] (In fact, Weobley remained in his post at the Palace until 1840, at which point he was transferred by the Office of Woods to the Brighton Pavilion—by then out of favour with Victoria.[26] This was nothing less than a Siberian exile, though it is hard to tell what was more shaming for him: having to liaise with Barry's men over the new building or being cast into outer darkness by the seaside where his life continued on its downward spiral.) Barry had employed a Mr Bennett to construct a sewer from College Street to Bridge Street for the new Palace on the same terms as the builder did work for the Commissioners of Westminster Sewers. By the time winter was coming on the architect was receiving complaints from Mr Jervis of 2 and 3 Old Palace Yard that his drainage was being disturbed by the new arrangements.[27] It was probably from this sewer that the antique coins emerged which Barry proudly exhibited to his professional colleagues at the Institute of British Architects' December meeting that year.[28]

Not everyone in the neighbourhood grumbled about the disruption. For the Navigation Committee of the City of London it provided the perfect opportunity to put into action plans to embank the Thames which had been under discussion since 1830, in order to make the course 'uniform and beneficial to the river, the Parliament Houses and the public'; a plan which continued into the middle of the century along miles of the bank and eventually enclosed the main artery of Joseph Bazalgette's sewerage network for London, still in use today.[29] Others were quick to seize upon the commercial opportunities provided by the arrival of a brand new building on the waterside. Later that year a new venture, the Westminster Steam Packet Co., appealed for shareholders in its innovative 'water-omnibus' service, which it planned to be 'running incessantly from the terrace of the new Houses of Parliament to the Greenwich railroad station, London-bridge, and touch off all the intermediate bridges, Hungerford and Temple-stairs'. Public safety, comfort, and convenience were to be the watchwords of this new enterprise which was offering a guaranteed 5 per cent return per quarter to investors.[30]

At the Office of Woods, officials were getting anxious about the impending Coronation and how it could be managed around the work underway at the Palace. If Westminster Hall were to be decorated for a feast then materials could be brought in on the same landing as for the cofferdam, but the contractor would have to erect his own crane and any additional platforms.[31] However, it soon became clear that the Prime Minister, Melbourne, had no intention of committing the government to pay out significant sums on what he regarded as a medieval fancy-dress party. William IV had set a precedent in 1830 by simply having a modest dinner at Buckingham Palace following the ceremony instead of the time-honoured banquet in Westminster Hall as his predecessors had done. He had also abolished many of the sacral elements of the enthronement that had been reintroduced by his brother, George. Some of the newspapers regretted the royal proclamation issued early in April confirming the lack of national celebration, and complained about the 'maimed rites' and 'dispensing with the services to be performed in Westminster Hall'.[32]

This worried some politicians. Without the procession from Westminster Abbey to the Hall, which had been immensely popular the last time it had occurred, ordinary people 'would be deprived of the opportunity of witnessing any part of the ceremony'. The Home Secretary, Lord John Russell, tried to soothe anxiety in the House by explaining there would be 'a public procession through the streets' from Buckingham Palace to the Abbey. But to Sir Frederick Trench's request that ladies at the Coronation 'should appear in articles of British manufacture . . . as there were at present 50,000 poor weavers in a state of starvation', the Home Secretary had no solution: 'the matter does not belong to my department'.[33] The primary purpose of the Coronation of 1838 was, felt the government, to 'amuse and interest' the young Queen's subjects—a startlingly modern departure from previous occasions based largely on medieval liturgical oaths and obscure ceremonial.[34]

On her Coronation day, 28 June, Victoria was woken at four in the morning by a gun salute in Hyde Park, and lay in bed at Buckingham Palace listening to the noise of the people and bands gathering outside for three hours. She stepped into George III's golden state coach, first used at a coronation by William IV, at ten and was driven to the Abbey as her uncle had been, amazed by 'the millions of my loyal subjects who were assembled in *every* spot to witness the Procession. Their good-humour and excessive loyalty was beyond everything, and I really cannot say how proud I feel to be the Queen of such a Nation.'[35]

As it rolled along Constitution Hill and through St James's, the coronation coach took Victoria not only to the site of Charles Barry's massive new Palace, but also past what was to become another of his most famous buildings. Barry's professional practice had not stopped simply because he had won the highest profile building competition in the country. In 1837, while all the wrangling over the Palace estimates and tendering for the initial contracts had been going on, Barry had produced a winning Italianate design for the new Reform Club in Pall Mall, that ultimate expression of Whig confidence of the 1830s, based on Barry's affection for the Farnese Palace in Rome, and to be built next door to his other clubland building, the Traveller's. What was more, as Victoria's coach trundled into Trafalgar Square before making its way down Whitehall to the deafening noise of the cheering crowds, discussions about a design for the empty plaza in front of Wilkins' National Gallery were underway. Two years later the work to landscape it was handed to Barry by the government on his former rival's death. Outside London, Barry had not been idle either, and in 1838 came a commission from the Earl of Carnarvon for Highclere Castle, subsequently known to millions as the eponymous Downton Abbey.

A month after the cut-price 'Penny Coronation', certain young noblemen were still miserable about Whig attempts to squash what they believed were their ancient rights (and rites) in favour of a joylessly progressive and utilitarian approach to monarchy and the public purse. Among them was a member of the House of Lords, Archibald Montgomery, thirteenth Earl of Eglinton, a man previously notable only for an appalling education and an excessive taste for fine claret, women, and horse racing.[36] A throwaway joke by him resulted in the *Court Journal* reporting in August that he was planning a grand tournament at his country seat in Ayrshire in revenge. What was then originally envisaged as a small entertainment at one of his race meetings soon blew up into a medieval jamboree of gigantic proportions.[37] Taking inspiration from a number of sources—Walter Scott's novel *Ivanhoe*, the sensational success of Samuel Pratt's armour showrooms in Belgravia, and his own half-brother's obsessive interest in building a giant castellated gothic hutch for his extensive guinea pig collection—Eglinton ended up presiding over a full-scale medieval pageant the following year. Admission was by ticket only and an estimated 100,000 applied from all over the country and beyond—including India, Brazil, France, and the United States. Those with known Whig sympathies were banned. Such was the frenzy that desperate applicants offered the most blatant of reasons for attendance. The Town Clerk of Anderston, near Glasgow, was sent a ticket because his wife had allegedly beaten a Radical with a candlestick.

On 28 August 1839 the crowds descended by road, by steamboat from Ardrossan, and by train from Irvine and filled the grandstands to watch, as they had once hoped to watch the coronation procession at Westminster. There was to be a full tournament followed by a medieval banquet and entertainments in the grounds of Eglinton Castle. The participants—whittled down from 150 to a dozen by reason of cost and fitness—were well-prepared and had been training intensively in the yard of the Eyre Arms, a public house in St John's Wood. Led by a Queen of Beauty, Lady Seymour, and her handmaidens, the parade of 13 fully armoured knights (including the future Emperor Napoléon III) appeared three hours late. This was due to the difficulty of manoeuvring the decorated horses and retinues into the required order to get to the jousting ground. One knight alone, Lord Glenlyon, had brought 78 men with him from his private regiment of Atholl Highlanders, to form his affinity. Then, the downpour came. The stands collapsed. The jousters got stuck in the quagmire. The banquet was ruined, including the traditional coronation feast dish of dilligrout, a runny porridge with whole plums floating in it. The soaked Queen of Beauty and her entourage were transported away in closed carriages. And perhaps worst of all, the thousands of spectators were left to shift for themselves in the torrents of chilly rain, their transport back home not expected for hours.

The Eglinton Tournament has gone down in history as a total wash-out. Yet Archibald Montgomery regrouped and after a few days the tournament was rerun, with repaired stands and the expected banquet and ball finally took place. Those who attended were delighted and enjoyed themselves immensely. The little Whig Queen, when she heard the news, was unimpressed. 'Talked of the horrid weather', Victoria wrote in her diary, 'Of it having poured so at the Tournament...I said it served them all right for their folly in having *such* a thing &c.'[38] Really the participants and audience at the tournament needn't have bothered about the demise of the Middle Ages and all that went with it: a Palace quite as grand as their imagined Camelot was about to rise on the banks of the Thames. And while the Eglinton Tournament marked the high-point of the craze for Romantic, Walter Scott-like medievalism which declined thereafter, its influence was seen in a new form of chivalry which took its place in the Victorian mind as a result—one based on the ethos of chivalric values in contemporary life rather than a historical 'sham'.[39] In the same way, the new Palace of Westminster marked the zenith of a particular kind of nineteenth-century Gothic, and though it was stylistically superseded long before it was completed, the influence of the building itself seeped into the lives and consciousness of every-one in the nation, and has stayed lodged there ever since.

Already at his side Barry had the talents of John Thomas as his super-visor of stone carving. Thomas, born in Gloucestershire to a hotelier's wife, and orphaned aged 12 or 13, had first been a local stonemason's apprentice working on the restoration of gravestones. In his spare time he also painted portraits and engraved brass, but a visit to his brother in Oxford persuaded him to concentrate his passion for design on drawing and carving architectural ornaments. His career had further blossomed with a move to Birmingham and, already in plenty of demand, he intro-duced himself to Barry during the building of King Edward VI's Gram-mar School in Birmingham. There, to overcome a shortage of wax models from which to carve bosses, the industrious 20-year-old made his own, and this resourcefulness and the quality of his work so impressed Barry that he turned to him again when he needed an expert craftsman to oversee the decorative stonework at Westminster. To hone Thomas's knowledge in preparation for the challenge of producing all the stone figures and heraldry inside and out, Barry sent him on a drawing tour of town halls in Belgium, just as he himself had undertaken when designing the original plans. From small drawings supplied by Barry's office, Thomas and his team in the sculpture workshop were to develop large-scale drawings which would form the models for the full-size plasters of royal and saintly figures, heraldic beasts, coats of arms, angels, and masses of delicious Gothic ornament from which the final work would be carved in stone. It was to become a triumph.[40] While that took care of the monumental stonework, there was still a crucial decision to be made about the material to be used to face the main superstructure of the Palace.

Early in July 1838 Barry proposed to the Office of Woods that he undertake a 'visitation of quarries…upon the subject of choice of stone'.[41] Once this became widely known, Barry and the Office of Woods were flooded with letters from industrialists and landowners offering supplies from their estates. Nothing could be more prestigious than to have the products of your own quarry adorning the new Houses of Parliament, glistening in the sunshine for all to see in the greatest city in the world. Solicitous enquiries into the progress of selecting the right stone were received from across Britain and Ireland, and even France; and seemingly disinterested musings flooded the correspondence columns of the national newspapers.[42]

For his expedition, Barry as usual gathered around him the best minds he could find to advise him. In August Henry de la Beche, the gentleman geologist who had been a patron and friend of Mary Anning, the most successful fossil hunter that ever lived, agreed to join him.[43] At the time, de la Beche was working as geologist to the Ordnance Survey having lost the income from his estates in Jamaica when slavery was abolished there in 1833.[44] A third member of the group came in the form of master mason and architect Charles Harriott Smith who was an expert on building stone. Cheerful, zealous, and intelligent, Smith was responsible for carving the capital of Nelson's Column some years later.[45] But it was the final member of the group who is most worth remembering. William 'Strata' Smith (1769–1839) had been born into a blacksmith's family in an Oxfordshire village. He had risen, by way of land surveying, to become the father of geological mapping, identifying for the first time fossil layers in coal seams and quarries, and challenging contemporary notions of the age of the earth—still largely at the time thought to have been created around 4000 BC. His lowly origins, mad wife, and lack of government backing, however, had led to his discoveries and methods being overtaken— even plagiarized—by gentleman-scholars at the Geological Society of London which for many years ignored his work and excluded him personally and he went back to being a jobbing geologist and surveyor following a bankruptcy. Happily, by the end of his life, Strata Smith had become reconciled to a new and younger generation of professional geologists and his work was now revered. He received the first ever Wollaston medal of the Geological Society and was awarded a doctorate from Trinity College Dublin. It was a long way from his beginnings at the forge in Churchill. His 1815 Geological Map of England and Wales—one of the most famous pieces of scientific advancement in the world—now hangs in the Geological Society's building in Burlington House off Piccadilly as a tribute.[46] Whether there was tension between him and de la Beche as they toured the country seeking suitable stone we do not know, but if there was it was likely smoothed over by Charles Smith, whom everyone agreed was the most cooperative and helpful person imaginable to be on the jaunt.

On Sunday 18 August 1838 Strata Smith joined Barry and the others at Scarborough from where they travelled to Newcastle. Their itinerary took the little expedition around some of Britain's most ancient and beautiful historic sites, and the quarries which had supplied them.[47] The trip generated some interest in the papers, and *The Observer* expressed the hope that it would prove useful, not only for the new Palace but also 'to the interests of building all over the kingdom'.[48] By the end of the month they had visited—among other places in Scotland and Northern England—Hadrian's Wall, Edinburgh, Glasgow, Brancepath Castle, Wolsingham, Barnard Castle, Ecclestone Abbey, Getherley, Richmond Castle, Northallerton, Thirsk, and the church at Coxwold. In September their road trip took them through Yorkshire, beginning with Rievaulx and Byland abbeys, Helmsley, and Pickering. They visited Eskdale on a return day trip using the new horse-drawn Whitby and Pickering Railway, then the quarries at Malton, Castle Howard, Kirkham Priory, and York. There they paused briefly to look at the museum antiquities and the stone in the Minster and travelled on to Beverley, Selby, Fountains Abbey, and the nearby millstone grit quarries, Ripon, Harrogate, Knaresborough, Spofforth, Wetherby, Thorpe, Tadcaster, Doncaster, Tickhill, Maltby, Leeds, Huddersfield, and Sheffield, where they arrived at nine at night on 14 September. On they went then, south to the Derbyshire moors, Haddon Hall, and Bakewell, into the Peak District, Matlock, Belper, Derby, and to magnificent Hardwick Hall, the ultimate Elizabethan prodigy house.

On 20 September they forged on into the English midlands to Southwell 'and examined the stone of the collegiate church' wrote Smith, '*remarkably good*...quarried in the vicinity of Bolsover, which we had not visited'. As in York, they paused at the Minster, there admiring the intricate and hardly worn foliage carving of its capitals and arrived at their overnight stop in Newark late as a result. On to Lincoln they travelled where they studied its magnificent gothic Minster, the Ancaster stone quarries 'said to be Roman', Grantham, Stamford, and nearby Burghley House. Once they had got through Kettering and Northampton by coach, they made their way back to London by the novel means of Robert Stephenson's thrilling new London and Birmingham Railway, which had opened along its whole length just five days previously on 17 September. This was the first London intercity rail line, and Euston station the first mainline terminus in a capital city anywhere in the world. Its magnificent Doric Propylaeum, or entrance archway, made of millstone grit, stood for 125 years until pulled down by modernist planners in 1962.

After a few days' rest and recuperation from their exertions, the stone-picking consultants launched into a western phase of their tour. Fortified by a hearty breakfast at Barry's house in Foley Place on 26 September, they set off westwards in a carriage and some 60 miles later found themselves amid the golden limestone of Oxford. The next day they carried on further west to Burford, Taynton, and Windrush in the Cotswolds, close to where Smith had been born. They explored Cheltenham, Gloucester (including its cathedral and new bridge), the Forest of Dean on 28 September, and arrived at Tintern Abbey 'but too late to see it distinctly'. The next morning they toured the ruins and further explored along the Severn and Avon valleys taking in Chepstow, Bristol, Bath, Frome, Shepton Mallett, Wells, Glastonbury, Montacute, Yeovil, and Dorchester. By now it was early October and the little band headed to the coast to view Weymouth and the Isle of Portland. There they stayed for two days, then relentlessly pursued their quest eastwards to Blandford, Shaftesbury, 'and the old quarries that supplied the stone of Salisbury Cathedral' before arriving at the cathedral itself by way of Wilton House, and 'examined the state of the stone in that fine building'. They returned by overnight coach to London on 5 October armed with many notes and ready to start writing up their report.

The memory of the honey-coloured and hardly weathered limestone of Southwell Minster stayed in Smith's mind. Over the following fortnight he could not shake off the sense that they had missed something important. This extraordinary man, born in the humblest of circumstances, whose brilliant scientific mind had reshaped the world and man's understanding of the deep past, now determined that the stone-pickers needed an additional visit. No one felt able to refuse. So it was that on 22 October they travelled north again on the Scarborough coach, to look at what they had bypassed before: the Bolsover freestone quarries which they believed had produced the 'exceedingly fine stone' of Southwell Minster. They went to the mill at Langwith which sawed the stone and 'obtained the prices and necessary particulars', returning home via Doncaster and York where they continued to deliberate on their findings.[49]

The work of Strata Smith in understanding that the surface of the earth was made up of layers, which could be identified by the fossils contained in each stratum, laid the foundations of modern knowledge about the age of the earth—estimated at four and a half billion years old. Then, on New Year's Day, 1 January 1839—four years, two months and fifteen days after the fire—the news came through that everyone had been waiting for. The cofferdam had finally been pumped free of water from the Thames. The great behemoth of a Palace was ready to rise up out of the mud and slowly emerge onto dry land.

5

A Bondage Worse than the Egyptians

1839 to 1841

A T THE END of January 1839 Barry and Walker were becoming increasingly concerned by the speed of their contractors. Although the cofferdam had been completed, the embankment foundation and river wall were nowhere near complete. Only when this was done could work on the superstructure begin. The Office of Woods ordered:

> you will express to Messrs Lee, the Board's displeasure at the repeated complaints that have been made of their slow proceedings in executing the works in question; and further inform them, that if they do not forthwith supply such additional number of proper workmen etc as you shall deem sufficient to complete these works within a fair and reasonable time, that this Board will be under the necessity of directing you to proceed without further notice to enforce the conditions of the contract which Messrs Lee have entered into for completing the works of the coffer dam included in the said contract.[1]

As a result, on 4 March, the foundation stone of the river wall was laid, excavations having taken three months. Throngs of the public and the steamboats arrived early in the morning, having heard a rumour it was to be the first stone of the Palace above ground, and were mightily disappointed to discover a notice at the site explaining that all that was happening was the lowering of the first stone for a wall that would eventually be under water. They returned home, 'rather chagrined at what they called a hoax'. There was no ceremony of any kind, though Duncannon looked on as First Commissioner of Woods and Forests, and as was traditional some gold and silver coins bearing the image of the new Queen were deposited in the centre of the first block.[2]

In return, the river obligingly spat out precious items of earlier times. Coins and other archaeological finds discovered were handed over to Barry as they emerged from the mud.[3] Large numbers of daggers and swords—from ancient hunting knives through to exquisite stilletos—some inlaid with gold, keys of various sizes and curious workmanship, antique copper coins, two or three small Roman pots, fossils 'of an ordinary class', one or two cannonballs, and several human skulls quickly emerged from the slime and into Barry's possession.[4] He had also been busy pulling together the final report on the building material to be selected for the new Palace. At the end of March it was sent to the government. One hundred and two stone types had been collected and analysed, with the help of two professors from King's College London (King's had been founded just ten years before by George IV, and had become, in 1836, with its godless rival University College, London's first university). Cubes of those geological samples were now lodged with the Museum of Economic Geology at the Office of Woods for future reference. During research into a suitable stone, Barry and the Commissioners had been approached by the Marquis of Breadalbane, a Member of the House of Lords, who offered a free gift of granite from his estates near Oban on the west coast of Scotland for the building. They had dismissed porphyries and granites at an early stage due to their immense cost and difficulty in use for ornamental carving and they now had to tactfully refuse.[5] The hundred or so options on their list provided an enviable colour chart from which to build the new Palace, among them 'dark, blueish-grey', 'ferruginous brown, striped', 'red, varied with green, brown and grey', 'whiteish-grey', 'brown-oliveish', and, most alarming of all, 'purplish-grey with occasional light greenish spots'.[6]

The experts had shortlisted a number from their travels and had then further ruled out certain stone types, notably a Carboniferous sandstone known as millstone grit from Darley Dale in Derbyshire, and the Upper Jurassic oolitic limestone of the Isle of Portland in Dorset used in St Paul's Cathedral, and were now homing in on rock from a relatively limited area stretching across South Yorkshire and into Derbyshire.[7] Today this mineral is technically described by geologists as the Cadeby Formation. It is magnesian limestone formed 260–50 million years ago during the Late Permian era which has, over time, had part of the calcium in its structure replaced by magnesium, turning its chemical formula from $CaCO_3$ into $CaMg(CO_3)_2$, that is, from calcium carbonate into calcium magnesium carbonate, a process known as dolomitization. (It will be no surprise to discover that this is the rock that makes up the eponymous mountain range in north-east Italy, named after the French mineralogist, Déodat de Dolomieu, who first identified the rock type in 1791.) This was the light-brown stone which Strata Smith and the others had so admired at Southwell for its carvability and seeming resistance to decay. 'In conclusion,' Barry and his colleagues wrote,

> having weighed to the best of our Judgement the Evidence in favour of the various Building Stones which have been brought under our Consideration...for crystalline Character, combined with a close Approach to the equivalent Proportions of carbonate of Lime and Carbonate of Magnesia; for uniformity in Structure; Facility and Economy in Conversion; and for Advantage of Colour, the Magnesian Limestone, or Dolomite, of Bolsover Moor and its Neighbourhood is in our Opinion the most fit and Proper Material to be employed in the new Houses of Parliament.[8]

Crucial to the decision of the commissioners was the ease of transportation of the selected stone from its quarry to London. Bolsover stone had an additional appeal to Barry because of the relatively straightforward route it would take to get to the wharfs at Millbank. The quarry near Worksop was only 8 miles from the Chesterfield Canal, and it would cost 6*s.* a ton to get by road to the canal, and then 10*s.* per ton to travel from the canal to London, via the Trent and Humber estuary.[9] Shortly afterwards, the first stone began to be quarried for the Palace.

At the end of March Barry also enquired of the Office of Woods exactly how they had arrived at the figure of £25,000 he had been offered for the work. A week later he received a cagey reply: 'this board must decline furnishing the particulars of the principle upon which the sum proposed for the remuneration of your services ... has been recommended'.[10] During May more buildings were demolished behind Abingdon Street to make way for the construction site. Black Rod's House on the river bank at the southernmost end of the old Palace—a familiar sight for all those travelling up and down the Thames, and which had survived the fire—was scheduled for demolition during the next parliamentary session. By the end of the month Lees had finally completed the foundation for almost the whole of the river wall.[11]

Time began to slip by. A builder was hauled before the courts for dumping mud from the site into the river, obstructing its use as common highway.[12] Compensation claims continued to arrive at the Office of Woods as a result of the disruption suffered by local amenities, including, on 13 June, the London Gaslight Company which sought £15 due to the construction of the new public sewer Barry had notified them about. The same day, Lees of Lambeth were informed by a clerk at the Woods on behalf of Barry that their operations to create the granite river wall of the Palace within the cofferdam had

> not been carried forward with the despatch required by your contract, and that they are still being proceeded with very tardily ... I am therefore directed by this board to express their extreme displeasure, and to inform you, that if the directions of Messrs Barry & Walker are not immediately and strictly attended to, the board will take measures to enforce the performance of the contract.[13]

Bad news then reached Barry from Bolsover. The shafts sunk to begin the quarrying of the stone had revealed that only small amounts could be extracted at a time. Charles Smith, the mason, went up to Yorkshire to investigate alternative dolomite. First a neighbouring quarry was identified at Stone's End, and then one at Mansfield Woodhouse in Nottinghamshire. Both were unsatisfactory. When the Derbyshire trial blocks arrived in London they were found to be full of vents, and the

Mansfield Woodhouse quarries again failed to produce blocks large enough.[14] The search continued, now in some desperation.

At the end of June Barry took the initiative and went ahead with inviting ten firms to bid for 'the works necessary in building the Carcase of the portion of the New Houses of Parliament which is towards the River'.[15] For proceeding with the tendering process without their approval, he was rapped over the knuckles by the Treasury which told him that in future all advertisements for bidders must be put to the Board of the Office of Woods with enough notice and particulars to allow it to clear the process with its paymaster.[16] The deadline for receipt of the bids slipped from the end of July 1839 to the end of September. But then there came good news from the stone front: the first full-sized trial blocks from a new supply. Anston dolomite from the Duke of Leeds's quarry began to arrive by the end of the summer and was transferred to the new landing wharfs created south of the cofferdam on Millbank.[17]

On the first day of October 1839 the firm of Grissell & Peto was awarded the construction contract for building the superstructure of the river front of the new Palace. The tender received from Lees of Lambeth was returned unopened: they had stupidly failed to attach a schedule as required by the Office of Woods.[18] Samuel Morton Peto and his cousin and brother-in-law Thomas Grissell were the most successful public works contractors of the age. They set up in business together in 1830, taking over the firm from Peto's much less successful uncle, building it up and quickly winning a series of highly lucrative contracts. In fact, they had undertaken the works at the Birmingham Grammar School and Reform Club for Barry, as well as a series of other London clubs. They had built the Lyceum and the St James Theatre in a matter of a few weeks.[19] The fact they won the contract for the superstructure was not a sign of favouritism or corruption by Barry (they had failed to get the contract for the cofferdam and river wall, after all), but rather a sign that they were the premier firm for public works in the country at the time—something which the Office of Woods had recognized by appointing them to undertake the building of Nelson's Column as the finishing touch to Barry's landscaping of Trafalgar Square.

Later that month Barry told the Office of Woods that he wished to consult with Dr Reid, 'both as to the principle and the detail of the system of ventilation which may be considered most advisable' for the new Houses of Parliament. He ideally wanted an experienced engineer, rather than a theoretical scientist, to undertake the work, but Reid had pushed himself forward on the basis of his experiments in the temporary Houses, and the Office of Woods had not prevented it. Following this approach, in November, Reid requested ground plans of all the apartments in Barry's design in order that he could advise him better.[20]

At much the same time, Lees of Lambeth were summoned to attend the Board of the Office of Woods on account of their 'extremely dilatory progress' with the river wall. There, they were sacked for noncompliance with the terms of their contract and replaced by Grissell & Peto, with whom—embarrassingly—they had only just had a handover meeting about the first stage of building the superstructure on the river front, the third Palace contract, for which the latter had bid £159,718.[21] The Lee brothers blamed the hold-up on their inexperience with that particular kind of construction and the number of casualties suffered among the navvies, but Barry identified it more accurately as 'want of proper management and the non-employment of a sufficient number of hands'.[22] The Lees' incompetence had not only significantly delayed progress, but also left Grissell & Peto with having to complete their predecessor's work as well as beginning the job of creating the 7-acre foundations for the site before they could commence the visible carcass on the river front.

Their solution was the 'Barry Raft'. This was a giant concrete platform spread over the whole area to level the site and provide a stable foundation for the new building, with the architect micromanaging the pouring of the base. Barry knew exactly what he wanted, declaring: 'the concrete forming the foundations is to consist of 6 measures of gravel and sand to one of ground stone lime mixed dry and then well worked together with water and in this state teemed and thrown into the trench from a height of at least 10 ft from the present surface of the ground, the top to be levelled'.[23] Sceptics scoffed at the time, but it stood the test of time and tide and eliminated the tricky problem of the shifting quicksands and sloping site below, allowing the ground to bear the weight of

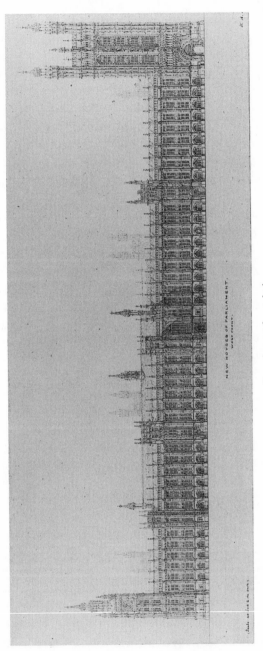

Barry's west front design

the Palace above and public expectations of it all around. The Barry Raft was of differing depth depending on the contours of the site. The House of Commons would rest on just 5 feet of concrete; the Lords 6 feet 3 inches; the Clock Tower 10 feet 1 inch because of its height; and the Victoria Tower, which needed a separate cofferdam to create a foundation trench in the floating gravel of Thorney Island in 1841, on a base 10 feet 7 inches deep—taking more time and money than originally anticipated.[24] Barry later described the conditions there as the worst he had ever known for building. Excavations today in the Palace precincts still reveal the rigid layer of concrete on which the Palace surprisingly balances.

By now the limestone from Yorkshire was starting to arrive on a regular basis at Westminster. Around five hundred tons were being shipped each month from Anston for the exterior stonework. Once quarried, using methods that had scarcely changed since Roman times, the free-stone blocks were loaded onto wheeled platforms called 'drugs', with 9-inch wide wheels, a foot and a half in diameter. Teams of eight horses then pulled each drug 2 miles over the hill from the quarry and deposited the blocks at the Chesterfield Canal storage pound at Kiveton Park from where they were loaded onto 70-foot long narrowboats at Dog Kennel's Wharf, with a capacity of 20 tons each. The barges took the stone 30 miles through Worksop to West Stockwith on the Trent, where it was transferred to 50-foot sloops plying the Humber Estuary. Then it was sailed several hundred miles down the east coast of England and up the Thames estuary, finally landing at the Millbank wharf beside the Palace where stonemasons cut and dressed the stone.[25]

On 10 February 1840 Queen Victoria married her cousin, 'dearest' Albert. The wedding took place at the Chapel Royal of St James's Palace and the bride departed from tradition by wearing a white satin dress, which set the trend for the 'white wedding' attire of British brides forever after. Victoria was utterly obsessed with her 'beautiful, angelic' new husband, not least because on their wedding night 'we did not sleep

much'.[26] One night the previous summer, after dinner at Buckingham Palace, the Prime Minister, the Queen, and her Mistress of the Robes, the Duchess of Sutherland, had fallen to talking about the Duchess's recent visit to Mount Felix in Surrey. This was a recently completed mansion near Walton-on-Thames, designed by Charles Barry, in the Italian style in 1836 for the fifth Duke of Tankerville. The Duchess considered it 'a fine house, though rather too large for the place', and Melbourne retorted, 'Mr. Barry always builds a Tower—it's exactly like the Houses of Parliament in small!' The Queen was amused.[27] Despite the joking, Barry became the Sutherlands' favourite architect. He rebuilt or remodelled all their major country houses: Trentham Hall, Staffordshire (1834–49); Dunrobin Castle, Sutherland (1845–50); and Cliveden, Berkshire (1850–51).[28] Trentham and Cliveden were Italianate; Dunrobin, Franco-Scottish Gothic. And as for Victoria, it is worth noting that Mount Felix—with its square Italian-style campanile tower and a double-height porte-cochère—looked not like the Houses of Parliament, but instead rather like a miniature version of Osborne House. Osborne, the royal family's retreat on the Isle of Wight, was built from 1845 by the building and property developer Thomas Cubitt to designs created by Prince Albert—and in it can be seen obvious, if unacknowledged, Barry-inspired architecture.

While Grissell & Peto spread the Barry Raft gradually across the river front, and with five hundred workmen on site, the Commons continued to chafe and squabble over the conditions in their temporary home. A new expert appeared on the scene at this point, namely the Cornish scientist Goldsworthy Gurney (1793–1875), chemist, engineer, and inventor of—among other things—the oxyhydrogen blowpipe, limelight, a keyboard instrument that worked by passing silk ribbons over glass, and an ammonia-powered steam carriage, which had made its first trip from London to Bath some years earlier, though proved not to be successful commercially. His most famous creation was the brilliant white Bude Light—produced by passing oxygen through an Argand oil lamp—an invention which had revolutionized the work of Trinity House, the nation's lighthouse authority. Gurney offered the Commons the chance to light their chamber with his invention for free, but instead the Exchequer had given him £100 to conduct the experiment, replacing the 280 candles with a number of Bude Lights in the ceiling, surrounded by ground glass shades to prevent heat and fumes from affecting the members.[29]

After a short time, Frederick Trench MP returned to his favourite subject. Described by a contemporary as 'a gentleman who fancies himself a man of taste', he put down a motion that the trial had gone on long enough and a return to wax candles would be 'preferable to the present forthwith'. He had long objected to the expenditure of money on 'scrambling, ill-concocted, ill-digested, inconclusive experiments' with the lighting. Many members disagreed, stating that the Bude Light made it easier to read, and the problem was that the light was almost too efficient—illuminating the motes of dust that blew up through holes in the floor when the House was ventilated from below. Mr Warburton 'found the greatest relief from the new mode of lighting, for, instead of numerous candles glaring in his face, the light was now above, and the hat formed a shade for the eyes'. A select committee deliberated; experts including Faraday were called in; they all agreed that the Bude Lights were working well, yet the vote was won by a majority of 19. A few weeks later one of the chandeliers carrying the replaced candles and their shades, weighing 6 hundredweight, fell down and seriously injured a workman. There was another debate. The Bude Lights had cost £700, but the chandeliers cost at least £500 (plus additional fancy decorations—as designed by Trench). Sir Charles Lemon MP complained that the House with the Bude Lights was striking, but by the return of the candles and their holders, 'flanked on one side with a petticoat, and on the other with an apron, the whole architectural beauty of the House had been destroyed'. Some members grumbled at being made guinea-pigs ('*corpus vile*') for the lighting of the new House of Parliament. Then the House voted again and reversed their decision of five weeks earlier.[30] The Bude Lights stayed.

Shortly after this particular scuffle, almost unnoticed, Sarah Barry, the architect's wife, laid the foundation stone of the new Palace, in a modest ceremony on 27 April 1840. This, the first stone of the superstructure, was positioned close to the site of the old Star Chamber in the Court of the Exchequer, where the tallysticks that had caused the 1834 fire had been stored. It was a modest ceremony, yet there had originally

been talk in the papers that Queen Victoria would be performing it—
The Times even reported in July that it would in fact happen the following year.[31] It seemed that no politician or official wanted to do it either.
Worry about public opinion and personal reputations may have been
the reason for this, because expenditure between 1837 and 1840 on the
preparations of the cofferdam, the masonry, the Barry Raft, and the
wharves had already reached over £150,000. The cost of additional
foundations alone on discovering more 'quicksands and springs' under
the Victoria Tower and for strengthening its underpinnings as well as
reinforcing the base of the Clock Tower had racked up £35,000.[32]
Marking the centenary of this moment in 1940, just as the Battle of
Britain was about to commence, *The Times* leader pointed out:

> For all its faults the building that was begun so secretly a hundred
> years ago is now one of the best liked and most distinctive in the world.
> To many it has come to symbolize the democratic system of government
> to which it was dedicated and which we are fighting to maintain. As we
> look up at the Houses of Parliament to-day perhaps we may be allowed
> to find a good omen for the hard task before us in the long, disheartening
> struggle of SIR CHARLES BARRY.[33]

By 1840 the Barrys and their six children were outgrowing their home,
Foley Place. This was just round the corner from the present location of
the Royal Institute of British Architects on Portland Place, of which
Barry was a founding member and whose library today holds significant
collections of his family papers and architectural plans. As a result, the
Barrys, their offspring, and their three servants moved to a more spacious mid-Georgian townhouse at 32 Great George Street in Westminster—in fact, a continuation of Bridge Street where Barry had been
born. This was not only to accommodate his family better, but also so
that he could be as close as possible to the site just a few hundred yards
away. Charles and Sarah's final child, Adelaide, was born there in 1841.
The house, like Ely Place and Foley Place before it, was rented. In fact,
Barry never built himself a home of his own, somewhat surprisingly; he
sometimes also rented second homes in south-east London, or Brighton
where he had made his name, and to which he and the family retreated
at times of crisis or illness.

Great George Street was at that time a smart residential quarter much favoured by politicians, civil engineers, and railway contractors, at one point including Morton Peto himself, and at number 23 lived and worked James Walker. Across the road from the Barry household was the original National Portrait Gallery, run by the Scharf family of topographical artists—and so this neighbourhood nicely encompassed Barry's career. These houses no longer exist, having been demolished at the beginning of the twentieth century to make way for the Whitehall Government Offices development (today occupied by HM Treasury and Cabinet Office among others)—a slightly poignant situation given that a number of Barry's own commissions involved new buildings in Whitehall. However, a vestige of the street's former self, as Barry would have known it, lives on, because today it is the location of the Institute of Chartered Surveyors, and the Institutions of Civil Engineers and Mechanical Engineers. In short, Barry was surrounded by contractors and fellow professionals in his new home. There was no getting away from the Palace now.

Thoughts turned to how the interior of the Palace should be decorated. By August 1841, Robert Peel was back in office as Prime Minister and proposed that a Fine Arts Commission be appointed to undertake this task. He was sure

> the House and the country would hear with great satisfaction, as this Commission would in no respect partake of a party or political character, and as also the new building, when completed, would comprise a part of her Majesty's ancient palace of Westminster, that his Royal Highness Prince Albert had willingly consented to become a member of such a commission, and to add to its labours the advantage, not only of his station and character, but also of his knowledge and taste in all matters connected with the promotion of the fine arts.[34]

The House was equally pleased to hear that none of the Commissioners, not even the experts, would be paid for their contributions. It also solved the problem of what to do with Prince Albert.

Sir Robert Peel

In the autumn Peel stood up in the House of Commons to inform the House that a further sum of £80,000–90,000 was needed for the new building, in relation to the work proposed by Dr Reid. 'The works connected with those buildings', he announced,

> are now advanced to such a period, that if the two Houses of Parliament shall determine that it is desirable that mode of warming and ventilating the new Houses, similar to that which has been provided for this House, should be adopted, it will be necessary that provision should at once be made for that purpose. The state of those buildings is such, that the flues and other works necessary to the carrying out of that design must be immediately provided. If these works are to be undertaken, they must, the House will perceive, be commenced without further delay.

Any modern architect, mechanical and electrical engineer, or building contractor reading that statement today would be flabbergasted. The idea that a building design could be finalized, let alone already be under construction, without its air-conditioning or heating services being fully integrated into it and costed would seem absurd, as would the confusion about who the actual client was. But the architectural profession—as a profession—was still in its infancy and project method-ologies such as those promoted today by the Royal Institute of British Architects were unheard of. Not for the first time at Westminster, Barry was having to undertake the biggest building project of the century while simultaneously developing new ways of working for the profession he championed.

The Prime Minister continued by telling the House he was minded to recommend the appointment of (yet another) select committee but—no doubt remembering how inclined certain members such as Hume and Trench were to derail attempts to move swiftly with decisions about the new building, even though they were from opposite ends of the political spectrum—he said,

> I can only express my hope and trust, that it will confine itself to the consideration of the object for which it will be nominated—that it will limit its inquiries entirely to the consideration of the proposed mode of heating and ventilating the new Houses—and that it will not extend it to anything which may cause inconvenience or interference in the progress of those works.[35]

Although Lees of Lambeth had buckled under the strain of the under-taking, Grissell & Peto's operation was not without its own problems. They got results by managing the whole of the supply chain required to provide materials for their work, including leasing the quarry at Anston, introducing innovative construction techniques, and above all, having a series of highly determined foremen in charge of operations at each of their building sites. The foreman at Westminster was George Allen, whose methods brought the firm into conflict with one of the most important skilled trades working on the Palace.

The Friendly Society of Operative Stone Masons had been founded in 1831, very much along the lines of a masonic organization. The members addressed each other at their regular meetings as 'worthy brothers' and there was a strongly mystical, religious slant to their initiation rituals. By 1838 it had nearly five thousand members—almost two-thirds of the masons in Britain at the time.[36] The secret ceremony, which all new members had to pass through, involved the reciting of the following verse by the 'Right Hand' of the President:

> Our commonwealth was like a savage land
> When the weak are slaves the Stronger bear command
> When tyrants rule with uncontrolled sway
> And degraded subjects must their will obey
> Such was our domestic lot our sufferings and our care
> Enraged our minds with madness and despair
> For when we had united and our rights obtained
> We found that only one half our rights was gain'd
> Our interests were so many and so various
> The tenor of our rights so frail and so precarious
> Had we not invented Lodges our rights to ensure
> All, All would have come to nought as it had done before
> Strangers the design of our Lodge is love and unity
> With self protection founded on the laws of equity
> And when we have our mistick rights gone through
> Our Secrets all will be disclosed to you[37]

Trades unions were still in their infancy and the fate of the Tolpuddle Martyrs in 1834 was still fresh in the popular memory, yet there had been a 'Great Meeting of the Working Classes' in New Palace Yard in 1838 when some sixteen thousand gathered to raise awareness of the People's Charter then circulating, and to hear speeches from the hustings there, which denounced—to loud cheers—how the 'waggon-loads of useless, sanguinary, and corrupt laws which disgraced the statute book were a standing memorial of the villainy and corrupt practices of the Legislature'.[38]

The following year the first Chartist petition was presented to Parliament by the Radical Birmingham MP Thomas Attwood. It comprised the signatures of 1,280,958 working men and women from 214 towns and villages, and from 500 political meetings, across the country. The six points of the original 'People's Charter' demanded a vote for every man over 21 years of age, provided they were sane and not in prison; secret ballots; the abolition of the property qualification for Members of Parliament; salaried MPs; equal-sized constituencies; and, finally, annual parliaments. When Attwood rose in the chamber to move that the Charter be printed, the MP for Colchester, Sir George Smyth, complained that he had broken the rules by making a speech on the presentation of, 'that ridiculous piece of machinery', gesturing to the immense document that had been rolled into the Commons. The Speaker, however, was indulgent of Attwood, given the public interest in the petition, and allowed him to carry on speechifying and to request that the petition be brought to the Table of the House. 'This produced loud laughter', wrote the Hansard reporter, pleased to have something novel going on to break up the monotony of his job, 'from the gigantic dimensions of the petition. The hon. Member unrolled a sufficient portion of it to enable him to place one extremity of it on the clerk's table.'[39] Another petition signed by 3.3 million people followed in 1842 and a third in 1848.

It was within this newly politicized context that the skilled and unskilled labourers on the Palace were working. There were stonemason union branches all over the country and the London one met every evening at the appropriately named Paviors' Arms, in Johnson Street, Westminster, just a few minutes' walk south of the Palace.[40] Two hundred and thirty of their members were employed by 1841 working on the superstructure of the new Houses of Parliament. Grissell & Peto's foreman, Allen, was known to many of them, and he was notorious for the methods he used to get work done on time.

On Saturday 10 September the stonemasons downed tools in protest at Allen's behaviour. On the Monday morning they stood outside the building hoping their grievances against him would be remedied. When they were not, they arrived the following day at the Westminster site, cleared up their tools and walked off, 'expressing their fixed determination not to return to work unless Mr Allen is dismissed from his employment as foreman'. Building was entirely suspended and 'not the sound of a hammer or chisel is heard in this immense range of building', *The Times* told its readers.[41] Allen's 'conduct of systematic cruelty has rendered him unfit to occupy a controling [*sic*] position among men', declared the strikers, passionately versifying as follows:

The second Chartist petition being presented in the temporary House of Commons, 1842

Shall one's despotic will
The hearts of working-men with torturing anguish fill—
Shall his relentless cruelty—his curses, d_____ms, and blasts
Embitter every working hour, make home a barren waste?[42]

Allen's alleged behaviour—besides verbally abusing them—took the following forms. He was arbitrary; refused compassionate leave for men whose relatives had died in other parts of the country; controlled which pubs they were permitted to use for their beer breaks; and he set them all to work at the speed of the fastest man, a process known as 'chasing', punishing them if they could not keep up.[43] Grissell & Peto soon posted notices on the hoarding around the building site addressed to the strikers, stating they believed the majority of masons had left work 'with reluctance and regret' and had been deceived by union officials, 'who have not honestly made known to them the proposals of their employers'. They claimed to have made strict enquiries into Allen's conduct, regarded it as unimpeachable, and refused to sack him, warning the strikers they would be welcome back on site, but that unless they decided speedily to return, their posts would be taken by others from all over the kingdom.[44] The MP for Westminster, Henry Rous, attempted to mediate but got nowhere.[45]

A week later *The Times* published a letter from Grissell & Peto in which they listed a series of rebuttals, stated that the charges made by the masons against Allen were without foundation and described how, 'we have only to regret that the tyranny of the union is such as to alarm the well-disposed workmen into a tame acquiescence with resolutions whose only tendency is to keep them unemployed'.[46]

They posted bills on the gates of their premises to reassure the public that the disruption was not serious, stating how *industrious and sober* the replacement masons they had found were. In response, the brethren produced a stinging rebuke in a reciprocal bill posting on the hoarding at Westminster:

> We do not wish to have the nomination of our superintendent, but we wish that a tyrant might not be appointed; for no man, possessed with a spark of manliness, can submit to have his feelings outraged in the manner in which Allen is constantly doing. The public will bear in mind that

we are not the first who have struck against this man's tyranny. The masons of Birmingham struck against him in 1837, and Allen, we are sorry to say, has not mended his temper, if he has in circumstances. It is not of the quantity of work required, or the rate of our wages, that we complain, but the unbearable insolence and oppression of a taskmaster, who resembles those of Pharoah; and who would reduce us to a bondage worse than that of the Egyptians.[47]

Then the 'roughers' and some of the carvers at the new Palace struck in sympathy, as well as the masons at Grissell & Peto's works at Nelson's Column and the Woolwich Dockyard.[48] Nine weeks into the action, the masons set up their own newsletter, *The Stone Masons On Strike*, to circulate news among their members across the country, and to raise funds for strike pay from sympathetic members of the public and other members.

To the delays caused by sourcing a satisfactory stone, and the Lees' inability to move quickly enough to complete the river wall, was now added this new menace to the timetable Barry had promised the Lords and Commons. In 1836 he had told them it would take six years to build them a new home. The events of 1840 and 1841 now made what was improbable, impossible. Under the leadership of its General Secretary, Thomas Shortt, the masons' union was brought to the brink of bankruptcy, yet the members remained determined. As the months passed, its fortnightly circulars revealed a steady process of radicalization and consciousness-raising as the industrial action went on. Lists of those who had 'wrought black' by breaking the strike began to be published in the newsletters to alert masons elsewhere to their fellows who had betrayed the cause, and to deter others who might have been tempted to work for Grissell & Peto in their place.

As a result of the strike, Barry stopped work on the Palace towards the end of 1841.[49] Neither the masons, nor the architect, had any idea when the strike would end, and by now he must have had a creeping sense of dread that the new Palace would be taking far, far, longer to complete than he had originally predicted.

6

A Very Heavy Expence

November 1841 to December 1843

O N THE EVENING of Friday 5 November (not the most auspicious date in the parliamentary calendar) a public meeting was held at the Crown and Anchor Inn where around three thousand five hundred gathered, 'crammed to suffocation' to support the strikers. They heard how the masons at Grissell & Peto's other major works in London were in fellowship with them, 'against the aggressions and sordid inhumanity of G. and P. their late employers, who persist in the retention of Allen in their employment'.

Thomas Wakley, the Radical MP for Finsbury turned up to tell them, 'in his opinion Allen was more fit to occupy a felons' cell than have the control of honest and industrious men'. He also declared—amidst much cheering—he thought it ironic that 'the spot from whence originated all the social evils of society was the spot the masons had so high-mindedly struck against, but before they could hope for any permanent redress, they must obtain admission within the pale of the British constitution'.

STRIKE

AT THE NEW

HOUSES OF PARLIAMENT.

Notice to the Public!

We, the Masons lately employed at the above works, having observed in the public papers of the Metropolis repeated attacks upon our character, relative to our recent strike, we therefore considered it our duty to defend ourselves through the same channel we were attacked; but to our surprise we found such channels only open to one side of the question, which must at once convince a discerning public that our opponents' position cannot be maintained by fair and just means. In consequence of a letter having appeared in the "Times" of Monday the 4th instant, signed Messrs Grissell and Peto, we felt ourselves called upon to answer the same through the medium of the same journal, and therefore sent the following letter, which was refused insertion, and which has also been refused by several of the daily press :—

(TO THE EDITOR OF THE TIMES.)

SIR,

A LETTER having appeared in the *Times* of this day, signed MESSRS. GRISSELL & PETO, stating that the charges made by the Masons lately employed at the New Houses of Parliament, against Mr. Allen, their foreman, are without the slightest foundation, and that the secession of the workmen has not originated in any oppression on the part of their foreman, we trust in your sense of justice to give insertion to the following reply in vindication of our rights as men, and to substantiate our charges:—

It would take up too much of your valuable space to enter *seriatim* into a refutation of their refutations; but, suffice it to say, that we regard them as mere glosses and evasions. Allen himself has not denied our charges, and Messrs. Grissell & Peto have merely made an attempt to shift the question, and to throw the blame upon what they are pleased to term our idleness and inexperience. This charge comes with an ill grace from them, after having posted bills on their own gates, declaring us to be sober and industrious.

We would also beg to remind Messrs. Grissell & Peto that they themselves virtually admitted the truth of our charges against Allen, for when we made a complaint to them on a former occasion they promised that Allen should alter his conduct. He did alter it. But how! He merely changed from one species of tyranny to another. He adopted the system of encouraging what they are pleased to term *chasing*, whereby one man who, might be gifted with greater physical ability than another, could be excited to do more work than his companions; his performance is then made a standard for the quantity of labour *demanded* from all the rest, who are bullied and abused if unable to come up to this mark.

We do not wish to have the nomination of our superintendent, but a spark of manliness, can submit to have his feelings outraged in the manner which Allen is constantly doing. The public will bear in mind that we are not the first who have struck against this man's tyranny. The Masons of Birmingham struck against him in 1837, and Allen, we are sorry to say, has not mended in temper, if he has in circumstances.

In conclusion, we beg to reiterate our charges,—we could add to them, were we disposed to do so, and are prepared to prove them by the evidence of the sufferers and eye-witnesses of his tyranny. Instead of shrinking from them, we court public enquiry and investigation into them; we challenge it, and are ready at any convenient time and place to meet it.

It is not of the quantity of work required, or the rate of our wages, that we complain, but of the unbearable insolence and oppression of a taskmaster, who resembles those of Pharoah; and who would reduce us to a bondage worse than that of the Egyptians; and because we complain of it, is it to be said—"Go to, ye are idle!"

We have all along separated our employers from the tyrannical foreman, for we believed that the conduct of the latter was not tolerated by them. We are therefore surprised and sorry to observe that they have now made common cause with him, and identified themselves with him. But they cannot justly constitute themselves arbitrators in their own case, any more than we do ours. All we want (and surely we do not ask too much) is that a more civil man than Allen be appointed as our superintendant, and in the mean time rest our cause upon the candid and impartial consideration of the public.

FROM THE OPERATIVE MASONS.

PAVIERS' ARMS, WESTMINSTER.

This has been thought unfit to appear in the "liberty loving" and impartial daily press of the metropolis. But mark their honesty: an article appeared in the columns of the *Times* of last week, containing the greatest amount of unprincipled falsehoods in so short a space it was ever our misfortune to behold. Mr. Jackson, of Pimlico, (to whom the said article principally alluded) was so disgusted with its audacious falsehoods, that he immediately contradicted it in the same Journal the following day, but nevertheless, it appeared in almost all the metropolitan press, both daily and weekly, although it must have been obvious to them all that they were promulgating the grossest falsehoods. Under these circumstances we have been forced to the alternative of placards, by which means we beg to state to Messrs. Grissell & Peto and the Public that we struck against a system the most degrading to the human character in existence. We have maintained our position hitherto peacefully and manfully; and however far they may have recourse to error and mystification—however far they try to persuade the public and us that injuries are not injuries, we have felt the lash, and have withdrawn from beneath its excruciating inflictions; and when they are prepared to remove the slave driver, then, and not till then, are we prepared to resume our employment. Resting our cause with an impartial public, we subscribe ourselves

Your humble Servants,

THE MASONS,

Lately employed at the New Houses of Parliament.

THOMAS CARTER, *Sec.*

SALISBURY & BATEMAN, Printers.

Poster publicizing the stonemason's strike

Wakley, a surgeon by profession (and founder of *The Lancet*) was a passionate supporter of the Tolpuddle Martyrs and Chartism. He donated £10 to the strike fund, and then swept grandly out of the meeting, in a performance which would not have disgraced Dickens's Mr Gregsbury.[1] On 8 November Lord Lincoln, the new First Commissioner of Woods and Forests, had an audience with some of the strikers' representatives. He had no intention of interfering in the strike and regarded trade unions as 'prodigious evils, calculated seriously to affect the wellbeing of society', to which the masons replied: 'Is it wrong for men to unite for the purpose of resisting the unnatural inroads of inhumanity?' Allen himself felt compelled to respond to the union's claims in *The Times* after the masons gave a letter to Lincoln with a list of complaints against him.[2] By December Grissell & Peto claimed that the numbers of masons were back up to strength on all three sites, the places of the striking workers having been supplied by non-unionized ones, while the strikers continued in their assertions that the strike was holding steady and no work was being undertaken.[3]

At this point, tragedy struck. Allen identified the bodies of three masons, among eight people killed in a railway accident—a fresh form of popular peril—on Christmas Eve when a train on the new Great Western Railway ploughed into a landslide at Sonning Hill near Reading. This was the earliest major railway accident in the UK and led to improvements to the carriage of third-class passengers.[4] But Grissell & Peto had other public relations matters to attend to. The King of Prussia, Friedrich Wilhelm IV, visited the site of the new Houses of Parliament on 24 January 1842. Accompanied by Lincoln, with Thomas Grissell and Morton Peto on hand desperately hoping there would be no mention of the strike, Barry showed the King his groundplan and elevations of the building, and also the plaster, wire, and mica model illustrating how the Palace would look once complete. The King was fascinated by the maquette. Barry had shown Victoria one in 1836 and others were regularly pressed into use by him to enable illustrious personages to grasp the magnitude of the undertaking. They were made by the premier architectural model maker, James Mabey, and today some survive in the Victoria and Albert Museum and the Parliamentary Estates Directorate. Together Barry and the King walked along the line of the eastern frontage, past the vast piles of stone, cement, and mortar which stretched along the site, where 'His Majesty frequently gave utterance to his feelings of astonishment and admiration at the magnitude of the undertaking.' Afterwards Barry accompanied the King and his entourage out through Westminster Hall, to the Prussians' delight and the curiosity of the barristers and judges who came out to watch the very grand visitor from the adjoining law courts.[5] The following day Friedrich Wilhelm stood as godfather at the christening of Victoria and Albert's first son, the future Edward VII, at St George's Chapel, Windsor. This was just the first of a series of visits by European royalty, for whom going to see the growing Palace fast became a much sought-after stop on their London itinerary. In February their Serene Highnesses, Princes Ferdinand, Augustus, and Leopold—Victoria and Albert's uncle and cousins—in town for a family wedding, took a tour.[6] It was a short but exciting trip by royal train to Paddington, and then by carriage across the parks to Westminster. Yet more Saxe-Coburg-Gotha relatives paid a visit to the building site in the summer, then on to see the celebrity chef, Alexis Soyer, and the state-of-the-art kitchens designed for him by Barry at the Reform Club before heading back to Buckingham Palace and Windsor.[7]

Throughout the first half of 1842, conflict was going on at Westminster on two fronts. Both Houses held anguished debates about the country's recent humiliations in the first Afghan War, while in building their new debating chambers the battle between the workers and their employers grew ever more acrimonious. By now thoroughly militant, the union told its members at the start of March that, despite the fine weather, 'comparatively speaking, little, very little progress is perceivable at the Houses of Parliament', with only 'three out of the two hundred and thirty who turned out from the building, that have betrayed us, during the long period of twenty four weeks'.[8] Its Brethren were

> struggling in an uphill fight against the combined efforts of a class-erected government, a class chosen legislature, and an ungenerous, an unfeeling, and rapacious host of indolent capitalists—men professing the precepts of Christianity, while practising the decrees of his Satanic majesty. At the Houses of Parliament, notwithstanding the report of the 'Surveyor, Engineer, and Architect', that 'the works of this splendid

pile are now in active progress' little, very little, is perceivable of the progress made since our members left and on Saturday night several of their most efficient hands, from about Dundee, left the works.[9]

In April it was reporting that only 'a few stones have been fixed, but those are chiefly coats of arms, and consequently prepared by the roughers and carvers in the employ of John Thomas. The Monument (of inhumanity) and disgrace to Grissell & Peto presents a still and death-like appearance. The saying respecting Solomon's temple is strictly applicable: "the sound of a (Mason's) hammer is not to be heard".' It was claimed that 150 new non-union masons were brought in, but their work was substandard and, 'they have been several nights seen engaged in taking down work which the architect has condemned'.[10]

It was, the union newsletter declared, a battle of 'moral welfare' and 'the most severe contest of Right v. Might on record... and the only one that has ever taken place in which pounds, shillings and pence have not been the principal matter in dispute'.[11] Yet in spite of this confident tone, by mid-May the strikers were having to forgo their strike pay on account of 'the embarrassed state' of the union's funds. In fact, the strike virtually ruined the union and it took years to recover its finances. Ultimately, all the masons who had struck found jobs elsewhere and in the meantime those brought in to replace them—'blacks' as they were ever after called—carried on the work without a drop in quality. For those members who had betrayed the union, however, the effects were long lasting. Elijah Philcock of Wolverhampton, 'the first traitor from the men that struck at the New Houses of Parliament', was named and shamed for years afterwards in blacklists, along with several hundred other men who had continued to work at the Palace of Westminster, Nelson's Column, and the Woolwich Dockyard from afar afield as Bristol, Bradford, Devon, Hexham, Wales, and Scotland.[12]

At the time he won the competition, Barry already had an excellently organized and efficiently run office with assistants and pupils. To these he added a 'superior clerk' (a Victorian project manager) and another assistant, who between them produced the working drawings from Barry's originals required for the new Palace. Towards the end of 1839, three 'practical clerks' were added to the firm, but were based on site at Westminster to oversee the works, taking responsibility for a third of the building each, while the Superior Clerk visited at least once a day to inspect progress and keep in touch with Grissell & Peto. Once the river front started to go up, two more pupils were taken on, including Barry's son Charles, aged 17 and destined for a career in architecture himself.[13]

Working alongside Charles junior in Barry's office was a young draftsman of much the same age called Octavius Moulton-Barrett (1824–1910), whose elder sister is much better known to posterity. Octavius was 18 years younger than Elizabeth, known as 'Ba' to the family: he the youngest, she the eldest of 12 children of a wealthy Jamaican plantation owner with a fashionable townhouse—50 Wimpole Street—in Marylebone. In the popular imagination, the story of the Barretts of Wimpole Street has become a byword for the stifling, tyrannical paternalism of the Victorian age, and yet the reality was somewhat different. Elizabeth Moulton-Barrett suffered from crippling ill health from childhood—variously spinal complaints and lung disease—which confined her on occasions (though not constantly) to a daybed in her room from where she achieved fame as a poet, critic, and translator. In the early 1840s she had recovered somewhat and had a lively correspondence with literary figures in Europe and America, as well as finding companionship with her spaniel, Flush, given to her in 1841 at the height of her mourning for another brother, who had died in a sailing accident the year before. Her many works at this time included *The Cry of the Children* in 1843, a poem in support of Lord Shaftesbury's Ten-Hours Bill amendment going through Parliament at the time, and intended to restrict the working hours of children in factories and mines. From 1842 onwards, Ba had admired from afar the work of a poet, Robert Browning, six years her junior, considering it 'undubitable genius', and describing in print his poetic heart to be like a blood-tinctured pomegranate despite never having met him. In January 1845 he plucked up courage to write to her in thanks for her reviews of his work and this led to a first meeting five months later followed by a passionate correspondence and over 90 visits to her divan in Wimpole Street before they decided to get married in secret. Precipitated by her father's refusal to let her visit Italy for her health, a mild winter allowed her early in 1846 to put on a cloak and walk down the stairs unaided to the living room. In strictest secrecy, she and Browning were married in September that year, and famously 'eloped' to the Continent with her maid Wilson and Flush, where they spent the rest of their lives in Italy, supported by her investments and their joint income from poetry following her father's disinheritance. Her sisters were sympathetic, but her brothers—including Octavius—were not, regarding their new brother-in-law as a rather common gold-digger. Expecting opposition only from her father, this shocked and distressed the new Mrs Barrett-Browning.[14] So throughout all this romantic escapade, Octavius had continued to work on the Palace of Westminster, while the gossip and scandal swirled around the family. His employer's reaction is not recorded.

A number of subsequent employees of Barry's office also became well known in their own right. On the payroll were not only Charles junior and his younger brother, Edward, (who also joined when he was 17), but others including John Gibson, later winner of the RIBA Gold Medal for Architecture; Alfred Meeson, his confidential assistant, and structural engineer of the Alexandra Palace and the Royal Albert Hall; and Julius Chatwin who founded an architectural dynasty that went on to reshape Victorian Birmingham. In 1847 Charles junior left his father's practice and set up in business with his father's first Superior Clerk, Robert Richardson Banks. They in turn employed Aston Webb as a pupil in their own firm, and between 1912 and 1914 Webb created Admiralty Arch and, at the opposite end of The Mall, one of the major ceremonial boulevards of London, the famous eastern balcony façade of Buckingham Palace, its current appearance.[15] Barry's office and the new Houses of Parliament bred a whole dynasty of Victorian architects who collectively reshaped the face of London and designed many of its most famous nineteenth- and early twentieth-century buildings, while his youngest son, John Wolfe Barry, became a distinguished civil engineer and was responsible for that other icon of London, Tower Bridge.

Despite having such an active and talented office at his disposal, Barry was a hands-on architect. Nor could he resist constantly refining his designs

with his 'itching pencil' until he got just the effect he wanted.[16] This had
begun as early as 1836 when the estimate drawings were being put together
and the groundplan of the Palace changed markedly when the main axis
of the building shifted westwards to run parallel to the river and not to the
walls of Westminster Hall, whose footprint inclined eastwards towards the
Thames. In this he had been encouraged and supported by the politicians
who had selected him. But his anxiety for perfection, coupled with a fertile
imagination producing a constant flow of solutions to the complexity of
the site, and the sense that an architect was an artist continually responding
to creative challenges in the creation of a new building, had led him over
the following years to tweak his designs so much that in some parts of the
Palace—though his alterations improved it—they also quite seriously devi-
ated from the approved and costed plans which the members had in their
heads. The most radical diversion from what the MPs and Peers thought
they were going to get occurred in or shortly after 1840, when Barry
decided on his own initiative to change the royal processional route into
the House of Lords at State Opening. His 1836 plan had the monarch
enter the Palace through the Sovereign's entrance under the King's—later
Victoria—Tower then directly up a giant three-tiered staircase straight
into a grand robing room behind the throne at the southern end of the
chamber. Barry's alteration—abandoning the profligate use of space in his
1836 scheme—turned the route into a short staircase of 36 untiered steps
at a right-angle to its original position, with a lobby (now the Norman
Porch) leading to the Robing Room and then into a giant hall known as the
Royal Gallery, and from there into the Lords chamber behind the throne.
In all this, Barry was taking a gamble that the Lords would acquiesce in his
changes, or simply not notice.

Having sneered at the Eglinton Tournament three years previously, by
1842 Victoria had undergone a transformation in her views of chivalric
spectacle. So much so, in fact, that in the spring of that year she was
planning a *Bal Costumé* to which, 'we have settled to go as Edward
IIIrd & Queen Philippa, & there is such trouble in getting the costumes

correct'.[17] In early May the costumes were ready, and Victoria declared herself most satisfied with her 'really very handsome' fancy-dress outfit.[18] The date of the ball was set for 12 May, and Victoria recalled that night how that morning she

> Went with Albert to look at the arrangement of the rooms for our great 'Bal Costumé',—which were progressing well, but are far from being finished yet. Tried on my costume once more...the Throne Room, which is really quite beautiful, the alcove & throne, all hung with dark blue cloth with gold crown & Garter printed all over the hangings...The procession walking up, slowly, 2 by 2, hand in hand, & bowing at the foot of the Throne, had a very fine effect. After this, our 'Cortège' was formed, which had (I hear since) a beautiful effect, as also the 'Coup d'Oeuil' of our group. We then went into the other room, where some of the Quadrilles were danced, returning afterwards to the Throne Room & the Throne, & I saw Mme Brunow & her Party dance a Mazurka. After we had been to the Closet, to rearrange my crown, we went to supper & then saw 2 Reels danced in the Ball Room, & I danced a Quadrille with George, I own, with some difficulty, on account of my heals. We did not return again to the Throne Room, & left the Rooms at ¼ to 3. Nothing could have gone better, than the whole did, &, it was a truly splendid spectacle.[19]

The change in thinking had been wrought by Prince Albert himself—her very own knight-errant—whose schooling and appreciation of European medieval history was far deeper than hers.[20] Albert was enjoying leading the work of the Fine Arts Commission of which he had been appointed chair in 1841, aided and abetted by Charles Eastlake as secretary, Barry's erstwhile acquaintance from his Grand Tour days. Barry however had been allowed only a role as an adviser, rather than a full member of the commission: a galling and worrying development. The Prince was deeply absorbed in plans for the painting and sculpture to decorate the new Palace, and for the cartoon competitions to decide on subjects and artists. Part of Barry's job was to brief him on progress with the building and on the spaces suitable for wall paintings, while at the same time trying to ensure that his own vision for the Palace's decoration was not compromised by the choices of the Commission over which he had little or no control.

All the activity at the Palace influenced Victoria and Albert's choice of Edward III and Queen Philippa at their fancy-dress Ball. Not only were those medieval monarchs archetypal royal lovers, but St Stephen's Chapel at Westminster had been constructed by Edward III as a cele-bration of his own dynastic ambitions. Now, with the ruins of the old House of Commons—once that very same chapel—cleared away by Barry in 1837, a new building was rising in its place, on exactly the same footprint and with the same dimensions—St Stephen's *Hall* (as it now was)—a splendid route from Barry's remodelled south end of Westmin-ster Hall to the octagonal Central Hall, planned as the crossroads of the new Houses of Parliament, and altered from Barry's original square groundplan. St Stephen's Hall, thought Barry, was one of many loca-tions where the Fine Arts Commission could consider painted decora-tions for the new Palace.

Barry had made clear to MPs the year before how he would have liked the fine art scheme of the Palace to proceed. 'It is my object, as an architect', he told them, 'to give the most striking effect to the building as a whole, and I think that the effect of architecture can in no way be so highly enhanced as by the arts of painting and sculpture.' Fresco had been proposed for the interior of his Reform Club, but had not yet been executed and he thought it would be difficult to find British or Irish artists capable of handling it 'owing to the want of experience with reference to that kind of painting in this country'.[21] Oil was also a pos-sibility, but overall he 'should prefer having it upon the wall itself, as it would then become an integral part of the building', and there was a limit to the size of wall a canvas could cover. If time and encourage-ment were given to artists to undertake the development of unfamiliar techniques, 'I see no reason', he said, 'why the efforts of our own artists should not equal those of any other country.' Given the purpose of the Palace and its state role, the subjects most applicable would be those which referred to famous events in British history and should 'most decidedly' not be allegorical. The purpose should be both decorative and celebratory, and the walls should not all be decorated at the same time: each successive generation should have the opportunity of adding its own persons and events to the scheme. The walls of Westminster Hall could be experimented upon, he thought, to give the effect of tapestry, or several of the corridors off the Central Lobby he had designed. Best of all he thought, would be utilizing St Stephen's Hall, better than any other location. One Member enquired as to whether he thought the Peasants' Revolt a good subject: clearly a trap. 'Any leading event in English history would be a good subject', responded Barry, mildly. There was another piquant exchange as well:

> 'Have you seen any of Mr Pugin's decorations?'
> 'Not to any extent, with exception, perhaps of Alton Towers.'
> 'Do you think the kind of decoration he has there applied ... is applicable to your style of architecture?'
> 'His decorations there are quite applicable to the style of architecture of the new Houses of Parliament,' replied Barry, drily.[22]

Free-standing monumental sculpture could also be employed 'with very great effect', he thought, but not reliefs, which was a Continental Gothic style, and he was 'not quite sure that I altogether approve' of the effect of coloured statues of the kind which Mr Pugin had introduced at Alton Towers.[23]

Albert, who had studied art history at Bonn University, was absolutely determined that the Palace should contain a monumental series of narrative wall paintings based on his knowledge of a new art movement gaining popularity across Europe, especially Germany.[24] Fresco, requiring paint to be applied directly onto a wet coat of plaster, was a highly specialist art little used in Britain because of the damp climate. Instead, Albert knew of a new technique using 'waterglass' (sodium silicate) which the Nazarenes—a sort of German Pre-Raphaelite movement—had used to stabilize such works in northern climes. Yet the decision to adopt it was to prove a terrible headache right into the twenty-first century when the techniques used proved unsuitable to the climate and also baffled later generations seeking to restore them. Royal fingerprints can thus be found all over the Palace, even today.

Barry's fertile imagination continued to run riot over the remnants of the old Palace as well. His plans for Westminster Hall were startling, despite having ruled out the possibility—suggested by one MP—of transferring all the burial monuments in Westminster Abbey and St Paul's there:

In the event of the law courts being removed, which is quite essential to the treatment of Westminster Hall as a whole, I should say that the Hall might be appropriated to the reception of statues of eminent public men of past times, to be arranged on each side, and at a short distance from the walls, and that they should be placed with reference to the ribs of the roof: that is, a statue might be place into sections or compartments, and so fitted for the reception of a distinct subject of painting. I merely mention this as an instance of the mode of applying the two arts with reference to architectural arrangement...Single statues I think would be most applicable in the situations which I have mentioned. With reference to further effect in Westminster Hall, if the proposed arrangements of painting and sculpture were adopted in connexion with a display of armorial bearings and ancient armour on the sides and above the windows, trophies and banners &c suspended from the roof, ornamental glass, and tessellated pavement and decorative painting, the whole would have a peculiarly striking appearance, and tend to awaken old and interesting associations connected with our national history.[25]

These thoughts seem in autumn 1842 to have inspired one of the rare holidays which Charles Barry took during his life, to the Kingdom of Bavaria. He enjoyed the mountains just as much as he had in the Alps 25 years before, and toured Munich, Regensburg, Nuremburg, and Constanz—sketching as he went. But he also took the opportunity to visit the newly opened Valhalla, perched on a cliff above the Danube at Regensburg.[26] This neoclassical temple, honouring the achievements of ethnic Germans since ancient times, contained a hall full of statues and plaques commemorating rulers, politicians, men of letters, artists, and scientists—exactly the sort of thing Barry had envisaged for Westminster. Happily, his plans for Westminster Hall were not executed, but instead a Valhalla of sorts was created by Barry in St Stephen's Hall, which during his lifetime was lined with monumental sculptures of Walpole, Pitt the Younger, Fox, and other notable parliamentarians. In the twentieth century, the *Building of Britain* murals completed the national celebration.

At much the same time that Barry's head was full of Bavarian glories, the papers were reporting that the new masons were receiving excellent wages and that Allen had been so impressed he wanted to fix their contracts for four years, but they refused to be bound for that time.[27] As for the stone itself, at its height between 1841 and 1844, around 500 tons of magnesian limestone was arriving at Westminster each month for loading up onto the wharfs at Millbank—some 456,495 cubic feet of it in total.[28] Just as Christmas 1842 approached, it was announced that the contract for the next phase of 'this national and truly magnificent work' had been awarded to Grissell & Peto who swept all before them. This contract, in the view of journalists, was the most important which had been entered into. Visible at last above ground, the public now began to grasp fully what the building promised, vastly helped by a new newspaper which burst onto the scene in that year. The *Illustrated London News* had launched in May, and timed its first edition to coincide with Victoria and Albert's *Bal Costumé* at Buckingham Palace. After a shaky start, its combination of royal gossip, sensational stories, and pictures—all for the price of a 6*d.*—ensured sales of 60,000 by the end of its first year. Barry immediately saw its potential as a public-relations tool if he could get the editor on side.

Trouble, however, was brewing for him in the Upper House. He had told the select committee of 1841 that the debating chambers of both Houses would be ready, 'I should say, within three or four years'.[29] The Lords had thus become convinced they would be in by 1844. Accordingly, the Marquess of Clanricarde asked a puzzled question in the Lords in February 1843 about a rumour that progress on the Lords chamber was not being addressed with the requisite speed in order 'to hasten the completion of certain ornamental parts of the building—he alluded particularly to the tower'. He by no means objected to those ornamental parts, but he thought that 'for no reason should one hour's delay be allowed in giving to their Lordships all necessary accommodation in their place of meeting', and if he didn't get a satisfactory answer he would request a select committee look into the matter. In response, he and the other Peers were informed that, 'as the Victoria Tower was the heaviest part...and there was, in the opinion of the architect, a probability of its settling, it was therefore, not deemed desirable that the rest of the building should be carried on until a certain portion of the Tower was erected'.

They were reassured that the Lords would be completed 'considerably before' the House of Commons and that their new home would be ready around 1845. Lord Brougham continued with his complaints of earlier years that the Tower was to be added 'for the sake of pure ornament'. There was 'not an atom of use connected with it' and it was a prime 'specimen of the bad gothic taste of the nineteenth century'. The necessity of proceeding, as was at first arranged, should be urged on Mr Barry. Resentment against the Commons was also uppermost in his mind; they 'had never been better off for accommodation than at present' (though he hadn't crossed the threshold of that place since he became Lord Chancellor). Lord Duncannon, First Commissioner of Works before and after the fire, considered that the appointment of a committee would be 'most satisfactory':

> It was now eight years since the building was commenced, and the architect stated at the time of the contract that within seven years the work would be sufficiently advanced to enable their Lordships to have all the accommodation necessary. Some two or three years ago he asked when it was likely that the building would be sufficiently advanced to enable their Lordships to sit in their own House, and was told by the Session of 1844.

The Peers noted that, 'the greatest inconvenience was felt by those of their Lordships who sat from ten o'clock till half-past four o'clock. The alternate heat and cold of the place made it at one time a cold bath, and at another a vapour bath.' There was no need to hurry in rehousing the Commons, 'the ventilation there was excellent, and the temperature agreeable'. So, a committee was appointed to inquire into progress.[30] A few weeks later, it reported that

> it was expedient that no delay should take place in preparing the new House of Lords beyond what was absolutely necessary for the safety of the work; that the architect should be directed so to conduct the works as to complete the new House, and fit it for their Lordships' reception, by the commencement of the Session of 1844; that if the architect apprehended any injurious consequence to the building from the course thus recommended, he should report the same to the House; that it did not

appear to the committee to be advisable that any expense should be incurred by an attempt to improve the present House.[31]

Perhaps provoked by this exchange, or maybe engineered by Barry himself, immediately after a meeting of the Fine Arts Commission on 7 April 1843, Prince Albert paid a late afternoon visit to the Palace, to inspect progress for himself.[32] Back in the Lords, three days later, Brougham returned to his favourite topic of the waste of money on the Victoria Tower which he had managed to convince himself had never been in Barry's original plan:

> This erection…must be a very heavy expence, and likewise a very heavy weight on the ground it was to stand on; and, if it should ever be erected as proposed in the plans he had seen, nothing, he would venture to say, was ever put upon the ground so contrary to good taste, or more completely devoid of all taste…Many persons whom he had seen, who were not at all unfavourably inclined to the architect, held up their hands in amazement at the plan with this tall tower on one side, and the smaller one on the other.

Duncannon told him in response that he was mistaken on all counts, and 'what his noble Friend meant by the small tower was the centre one, which was intended for the purpose of ventilation, and had been added since the original plan was drawn'.[33] Of ventilation they were to hear more shortly.

The increasing public appetite for a flavour of the new Palace's interior was briefly satisfied at the start of June. 'Much interest was excited', the readers of *The Observer* were informed, by the works to install the prize designs for the frescos to be exhibited in Westminster Hall. These arrived on 1 June 1843, and were carried into the boarded off space to much curiosity. The cartoons were in chalk or charcoal—without colour—and the lifesize subjects were to be from British history, Shakespeare, Milton or Spenser.[34] Through the week the work continued to hang them, this 'national trial' of artists occupying the whole space of the Hall except for a narrow passageway left for those wanting to get to and from the Law Courts.[35]

Prince Albert paid another visit to see the completed installation of the designs before the public was let in, reporting back to his wife that,

'Many doubted the possibility of any drawings being executed here, therefore he was much pleased to see that 50 drawings had been sent out & 10 very fine ones amongst them. The others were not at all good.'[36] The Queen herself visited the exhibition at the end of the month:

> At about 1, we went to Westminster Hall, where the cartoons, I mentioned before, are exhibited. The Gentlemen of the Commission were all there, including Ld Melbourne who I thought was looking very well, particularly with his hat on, but he has still rather a vacant look, which changes the expression of his face. The Exhibition is a very interesting one, & there are many very clever drawings, almost all by persons one knows nothing of. The finest, are, the 1rst landing of Julius Caesar & Caractacus, these have got the 1rst prizes. I am proud to think that it is chiefly, if not entirely, owing to my beloved Albert, that this Exhibition has taken place.[37]

Of the cartoons a number stood out. A hasty but powerful rendition of *St George after the death of the Dragon* was by Richard Dadd, who in August that year—even while his artwork was on display—slew his own father while suffering from voices in his head, which he believed came from

The exhibition of fresco designs in Westminster Hall, 1843

125

the Egyptian god, Osiris. Dadd was confined to Bedlam for the rest of his life.[38] Edward Armitage's *Julius Caesar's First Invasion of Britain* won one of the three £300 prizes for the best cartoon. Coincidentally his entry was lucky number 64, just as Barry's had been in 1835. Armitage, aged just 26, went on to win a £200 premium for his cartoon *The Spirit of Religion* in 1845 and a £500 first-prize premium for his meticulously researched oil painting *The Battle of Meanee* in 1847, which Queen Victoria purchased for £400 and is now in the Royal Collection.[39]

A month after her first visit, Victoria went again to Westminster. It was becoming quite the royal entertainment:

> At 1, we went with our Suite to the new Houses of Parliament, where Uncle & Clèm met us. I was, & so were they, in the greatest admiration, of the grandeur, magnificence & good taste of the whole. Mr Barry met us there. Parts, are in a very forward state, & the carving of the stone is quite beautiful. All the Saxon Kings & their wives are sculptured in stone, & the arms, &c wonderfully carried out. We went all over the building & had all the details shown to us. The sculpture of the interior is equally fine. On one side are figures of all the Kings, beginning with William the Conqueror, the names carved under each.

But, she noted: 'We then visited the Houses of Lords & Commons now in use, which are certainly very inadequate.'[40] Even the Queen had heard of the chafing of the members to move into their new homes.

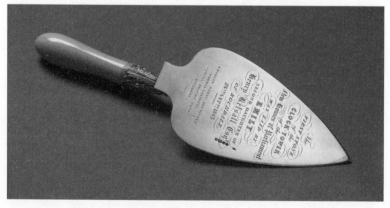

Commemorative silver trowel used to lay the first stone of the Clock Tower

The first stone of the Clock Tower was laid in September 1843 with a dainty silver trowel with an ivory handle, by Emily Kelsall, sister-in-law of Morton Peto.[41] It would be another 25 years before the tower, clock, and bells were all working together as they should. The cartoon exhibition closed at the beginning of that month, but the exhibition structures were retained because Albert and the Fine Art Commissioners were already planning another competition for 1844 to test artists' fresco technique against their cartoons.[42] There followed another flurry of high-profile visitors to the building site in the autumn. The recently deposed Spanish Regent, General Espartero, came to visit with his wife, and was received by Eastlake and Barry; while on 2 October 1843 Grand Duke Mikael of Russia paid a visit and met with Barry, occupied a considerable time in minutely inspecting the entire works which he had only previously seen on paper, ascended the scaffold, and walked along it very pleased with the heraldic ornaments already completed, which surrounded the west front of the building. The viewing and explanation by Barry took two hours, after which the Duke scurried through Westminster Hall and the temporary Houses, arriving late for his visit to the Surrey Zoological Gardens and missing feeding time.[43]

For the architect this was all a horrible distraction. The Palace lay, like a great stone crocodile along the bank of the Thames, gobbling up money, time, and patience in equal measure. Money continued to be poured into the hole in the ground at Westminster: almost £300,000 from 1840 to 1844, and the number of men working on the building had risen from under 200 to nearly 800 in the same period. With time pressing, the Lords becoming fractious, and the interior of their chamber not even begun, Barry was under tremendous pressure to produce what he had promised the Peers despite all the delays and complications. But a new, more dangerous phase of the struggle was about to begin.

III

AIR
1844–1852

And the posts of the door moved at the voice of him that
cried, and the house was filled with smoke.

Isaiah 6:4

7

A Regular Fix

1844

THERE THEN FOLLOWED one of the worst years of Barry's life, and to understand what went on at this time is to understand better his later actions towards Pugin. He had assured the Lords that if their chamber received a wooden instead of plaster ceiling and temporary fittings then they would be able to move in during 1844. Early in March that year the ever-competitive peers were informed that the walls of their new chamber had grown a further 25 feet while the Commons was only 9 feet further along. In just two months' time, they were promised, the roof would be on and the architect had undertaken that it would be ready for the next session, albeit with temporary interior fittings. Some of the Lords felt this would incur even more cost and delay, and queried why matters could not be completed even in the current session, for 'nothing could be more simple', and they 'saw no reason why the building should not be rapidly completed, at all events for all practical purposes'. The Lords' committee on the progress of the building was resurrected to find out more.[1]

Expecting trouble over the delays, Barry attended the committee hearing on 21 March prepared to answer the attack.[2] He offered timescales and costings for a temporary fit-out for the Lords chamber if that

131

was really what the Peers wanted, and batted away fairly successfully some challenges about the design of the Victoria Gallery (today the Royal Gallery) and whether its huge space would make sittings draughty for their Lordships next door. Without drawings in front of them for how a quick and dirty fit-out might look, the Peers asked Barry to return after Easter to show them.

On 20 April Prince Albert and five of the Fine Arts Commissioners paid a two-hour formal visit to the Palace to view progress and inspect the likely locations for wall paintings and sculpture. They first took in the river terrace and the carvings on the elevation there, and then walked round to the Victoria Tower which had reached 30 feet in height, 'the majestic beauty of which called forth the admiration of the Prince', reported *The Times*. They admired the Victoria Gallery as a likely location for some murals, Albert paying close attention to Barry's explanations. Then they mounted some scaffolding and peered down into the Lords chamber—its walls were currently 60 feet high and the windows fixed. Albert heard how the lower parts were to be panelled and carved in wood, while the upper parts were to be in Caen stone. He even asked one of the masons to stand in a completed stone niche to demonstrate how the sculpture might look, and was delighted with the effect. He admired the central lobby, and the library and committee rooms, and noted the 700 men constantly at work on site. The party went on to the model rooms of Messrs Thomas and Dighton, inspected the one for the interior of the Lords, and then on to Barry's site office (today the Parliamentary Sports and Social Club) where details and drawings were laid before the Prince. Finally the Prince 'expressed his extreme gratification' at progress and the Commissioners were similarly warm about 'the activity which had been displayed, and the talent which had been brought into requisition'.[3]

Buoyed up by the royal visit and not scenting danger, Barry returned to the Lords on 26 April to face the committee. There the questioning took an unexpected and altogether more hostile turn. Lord Sudeley had appeared before them earlier that day. This was none other than the ennobled Charles Hanbury-Tracy, Chair of the original competition judges in 1835. Having staunchly supported the panel's choice of winner in 1836 in the face of criticism from all quarters, he was now dismayed to discover from a plan lately published in the *Illustrated London News* that Barry had substantially altered the particular layout which the committee had approved some eight years before. Furthermore, while the Lords were bemoaning a supposed lack of progress, Sudeley pointed out that stairs from the Sovereign's Entrance, the walls of the Victoria Gallery, and the passage behind the throne in the chamber (in fact, most of the south block of the Palace) were so far advanced that to alter them back to what was approved in 1836 meant the Lords 'must either put up with what we consider a Defect in the Plan or pay the expense which its Removal may occasion'.[4]

Barry was not at the earlier session and on taking his seat, was told that the committee understood that there had been considerable alterations made in the plan which was submitted by him in the year 1836. Would he be kind enough to state what authority was given for making those alterations? 'There have been no Alterations in the leading Features of the Plan; the Alterations have been principally in the Details', said Barry, employing his familiar admixture of soothing reassurance and disingenuousness which had worked so well in the past to sedate over-excitable committees. It did not work:

'Those Alterations which have been made, have they been made by any Authority or not?'
'No; upon my judgement.'
'Without any Authority?'
'Without any Authority.'
'Before being made were they described to any Person?'
'To no Person.'
'Neither to the Commissioners, not to the Woods and Forests, nor to the Government?'
'No.'

The Lords went on. Did he consider the creation of the Victoria Gallery, the new position of the Royal Staircase and the displacement of the Robing Room '140 odd feet' from its original position a mere alteration of detail? How was the diminutive Queen to process such a long distance comfortably at State Opening? Was he not aware of the 'inconvenience of any Person going that Distance under the Weight of heavy

Robes?' Taken unawares, Barry was uncharacteristically flustered: 'I can hardly speak from Recollection accurately, because I have not the original Plans with me.' The session ended with Barry being forced to hand over a printed copy of the Lords' original competition specifications for inspection—which the members appeared not to have to hand, or even to have consulted in the previous eight years.

Barry was shaken. Three days later he was on the rack again, challenged about the size of the site as extended in 1836; on the adaptations he had been forced into to accommodate the increasingly eccentric ventilation and heating requirements of Reid (from whom naturally he received no support); about the turning circle required for the Royal Coach inside the Sovereign's Entrance; endless discussions about the wretched staircase rising from it; and just why he had taken it upon himself to make decisions without involving their Lordships, the government, or the Office of Woods and Forests.

As well as countering all the questions at this and two more draining sessions, and providing further documentation, Barry had by now collected himself enough to read out a pre-prepared statement which included the declaration:

> Your Lordships can scarcely, I think be aware of the enormous Extent of Labour, Responsibility, as well as Anxiety of Mind, which I have to endure in conducting this Great National Work, in which, when complete, if there should be any thing faulty I shall be sure to be visited with the entire Blame. I am not, however, disposed to shrink from the almost appalling Task imposed upon me, as I am firmly persuaded that all Great Undertakings are best accomplished under an undivided Responsibility. On the contrary, I am ready, as I have hitherto ever been, to devote the best Energies of my Mind to the Perfection of a Work which it is my Earnest Desire to render an Honour to the Country, but unless I am supported, nay, encouraged in the Performance of my Tasks, by the cordial and kind Support and Indulgence of your Lordships, and all who are interested in the success of this, the greatest Undertaking of the Kind of the present or any former Period, it is quite clear to my Mind that it cannot be brought to a satisfactory Termination.[5]

Back me, or sack me, in other words. He had made alterations, major ones, both practical and aesthetic. He was the person best placed to put them into effect, 'being better acquainted than anyone else with Principles and Details of the Plan of the entire Building'.[6] What, in addition, the Westminster stationer's son was saying, of course, was that in the face of the squabbling, indecisive, politically motivated, contradictory, and largely self-regarding views of the hundreds of aristocrats who were his clients (not to mention their equivalents at the opposite end of the building) he had long ago determined to complete the building on his terms, for the national good, and despite—not because of—their requirements. When a couple of members of the committee suggested that he consider stopping work on the Victoria Gallery until such time as they had considered the plan, he took the wind out of their sails:

> I have the Pleasure to state that I have anticipated your Lordships Wishes in that respect, by stopping that Portion of the Work; but it is right that I should at the same Time state that I have done so at considerable Inconvenience to the Contractors, in consequence of the Number of Hands they have now in Employment, and the vast Quantities of Stone which are continually pouring in; and therefore if any Change is to be effected in that Portion of the Building it is of absolute Importance that it should be decided upon as speedily as possible.[7]

Barry had put the Lords on the spot, for it was always easier to criticize others' tough decisions than to take responsibility for a difficult course of action themselves. With the pressure on them to determine what they wished to do, their report was published on 13 May. Three days later, the Commons published all the correspondence between Barry and the Office of Woods relating to his fees.[8] The threat was clear. Barry was hauled before the Lords committee once more on 21 May, and by then the Commons had set up their own investigation.[9] This had been instigated by Peel and Lord Lincoln, both staunch supporters of Barry who intended to clear his name. It was nevertheless gruelling. Barry appeared four times before them over the next month. Later, Lincoln himself described the committee as including members who 'acted with great suspicion' towards the architect and who only 'after a most minute investigation came to a deliberate conclusion completely exonerating Mr Barry'.[10]

Challenged on the six-year timescale he had given in 1836, Barry came clean. 'It was perhaps very unwise of me,' he confessed, 'as there are so many contingencies upon which the completion of the building depends; it was however a mere conjecture.' The Commons tried to pin down how much longer it would take. 'That question would be very difficult to answer', the architect explained. There were so many unknowns: the pulling down of the temporary buildings and the decant of activity from one portion of the building to another. 'Therefore I would rather not give any answer to that question because I feel I could not do so with any degree of certainty.'[11] One thousand men were now working on the rebuild, including three hundred at the quarry.[12] Barry was 'decidedly of the opinion' that it would have been injurious to the 'building as a building' if any of the matters which he had decided on for himself had been handed over to others to determine, 'and would have created delays without end'. In the words of one sympathetic MP, it would have been deposing him from his position as architect. They queried the propriety of having suspended work on the say-so of just one or two difficult members of the Lords committee. Barry responded, 'it is questionable, but under the circumstances I have considered myself justified in meeting their wishes'.[13] Of the Lords' suggestion that the committee rooms should be expedited, he told the other House, 'I would rather not fit up any portion of the building in a temporary way.'[14] Barry was turning it from a fight between him and the Lords, into Lords versus Commons.

In the midst of this crisis, the Tsar came to visit. Nicholas I arrived in London at the beginning of June in an attempt to mend diplomatic fences following the latest round of the Great Game in Afghanistan. He had travelled incognito to England, fearing assassination by Polish terrorists, but 'the Autocrat' (as he was called by the press) was not recognized on the streets of London.[15] Accompanied by the Russian Ambassador, Baron Brunow, he was joined by Albert and Lincoln on a morning tour of the new Palace on 8 June, taking the now-familiar route around the site, the model room, and the architect's office. Barry and Grissell were delighted to discover that the Emperor took the highest interest in the progress of the works, minutely examining the quality of the stone and its workmanship, and was much pleased with the regularity and orderly procedure of the immense body of masons and other workmen, as well as with the ingenuity displayed in moving the various materials.

'His Imperial Majesty', reported *The Times,* charming and a hit with the ladies, 'evinced the liveliest interest in the whole of the works, and it was exceedingly gratifying to observe the freedom and condescension with which His Majesty conversed with Mr Barry upon the design and arrangements of the various parts.'[16] His afternoon entertainment was far less successful. He visited Chiswick House for a political lunch in a Gothic pavilion in the grounds, but when a group of guests decided to inspect the pet giraffes in the garden, this led to a stampede across the water by the animals (already spooked by the gun salutes and bands playing for the Russian party) who then charged into the Tsar's party on the opposite lawns.[17] Yet the visit left Barry with a new friend and unlikely ally. So delighted was the Tsar with the Palace designs that Barry commissioned two large painted perspectives of the buildings by the watercolourist, Thomas Allom (like Barry, a co-founder of the Institute of British Architects). These were subsequently presented to Nicholas I and are now in the Academy of Arts, St Petersburg.[18] Further royal visits followed that year: the King of Prussia in August, and more German princelings in November, anxious to be seen at the hottest attraction in London.[19] It was gratifying then, for Barry to receive a personal present from the Tsar the following January. Baron Brunow, Barry recalled in his diary, 'by the express command of the Emperor of Russia and with a highly complementary message from His Majesty presented me with a valuable gold snuff box studded with Brilliants' and at Ashburnham House, the Ambassador's London home, Barry was introduced to the Emperor's personal architect.[20] Professional and public opinion also came out in favour of Barry against the politicians. The *Illustrated London News* declared him 'the only directing mind in the whole business', while the *Civil Engineer and Architect's Journal* quoted Barry's view that 'all great undertakings are best accomplished under an undivided responsibility' as almost incontrovertible.[21]

Back in the Commons committee, Lord Lincoln stepped down from the chair and allowed himself to be examined on 17 June. As ever, he was a loyal defender of Barry:

> I am quite sure that any practical course, which in a great national build-ing of this kind removed the responsibility from the shoulders of the architect, who ought to bear it, and is the most competent judge of all the details of the building, to the Commissioners of Woods, who are not practical architects, who may be men of no taste whatever, and, as a fluctuating body, are quite unfit to superintend, in all its practical details, the erection of a building which must extend over a great many years, would be extremely inconvenient and prejudicial.[22]

He launched a broadside against those members who fancied them-selves as experts:

> if I had been a private individual, employing an architect for the con-struction of my own private residence, I should have been at perfect liberty to exercise any criticism, however unjust, and to have pleased my own whims and fancies, however absurd, and to have controlled my architect, however good, in any manner I might think fit; but in the case of my performance of my public duties, as superintending the execution of a great national work, I should have considered myself greatly depart-ing from my duties had I interfered in any such way. Again, if I had been employing an architect in the construction of my private residence, I should have a right to fool away as much of my money as I thought fit; but in the case of a public building, I consider myself acting, to a certain degree, as guardian of the public purse, and to have no right to sanction any expenditure, either for the gratification of any pride, or the indulg-ing of any fancy I might entertain, as to the proper and efficient con-struction of the building.[23]

Furthermore, it would, 'tend neither to the advantage of the building nor to the public service' that any member of either the Commons or Lords, 'who conceives himself to be as good an architect as Mr Barry, should interfere in these matters of taste'. At last, he felt confident to resume works in the Lords.[24] On 27 June he made a third exhausting appearance before the Commons committee, setting 1846 as the date for the completion of both chambers, enabling the Queen to use the processional route for State Opening that year and for both Houses to be operating out of them. But he was not prepared to be drawn on timescales for the remainder of the carcass of the building and the completion of its three towers.[25] Posterity has also vindicated Barry's changes to the design. By substituting the 'long and tiresome staircase' to the Principal Floor with the Royal Gallery he created one of the most spectacular parts of the Palace, familiar to anyone who today watches the monarch process down it at the annual televised State Opening of Parliament.

The day after this, Queen Victoria went to see the cartoons, frescoes, and sculpture in Westminster Hall. All the Commissioners were there. In her opinion, 'there were not many good Frescos' but she noted among the cartoons, 'a very clever one' by Daniel Maclise, 'beautifully executed' and among the sculptures, 'a small figure of Richard, Coeur de Lion by J. Sherwood West, which we admired very much'.[26] Maclise (1806–70), an Irishman from Cork, had already established a successful career as a portrait painter. The competition at Westminster became the catalyst for his move into monumental historical subjects. His drawing, *The Knight*, had caught the eye of the commissioners as well, and he with a number of others were invited by Albert to experiment with the waterglass technique (coating the murals with a solution of sodium silicate), in the Garden Pavilion of Buckingham Palace before employing it in earnest at Westminster. As a result, 'he is in great favour with the Queen', gossiped close friend Charles Dickens subsequently, 'and paints secret pictures for her to put on her husband's table on the morning of his birthday, and the like'. Another exhibitor, William Dyce, was commissioned by Albert to produce a rather erotic painting for Victoria three years later, as was Charles Eastlake, the secretary of the commission. The Queen also liked a piece by C. W. Cope, the history painter. All three were shortlisted to produce cartoons for the decoration of the building and, over the next 20 years, Cope, Dyce, and Maclise went on between them to create the best painting cycles in the Palace.[27]

The Commons reported on 4 July, imputing 'no blame to Mr Barry' for his decisions in the past, but for the avoidance of doubt in the future required him to make six-monthly reports on progress to the Commissioners of Woods and Forests and to submit to the board details of alterations proposed with plans. They felt that 1847 was a realistic date for completion of the chambers, given the ventilation requirements of the building. The Treasury agreed. But the Lords, when they reported, stated that while temporary fittings were not to be used, they expected their chamber to be completed by April 1845.[28] Barry had won this battle, albeit with some permanent scars. 'Not only the decision of the Committee itself,' his son later recalled, 'but also the tone of much of the examination, naturally caused Mr. Barry the greatest possible mortification.' But the 'cordial and generous support' of Lincoln 'set him right in public estimation, and gave him personally the greatest encouragement and comfort'.[29] Nevertheless, from this time onwards he became more watchful of his reputation, and more ruthless towards anyone or anything which would hinder him in the task he had set himself of creating the perfect new Palace of Westminster. The pressure was still on and Barry recognized he now needed help from an ally as visionary as himself if he were to have any hope of meeting the deadlines of either House. There was only one man for the job.

In the eight years since the two had worked together Pugin had become famous. Aged 32, he was living in Ramsgate, by his beloved sea, with his second wife and six children. He was now well known as the author of *Contrasts* and *True Principles*, and much sought after as an architect of new Catholic churches including major works at Birmingham, Newcastle, and Nottingham. He had undertaken some notable private commissions including Scarisbrick Hall in Lancashire, with its striking Gothic clock tower. With public recognition and success, however, had come increasingly poor health. He had recurrent attacks of his former eye problem, for which he was treated with mercury, temporarily rendering him almost blind. On these occasions, his skin was bled and he was deliberately and painfully 'blistered' to release the toxins.

At some point over the summer—it is not entirely clear when—Barry wrote to Pugin asking for help with devising a scheme for the Lords chamber. This had been further complicated by a request from the

Lords in committee that the royal seating in the chamber should be extended from one throne to three, to accommodate Prince Albert and the new Prince of Wales. It is possible that Pugin had sent Barry occasional notes and ideas for the interior design of the Palace in the intervening period, but now Pugin—suffering from 'English Cholera' or gastroenteritis when Barry first wrote to him—made clear that, 'it is next to impossible for me to design any abstract portion of a great whole in the same spirit in which you have conceived the rest, and I know it is only a waste of time for me to attempt it'. Barry should take a look at the carving at Amiens and Leuven—Pugin could go with him on a trip—but, 'as I said before, I can do you no good except in actual detail, and in that more by ferreting out the fine things that exist than composing new ones'.[30] Barry must have been desperate, frantic even, at being turned down. He had been dismayed by the poor quality of the designs entered for an exhibition of decorative arts in the Palace exhibited that April, and the watercolours of sculptural details produced by his assistants fell far short of the Gothic perfection he was aiming for.[31] Now there was the worry that if he did not take steps, the Fine Arts Commission would seize control not just of painting and sculpture, but of all the interior design: glass, panelling, flooring, furniture, textiles, the lot. He vetted and, where necessary, changed every stroke of the designs for the Palace, as they were churned out by his office, but it wasn't enough to satisfy his insatiable quest for perfection. *The Builder* magazine informed its readers that every yard of the Palace's design required as many detailed drawings as for a single ordinary house, and 'over all of these does Mr Barry's pencil pass...we will venture to say that the architect of the Houses of Parliament finds little time for other occupations or recreation from early on Monday morning till late on Saturday night. The wear and tear must be immense.'[32] It was. The strain of the *annus horribilis* of 1844 took its toll on the normally stoical Barry: he even took to being a vegetarian to overcome his symptoms, much to his devoted family's puzzlement and worry.[33]

141

'The Great Ventilator', David Boswell Reid, was by now a major cause of heart-clogging stress and frustration for Barry. When Reid had first proposed his grand plan for heating and air-conditioning the Palace to members in 1841 it was with his customary verbosity and bullishness. His scheme may be summarized as follows. Unpolluted air would be sucked into the building from the top of the two towers in Barry's design—the Clock Tower to the north, and the Victoria Tower to the south. This would be carried by means of coke-fired steam engines through the flues to the basement of the building, where it would form a reservoir of cool air, particularly useful in the summer. It would then be exchanged with the 'vitiated', or stale, hot air of the building, particularly in the chambers and committee rooms. Fireplaces in rooms could be abandoned and all the heating become dependent on a giant network of shafts through the whole which would finally expel the foul breath of the Palace out through a single exit. This was to be in the form of a third, giant tower over the Central Lobby or Saloon, whose octagonal shape Barry had so cleverly designed to hide the fact that the new building was not truly aligned with the former St Stephen's and Westminster Hall.

Barry had obligingly designed this giant central spire to act as the Palace's exhaust pipe and estimated that it would cost an additional £86,000 to construct, including nearly £42,000 to ensure the Palace had the necessary fireproofing to accommodate Reid's crackpot plan. But he seems to have gone along with it at first because he was tempted by the opportunity which the new tower gave for enhancing his design yet again: 'I have no hesitation in saying that I think the tower would be an important feature in the building, and would improve materially its general effect.'[34]

Things soon started to go wrong. Reid increasingly viewed the ventilation system as the main purpose of the Palace and his wish to vivisect Barry's creation got the better of him in the following months. By 1842 his scheme for the flues had changed. He favoured trying out both gas and hot water as a means of heating rather than coke, and his design now involved the converging of all fireplaces on a single 800 foot horizontal flue the length of the building through which the halitosis of the Palace could be relieved. Barry had been more cautious when

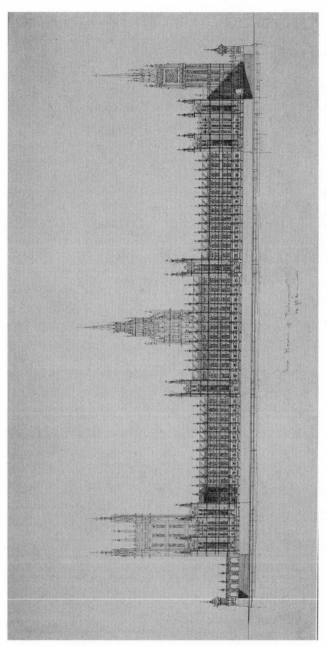

Barry's design with the new spire over the Central Lobby required by Boswell Reid's ventilation schemes

commenting on this revised plan and the way it further compromised his fireproofing. Members on this occasion concluded, 'serious doubts may be entertained as to the success of such an experiment, of which...there has not as yet been any adequate trial in any building of corresponding magnitude'. The select committee decided cautiously to adopt a 'double provision of flues' so as to make the 'ultimate arrangement open for future consideration' and ensure that fireproofing extended everywhere it was required.[35]

Nor had Reid been forthcoming with support of Barry during the committee sessions of 1843, and then in 1844, at the height of the controversy over the Victoria Gallery, Reid had offered the time of one of his clerks to finish plans for certain alterations which Lord Sudeley was proposing to impose on Barry.[36] This was ironic, given that Reid himself admitted he was largely unable to decipher architectural plans.

Yet giving evidence to the Commons in June 1844, even he declared he was finding it impossible to work with two masters, the Lords and Commons, citing his biggest difficulty as being 'the different temperaments

Dr David Boswell Reid

144

of different members, and the different demands made in the same bench at the same moment'. On this, at least, Barry and he could agree. Though he still managed to take a swipe at Barry by telling the committee: 'I have recast some parts of my plan four or five different times, in consequence of alterations.'[37] His latest mad scheme was to fill the ground-level area Barry had designed for parking members' carriages with new shafts, but such was the quantity of gases emanating from either end of the horses there that he proposed the open-air courtyards (to which he proposed they should be removed) would also soon need his ventilation skills.[38]

A few months later Barry tried again with Pugin. It was 3 September 1844. In the interim, disaster had struck and Pugin's wife, Louisa, had died suddenly on 22 August. He was also infatuated with a young woman called Mary Amhurst whom he was already eyeing up as the third Mrs Pugin. Into the middle of this personal crisis Barry made a second appeal. If he was aware of Pugin's vulnerable state, it did not deter him, so anxious was he to secure help. He may even have regarded it as a way of distracting his old collaborator from his grief. 'Dear Pugin', he wrote,

> I am in a regular fix respecting the working drawings for the fittings and decorations of the House of Lords, which it is of vital importance to me should now be finished with the utmost possible dispatch. Although I have made up my mind as to the principles and generally, as to the details of the design for the throne, which is at last perfectly satisfactory to me, I am unfortunately unable to get the general drawings into such a definite shape.[39]

This was because of a railway accident which had resulted in 'a lameness in one of my legs, which has laid me on my back, either in bed or on the sofa, for the last ten days' and he feared it would continue for days or even weeks. He was convalescing in a Brighton hotel, 'for the advantage of change, sea air, bathing, &c., &c.', and invited Pugin to join him for a few days to work on the drawings as 'as I know of no one who can render me such valuable and efficient assistance, or can so thoroughly relieve me of my present troubles of mind in respect of the said drawings as yourself'. He wanted to consult Pugin generally, but also proposed entering into 'some permanent arrangement that will be satisfactory to you as to occasional assistance for the future in the completion of the great work'. He felt 'quite sure' that if 'we were here together quietly for a few days, we should be able to make out definitively every portion of the design', in general drawings which Pugin could then afterwards supplement with detail 'from time to time, according to your leisure and convenience'. Barry had all his designs with him as a starting point,

> together with a good supply of drawing-paper, tackle, &c. It would really do me good both in body as well as in mind, to have you with me; therefore, pray do not disappoint me if you can in any way help it. Believe me, dear Pugin, yours very truly, Charles Barry.

Despite the flattering and relaxed tone of the letter, Barry was putting on a brave face. He was quite as much in despair professionally as Pugin was personally. But the solution for both men was the same—to throw themselves into the work together, being of like minds and understanding each other's motivations surprisingly well. In a postscript, Barry dangled a final temptation to Pugin—suggesting that he did indeed know of the recent bereavement: 'The weather here is delicious and exhilarating, and the proposed change would be sure to do you good.' Work with a sympathetic collaborator beside the sea was the best antidote for the bruising both men had experienced that year. This letter, probably the most important Barry sent in his life, worked. Pugin travelled round the coast and stayed with Barry from 12 to 16 September.

Back at the Palace a 'most singular feat' was about to take place on the river outside. One of the clowns at Astley's Circus (known for its performances by trick horse riders) announced that he was going to sail between Vauxhall and Westminster bridges in a washtub drawn by two geese. The hour arrived and at half-past three he boarded his makeshift craft and headed down river in stately fashion, cheered on by the crowds up and down the riverbanks and escorted by an immense number of boats. He emerged unscathed at his destination, disembarked, and

1. Charles Barry in the 1830s

2. The old Westminster Barry knew, as rendered by Pugin's father in the 1820s

3. J. M. Gandy's classical fantasy of the House of Lords in St James's Park with the old Palace burning in the top left corner

4. Charles Barry in 1851

5. A. W. N. Pugin in 1845

6. Charles Barry at the end of his life

7. The Fine Arts Commissioners. Barry is standing in the foreground, demonstrating a model of the Palace to Prince Albert, seated centre

8. The House of Lords chamber in 1857

9. The House of Commons chamber in 1858 with its lowered ceiling

10. View of the Palace from Millbank, with the stone wharfs in the foreground during the mid-1850s

11. Old Palace Yard under construction, showing the rails and steam engines used to haul the stone around the site

12. View of the Palace with the incomplete clock face, 1858

13. State portrait of Queen Victoria by Winterhalter with the towers of her new Palace in the background

proceeded to some acclaim to the home of the circus at the self-styled
Royal Amphitheatre in Lambeth.[40] If the architect of the new Houses
of Parliament read of this anserine feat in the papers at Brighton, he
can have been forgiven for suspecting that this was some cruel satire on
his recent travails, for the name of the clown, well-publicized beforehand, was Mr Barry. Four days later (as if a reminder were needed that
building the Houses of Parliament was a matter of life and death for
some), a mason's labourer fell 30 feet from a scaffold onto a pile of stone
rubbish below. Taken to Westminster Hospital with blood gushing from
his mouth and ears, and fatal brain injury, Edward Carter left behind a
widow and two children.[41]

Barry continued to reel in his old ally. Early in November Pugin wrote
to J. G. Crace, the royal decorator who became his regular collaborator.
He urged him to post the remaining wallpaper and window dressings for
his drawing room to complete his new house, The Grange at Ramsgate,

Encaustic floor tile with VR monogram designed by Pugin, manufactured by Minton

for I expect some persons to come to see me very shortly & am most anxious to have everything to rights for them to see. I am sure if you make a little Exertion you can do it...I would not press you if there was not necessity—but—it is of *consequence to me*. I may say *GREAT Consequence* & perhaps to you—in the long run—for if this sort of thing takes we may do wonders.[42]

Barry arrived there five days later. It is clear that Pugin had wanted to impress him with the interior decoration of his own home as they worked on the throne designs together over the next three days. That worked too. In December Barry arranged the appointment of Pugin as 'Superintendent of Wood Carving'. Pugin's patron, the Earl of Shrewsbury, was jubilant. Barry's appointment of Pugin had settled the argument against his anti-Catholic detractors, 'by picking him out from the whole kingdom as the only man to carry out the details of the Parliament Houses'.[43] Pugin himself set out the terms of their relationship, for the avoidance of doubt. For £200 a year he would supply all the drawings and instructions for the wood, working from Ramsgate, all travel expenses to be charged on top, as were models, and drawings of metalwork, tiles, and glass. He was responsible to Barry 'in all matters connected with the work. I act as your agent entirely, and have nothing to do with any other person. I mention these things that we may have a perfect understanding at starting, for it is a great work and will occupy the great part of my time.'[44]

8

A Very Difficult Work

1845 to 1846

W ITH PUGIN ON board, Barry now moved swiftly to arrange suitable premises for the creation of the Palace's interiors. By the end of 1844, the Thames Bank workshops by Vauxhall Bridge had been leased by the government and there Pugin's woodwork designs were to be put into effect. Several hundred men worked there at a time, using the latest in modern technology to speed the processes. Pugin himself supplied some hundreds of examples of medieval work for the carvers to model from, gleaned from architectural salvage, and from plaster casts of originals—including a full-sized set of the choir stalls from Lincoln Cathedral. The work took place under the watchful eye of Richard Bayne the resident superintendent; Mr Potts, the woodcarver in chief; and Mr Jordan, inventor of a patent woodcarving machine. Barry visited several times a week to assess progress and Pugin was also often to be found there, regularly travelling up from the south coast to do so. Barry unhesitatingly allotted the production of the ornamental metalwork from Pugin's designs to the Hardman manufactory of Birmingham ('the only one in the Kingdom where such work is properly executed'), the encaustic tilework to Minton of Stoke-on-Trent, and the decorative paintwork to Crace. All of them had already worked with Pugin on other projects and Barry concurred that these were by far and away the best suppliers for the high-quality finish he needed.[1]

The Royal Throne, the centrepiece of the House of Lords scheme, was a different matter. Barry had previously told a Commons committee that it was 'decidedly his opinion' that control of the interior design should be under one person: him, not the Fine Arts Commission. And as for the Throne, one of the highlights of the Palace, that was an integral part of the architectural scheme.[2] Barry contracted the well-known cabinetmaker, John Webb of Bond Street, to undertake the work required, while Gillows provided later furnishings which had to be made at Thames Bank, not in their West End or Lancaster showrooms.[3] There were of course numerous other contracts—including the metal window frames, plain glazing, and the giant fireproof cast iron roof tiles—all let to firms in London and throughout the country.

At the start of the year many workmen at the Palace were observed busily constructing ten new temporary committee rooms in New Palace Yard. Select committees until then had been meeting on site in the old Speaker's House, to the east of Westminster Hall, which was now demolished. The temporary restaurant and tearooms were also shifted elsewhere to allow the clearance of the site which became St Stephen's Hall. Two survivors of the fire, the Speaker's dining room—the undercroft chapel of St Stephen's—and its gorgeous Tudor cloisters, Barry intended to renovate to their 'original architectural elegance'.[4]

Pugin was swiftly in touch with his friend, John Hardman, with whom he had worked on the supply of ecclesiastical ornaments for St Chad's Cathedral in Birmingham. Hardman's, originally a button-making business, met Pugin's rigorous standards and its proprietor shared his faith. Pugin was already discussing different methods of manufacturing metal plates for the Lords Throne with Hardman—though 'let Mr Barry decide', he advised, on the preferred effect—and made his friend aware just how 'very anxious' Mr Barry was for the railing compartment to go around it, and how the estimates and tenders should go to Barry as 'he will then get Woods & forests order [*sic*] & everything will proceed'.[5] By the start of February, Pugin was telling Hardman that he and Barry 'had at last hit on a crown that will do', but the design of the four brasswork upright gasoliers for each corner of the dais was a struggle. 'I think it would not be prudent', Pugin confessed to Hardman, 'to cast much of the railing till Mr Barry has finally approved of it as he is such a man for alterations that one is never safe till the final order is given.'[6] Wood carving for the interiors of the House of Lords began in February 1845.

At the end of the month both Pugin and Hardman had to start all over again with the Throne compartment as Pugin had feared, explaining to Hardman:

> We shall have to begin quite afresh with the railing for Last night Mr Barry altered all the rose work at the bottom & we must start quite a new pattern, he is aware of the great loss of dies &c. for I have explained it to him & he says he cannot be helped for he must have it perfection to his mind...the moment the railing is quite to Mr. B.mind you may put as much strength as you like or can on it.[7]

Pugin hated travelling to the London workshops and longed for the sea. The city made him ill. 'I suffer dreadfully. it rouses up all sorts of wreched associations & I cannot bear it,' he told Hardman. A few weeks later he was 'very unwell indeed but do not relax a moment from business' and 'more miserable in London than ever' because it reminded him of his late wife and his dead parents. '[I]t quite increases on me. God only knows how much I suffer in my mind. every place is associated with miserable ideas for me. I am quite unhappy at being forced up so much.'[8] A week later, however, he was in cheerier spirits, as was customary with his mood swings: 'things are looking up at Westminster. I expect we shall soon start on the *Throne chairs*. 3 of them. I shall send you very shortly all the shieds & banners for the Throne. it is an imense job.' But, he had noticed he wasn't the only one under strain as he and Barry went to and fro to the workshops at Thames Bank: 'Mr Barry looks ill & harassed. it is a very difficult work & I think he finds me a great comfort to him. I assure you I have enough to do & must give up almost everything else.'[9]

Barry's grip over the whole design, his perfectionism, and concentration on both the smallest item and the larger picture were exhausting for both those he worked with and himself. Two days after Pugin expressed his concerns, Lord Lincoln told the Commons that the cost of the building had slightly exceeded the original estimate and had risen to £928,913. Having recently met with the architect he had been assured that Barry 'saw no reason to withdraw the declaration which he had made last year, namely, that the New Houses would be ready in 1847'.[10]

On the afternoon of Friday 7 March Prince Albert and the Commissioners came to inspect progress and this time the areas set aside for fine art. Barry and Grissell were, as usual, the tour guides. After the delays of 1844, progress was now evident. The Royal Gallery on the Principal Floor was half its final height. The Victoria Tower was proceeding rapidly and at its base the 60-foot archway of the Sovereign's Entrance was almost complete. Its walls were expected to rise another 10 feet over the summer. The Lords chamber was entirely roofed in, with wrought and galvanized cast iron. Work on fixing the coffered ceiling and wainscoting went on apace, to be 'elaborately carved, and emblazoned with the arms of the different peers'. The Prince and his entourage spent much time browsing the lobbies, corridors, and public entrances, to understand where wall paintings and more sculpture might be positioned and, it was noted by reporters, the roofs of these spaces 'would long since have been fixed but for the delay occasioned by arrangements necessary for the ventilation, the complicated nature of which has very much retarded the progress of these works'. The party moved on to St Stephen's Hall, eagerly anticipated as 'one of the grandest edifices in London', to be lavishly decorated with artworks on historical themes.[11]

Into the crypt of old St Stephen's they went, where the partition walls and plastering of the former Speaker's dining room, with its neighbouring coal holes and lumber rooms, 'which had so much disfigured this exquisite piece of architecture', had been removed—and the thirteenth-century vaulted structure was revealed once more. There had been gruesome discoveries down there during the strip-out, as probing the foundations had revealed several skeletons which had 'belonged to men of immense proportions and gigantic stature', their giant jaws containing perfect sets of teeth. On the river front the committee floors on the first and second levels were now complete and the whole roofed in; the towers of the new Speaker's House by Westminster Bridge nearing completion; and the scaffolding starting to come down on that side. The

House of Commons chamber, however, was not so well advanced, being only 20 feet above the Principal Floor. Albert went to Barry's office to look at the models, drawings, and plans once again; questioned him as usual, closely but amiably; warmly congratulated him and Grissell upon the progress made and the admirable manner in which the work had been executed so far. As usual, royalty was much more impressed than politicians by the building. But that did not stop new ideas from emerging which Barry had to incorporate into the building: the Commissioners decided that they wanted stained glass in the windows of the House of Lords.[12]

Then at the start of June, a new and very personal attack on Barry's reputation began. The Maynooth Bill debate of early June 1845 was the catalyst. Nights of protracted and overheated argument in the Lords chamber about Peel's controversial grant increase to the Catholic seminary near Dublin had brought things to a head. The bill eventually passed and, coincidentally, Pugin was soon after commissioned to design the new seminary building. Parliament would shortly have more pressing Irish issues to think about when *Phytophthora infestans* began eating its devastating way through the potato crop that year and the next. But in the meantime Lord Brougham, whose antipathy to the new Palace continued unabated, returned to a favourite theme, provoked by the air quality in the former Painted Chamber, now poisonous from the stink of four hundred peers who had debated there for a solid 18 hours in an attempt to prevent the bill's passage. The suggestion that all would be well now that the peers had a definite date for the opening of the new chamber failed to placate the former Lord Chancellor. 'I don't regard the assurance of Mr. Barry as worth the value of the paper on which it is written', he thundered on 5 June. 'Mr. Barry is all but resisting the authority of this House, he is fencing with the House. He foolishly, short-sightedly—and, as he will find to his cost, most ignorantly—fancies that he has high protection out of this House. He will find himself mistaken, completely mistaken.'[13]

This was subsequently reported in *The Times* as simply 'a lively conversation respecting the new Houses of Parliament'.[14] Then, two days after Brougham's attack, Barry received a note from Pugin, containing excruciating news, which could not have come at a worst time:

Lord Brougham

My dear Mr Barry

Since I saw you last night, I have been informed that some most exaggerated statements respecting the nature of my employment at the Palace of Westminster have appeared in one of the papers. I need not tell you how distressed and annoyed I feel at it, for I have always been most careful to prevent any misconception on this head. I have most distinctly stated that I was engaged *by you and for you* to carry out in to practical execution the minor details of the decorations according to your design, that I did nothing *whatever on my own responsibility, that everything was submitted to be approved or altered by you*; that in fine, my occupation was simply to carry out your views in the practical execution of the internal detail. I can assure you, I wish to serve you in this work with the greatest fidelity; no one can better appreciate your skill and judgement than myself, and no man has ever born more sincere and willing testimony to them than myself. Now, if you think right, I will make a formal denial of these statements to put an end to all nonsense. I have not seen the article, but Mr. Crace told me that one of your clerks had mentioned it to him; it will therefore be easy to know when and where it appeared, and I really think it would be as well to state the real state of the case. I will send you my contradiction for your approval. I am sure that you know me too well to imagine that such statements would give me anything but great pain and annoyance; but I should like at once to disabuse the public, and let them know the true nature of my employment at the Palace. Pray let me here from you about this.

With misplaced jocularity, Pugin added a postscript about the debate: 'I see in the *Times* this morning that Reid and Barry (!!!) came in for their share of blame in the Lords.'[15] In the years since they had last worked together, Pugin had made enemies among those jealous of his talent and success, just as Barry had. But, unlike Barry, Pugin was noisy and opinionated in public, and this came back to haunt him. An article had appeared in *The Builder* at the end of May stating that the decorative portions of the interior had been 'intrusted' to Pugin, and then in June a much more intemperate one in *The Artizan* with even more awkward claims in relation to Pugin's role at Westminster followed. 'Charles Barry and His Right-Hand Man' made out that Barry was covering up his employment of Pugin to hide his own inadequacy as an architect, and that Pugin (whom the magazine also treated to some nasty anti-Catholic prejudice) had been spreading it about in the 'most cock-crowing tone' as well as 'modestly insinuating that he is the only person in the world—at least in this country, who possesses the requisite taste and knowledge' to undertake the work.[16]

Having difficulties with a particularly complicated pattern, Pugin tried a feeble joke with Barry: 'I wish Lord Brougham had to set it out himself'.[17] A few days later Pugin drafted a letter to the editor of *The Builder*:

> My attention having been drawn to an erroneous paragraph, which appeared in your journal, relative to the nature of my employment at the New Palace of Westminster, I take an early opportunity of stating that I am not engaged in any work connected with that building on my own responsibility, but am simply superintending the practical execution of the internal details and decorations of Mr Barry's design. Nothing is done without his entire knowledge and approbation, nor is anything put into execution that has not been previously arranged and designed by himself.[18]

It was not sent. In the meantime, Barry, beset on all sides, had arranged for a rebuttal of his own in a total breach of parliamentary procedure. He arranged for a letter responding to Brougham's invective to be read out directly in the chamber by Lord Wharncliffe, the Leader of the

House. This tactic shocked some of the Lords, who declared it 'a most irregular proceeding', but it indicated the degree to which Barry had felt it necessary to go to protect his reputation, and to manage the pressure on him from both inside and outside the project.[19]

At the end of the month Victoria went once again to see the short-listed fresco cartoons and samples in Westminster Hall to be painted in the House of Lords:

> viz: Abstract representations of religion, Justice & the Spirit of Chivalry. The other subjects are: the baptism of Ethelbert. P[rin]ce Henry acknowledging the authority of Chief Justice Gascoigne, & Edward the Black P[rin]ce receiving the Order of the Garter from Edward IIIrd:. Of each there was a large cartoon, a small coloured sketch & a piece of fresco. The Exhibition was really a very fine one; the best of the frescos was, I thought 'the Baptism of Ethelbert',—quite like a Raphael. 'The spirit of Chivalry' was also very fine, but a little confused.[20]

Was the 'Spirit of Justice' cartoon by Daniel Maclise the Queen saw that afternoon a development of the 'very clever one...beautifully executed' she had admired the year before? If so, then Victoria was aware and approving that Maclise had used as his model one of the most controversial campaigners for women's rights of the age. For the statuesque, black-haired, female figure of 'Justice', holding aloft a brass scale, which today looks down on the lawmakers below, was none other than Caroline Norton, whose abuse at the hands of her husband in the 1830s led her to campaign for reform of the law in relation to married women. As a result of her prodigious talent at lobbying, the Custody of Infants Act had already been passed in 1839, and this was to be joined by the Matrimonial Causes Act 1857 and the Married Women's Property Act 1870, which together modernized divorce law and transformed married women from being their husbands' chattels into independent beings in the eyes of the law over Norton's lifetime.

By this time, Pugin was finding himself 'so driven for time with my *parliamentary business*' that he was scarcely able to deal with any other clients.[21] Barry had visited various Birmingham manufacturers—Hardman, Hodgson, and Messengers—to decide who should make the ornamental brass gates for the Lords chamber doors. Pugin reported to

Hardman, 'he was deligted with your place. he says you are the only man & yours the only place—Messenger wished him to see some beastly Cast gates & disgusted him beyond measure.'[22] Barry had 'finally passed' Pugin's design for the big and little vanes for the roofline of the Palace and now wished Hardman to proceed with them 'as fast as possible and *mind the gilding*', said Pugin.[23] Pugin's health—and particularly his eyes—continued to wreak havoc with his productivity and morale: 'the worst thing I have to contend against is this dreadful disorder. the agony is sometimes past bearing.'[24]

Still, he had time to seek inspiration from the Gothic Continent. Writing from a tour of Europe in August 1845, Pugin enthused to Barry on his finds:

> There is nothing I have seen to compare with Basel, except Nuremburg. Lots of fine iron work—such clocks in leaden turrets! Do not you envy me?...I have seen much that will be applicable to the great work. After all there will be nothing like it, for the largest of the old works are small in comparison, and not half so well carried out; and *I must own you are right in the principle of repetition of bays*. All the great town-halls are certainly so, and I have paid particular attention to this point. *You know I never hold out after I am convinced, and now I can advocate it conscientiously*.[25]

Pugin had also admired the railway stations on his trip up the Rhine:

> The best modern architecture I have seen is the railway from Mannheim to Strasbourg. The stations are beautiful—all constructive principle. If the roofs had a higher pitch, they would be almost perfect. I have seen some splendid metal-work in brass and iron, and have taken a fresh supply from the fountain of medieval antiquity; you ought really to be forced away for two weeks to this country, it would do you the world of good, and you would fetch up the actual time afterwards. Remember, life ebbs away, and every year some fine old thing is destroyed. You ought, as a positive duty, to come to these countries now and then. I am so up to everything that I could give you such directions that would enable you to see a vast deal even in two weeks...There is a great deal of fine old heraldry about the buildings in Basel and in Alsace. I see so much that I did not know of at all, that it really appears as if we know less the longer one studies; and I suppose, by the time one is very knowing indeed, we shall almost be past profiting by the knowledge.[26]

The letter is typically Pugin at this time—enthusiastic, bubbling over with new ideas, generous in his appreciation of Barry's judgement on the overall design, and sympathetic to his struggles. Pugin always cut a noticeable and eccentric figure. Well-built and quite short, with flowing hair, a booming voice and large hands and feet, his favourite attire was a scruffy sailor's tunic or a canvas short jacket, accompanied by a battered shiny hat and coarse socks showing in a wide gap between trousers and shoes. He frequently broke out into singing favourite opera tunes when in a good mood, or cursing ripely when things were not going well. When his mental state deteriorated, he stopped washing.

Barry was the complete opposite—taller, all black velvet waistcoats and green silk dressing gowns, West End tailoring, smoother, sleeker, cleaner, and above all more willing to tell people what they wanted to hear to achieve his ends. As a young man he had been deeply embarrassed at being turned away from the Chapelle Royale at the *Tuileries* in Paris for wearing Nankeen trousers (a sort of Regency chino) rather than black breeches and silk stockings. When he visited Canova in Rome, he noted that, 'like most great men, he is not very attentive to his dress'.[27] He took especial care with his wardrobe in future, all part of his attempts to pass unremarked in polite society. Portraits of Barry by fashionable artists, which by the mid-1840s were starting to appear, show his open and friendly countenance with a receding hairline and brown curly hair, but matched with a firm gaze. Here was a man whose friendly appearance and polished manners in public belied an utter determination to finish the task he had allotted himself.

It would be wrong to imagine that the Houses of Parliament occupied all of Barry's waking hours at this time (or indeed Pugin's). The point was that he was working around 19 or 20 hours a day to keep on top of the huge workload from his professional practice as well as the Palace (he was even working on drawings for the Palace on the day of his daughter's wedding in 1845).[28] That year he was alternating work on the Palace (neatly noted as 'NPW' or 'HOP' in his leatherbound pocketbooks) with other commissions. At Westminster he was always refining the plans and drawings, making site visits, appearing before parliamentary committees, corresponding with suppliers, liaising with Grissell &

Peto, attending meetings of the Fine Arts Commission, visiting the
stone and wood carvers at the Thames Bank workshops several times a
week, directing his own office staff, and consulting with the Office of
Woods on any number of issues. On other days, his prodigiously busy
professional life included work on Trentham Hall in Staffordshire and
Dunrobin Castle, both for the Duke of Sutherland; on the Board of
Trade building in Whitehall; on the new Public Record Office with its
Keeper, Francis Palgrave; on Harewood House in Yorkshire; on a proposal for the removal of the Lawcourts next to Westminster Hall; on
Bridgewater House in St James's; a plan for widening Piccadilly; and on
smaller projects in Brighton and nearby Hurstpierpoint for private clients. To all of this he added a trip to Scotland to see more prospective
clients and to judge an architectural competition, and allowed himself
a 16-day holiday in September to Paris, one of his favourite cities.[29]

The Palace's design was now ten years old, and despite Barry's constant tweaks and alterations to it was now in danger of being overtaken
by a new generation of Victorian Gothicists, led by the art critic and writer,
John Ruskin, who took as his inspiration not the fifteenth-century civic
models of North-West Europe, but those of thirteenth- and fourteenth-
century Venice. Ruskin set down his own unimpressed view of the Palace
in the second volume of *Modern Painters* in 1846:

> it may be well to note, in our own new houses of Parliament, how far a
> building approved by a committee of Taste, may proceed without man-
> ifestation either of imagination or composition; it remains to be seen
> how far the towers may redeem it; and I allude to it at present unwill-
> ingly, and only in the desire of influencing, so far as I may, those who
> have the power to prevent the adoption of a design for a bridge to take
> place of Westminster, which was exhibited in 1844 at the Royal Acad-
> emy, professing to be in harmony with the new building, but which was
> fit only to carry a railroad over a canal.[30]

Barry had in any case fallen out with James Walker over the refurbish-
ment of Westminster Bridge, Walker having publicly involved the
Speaker in the proposals for renewing the piers. Barry considered the
bridge was now in such an unstable state that a completely new one was

required, and it was essential that he got the contract to design it so as to ensure it blended sympathetically with the Palace when viewed from downstream.[31]

By the end of the summer, new rumours were circulating about Pugin's role in the Palace, and early in September a letter appeared from him in *The Builder*:

> A misconception prevails as to the nature of my employment in the works of the new palace of Westminster, I think it incumbent upon me, in justice to Mr Barry, to state that I am engaged by him, and by him alone, with the approval of the Government, to assist in preparing working drawings and models from his designs of all the wood carvings and other details of the internal decorations; and to procure models and drawings of the best examples of ancient decorative art of the proper kind, wherever they are to be found, as specimens for the guidance of the workmen in respect of the taste and feeling to be imitated; to engage with artists, and the most skilful workmen that can be procured in every branch of decorative art, and to superintend personally the practical execution of the works on the most economical terms compatible with the nature of it, and its most perfect performance.

But it was the next passage that echoed down the years:

> In fulfilling the duties of my office, I do not do any thing whatever on my own responsibility; all models and working drawings being prepared from Mr Barry's designs, and submitted to him for his approval or alteration previous to their being carried into effect; in fine, my occupation is simply to assist in carrying out practically Mr Barry's own designs and views in all respects.[32]

Some later commentators believed that Barry had a hand in dictating it, but more likely is that Pugin was overly modest about his own input, and went to the opposite extreme, embarrassed by the ongoing pickle he found himself in, and distracted by his desperate infatuation with Mary Amhurst.

However, things were soon back on an even keel and, later that month, the two men went to see Pugin's work at Alton Towers.[33] The Fine Arts Commission had now decided that the 18 sculpture niches between the windows of the House of Lords should—on the suggestion

KEY TO THE PICTURE OF

THE MEETING OF THE FINE ARTS COMMISSION. 1846.

The Fine Art Commissioners in session

of Prince Albert—be filled with statues of the barons and bishops who forced King John to agree to the terms of Magna Carta in 1215. *The Times* foresaw trouble about the exclusion of the Archbishop of Dublin, which might cause a grievance among 'the Irish agitators' but otherwise thought this a fine idea, except that the poses of the barons being feudal might present 'little or no variety of attitude'.³⁴

Money continued to cause Pugin worry and, in order to calm him whenever he failed to get prompt payment from the Office of Woods, Barry would encourage him to think of a higher cause:

> I will not do you the injustice to believe that filthy lucre only is the main spring of all your efforts on behalf of the great work, but that like myself you are prepared to make a sacrifice for the glory of making it the means of establishing for the future what you believe the one and only true style of art.³⁵

As the New Year came round and the pressure to complete the Lords chamber ramped up even further, Pugin continued to publish refutations of his role in the Palace. In a letter to *The Ecclesiologist* he wrote:

> I have repeatedly stated, and now again repeat, that I am not in any way engaged as a responsible architect as regards the new Houses of Parliament. I design nothing. I superintended the execution of the decorative details in wood, metal, and glass; but everything is, arranged by Mr. Barry and subject to his approval, and I do nothing more than carry out his views in the execution of the work.³⁶

Pugin did not react well to the stress of the Palace, or the timetable being imposed by the Lords through Barry. And, gradually, the intense pressure of the Palace's creation was turning him, in Barry's eyes, into a supplier and subordinate, rather than the colleague and partner he had been ten years before. In February Pugin was reassuring Crace, who was carrying out all the painting, gilding, and carpetmaking, about some query regarding Barry's approach or manner: 'what you say about Mr B. I think nothing of. he is often so.'³⁷ Throughout 1846 his letters are peppered with comments about the increasing pressure he felt: 'the new Houses of Parliament occupy a great deal of my time, and I work incessantly'; Barry 'is at me every day'.³⁸ When Barry brought him the details required for the Commons his response was, 'it seems I am to die in harness. I am getting very weak. It seems to me I am quite altered. I know I feel 20 years older.'[39] Yet his new work at Chirk Castle in the Welsh border country was 'enough to drive any man Mad...it is worse than the House of Lords'.[40] All this while he was plagued with painful and distressing symptoms which severely pulled down his mood, and caused hysterical outbursts such as, 'I am torn to pieces. I shall get as bad as ever. by George I will leave off all together...the tide has turned. I know I am going down every day. everything is unfortunate.'[41] By the autumn things were being missed or misunderstood. Hardman told Barry he didn't know he was to make railings for the ends of the Lords chamber. Pugin felt his memory was going and began to send designs with errors in them which Hardman had to point out.[42] He started to realize that the salary he had agreed did not reflect the amount of work he was putting in compared to others, and that the travelling costs and other expenses he incurred were also to come out of his fees. Payments continued to be well in arrears, and Pugin pleaded with Barry to intervene on his behalf with the Office of Woods about his cashflow:

> You must know in your heart as a great man that I am entitled to a great deal more even what than I ask but all I do ask is the fulfilment of the terms originally agreed...you know I hold you in just honour and am a most faithful Lieutenant but unless the money is instanced I must resign my commission—for I won't fight at the price.[43]

In March 1846 another Lords committee reported that, 'for the last nine months or more there positively had been no advance made towards the completion of the House designed for their Lordships, notwithstanding that they had repeatedly expressed their impatience to get into it'. They had been informed that 'some difference of opinion had unhappily arisen between the architect and the scientific gentleman to whom the duty of ventilating the new building had been confided, and the consequence of this difference had been a total suspension of the works'. The committee was unable to apply any remedy. The Postmaster General, the Marquess of Clanricarde, moved that, due to the delays, the Queen might be asked to place the building under the direct superintendence of the Office of Woods, and 'this wish was approved by the house, which has evidently lost all patience at the interminable delays opposed to its establishment in its new abode'. The Duke of Wellington, however, persuaded him and the House to step back from the brink and not get the Queen involved, but to delay until the Commons could join in the discussion.[44]

Meanwhile, the mid-1840s were the height of parliamentary activity on a new type of legislation. As the Palace rose into the sky above the capital, so a network of railway tracks was spreading rapidly across the surface of the land, cutting through sleepy countryside, connecting towns and cities previously only linked by horse-drawn transport, and causing a revolution in standardizing time across the country because of the need to publish accurate schedules of services. Because the new passenger and freight locomotives would steam right across private land, Parliament had to approve plans to build these new iron roads and allow owners to be compensated accordingly, through a tortuous legislative procedure quite unlike the passing of an ordinary Act. Early in 1845 Barry erected some rather superior wooden shacks in New Palace Yard, outside Westminster Hall. With double-boarded walls lined with felt for warmth and skylights for illumination, they were pronounced 'very convenient' by the *Illustrated London News*.[45] Rather than being rooms for select committees, these were temporary committee rooms for the hearing of evidence and inspection of plans for railway bills as railway-mania took hold.

To deal with the vast increase in parliamentary bureaucracy, a guide was needed for the railway companies and their agents who wanted to understand the intricacies of Westminster. To meet this challenge, a dedicated but humourless assistant librarian in the House of Lords called Thomas Erskine May stepped forward. His handbook, *Parliamentary Practice*, first published in 1844, was a bestseller and he edited a further eight editions in his lifetime during which it was taken up in colonial parliaments on the Westminster model, including Canada and Australia. It was also translated for use in the

The temporary committee rooms for railway bills in New Palace Yard

various German diets, and the French, Spanish, Italian, Hungarian, and Japanese legislatures—though quite how useful it would have been in those very different parliamentary systems is questionable.[46] Ever since, 'Erskine May' has been the informal title for this bible of parliamentary procedure, kept close at hand on the table of each House and in many offices across the Palace as the essential book of reference at Westminster.

It was this that was driving the pressing need in 1846 for Barry's airy new committee rooms, replacing the New Palace Yard lean-tos. Those on the first and second floors of the river front commanded splendid views over the river along its entire length. Temporary windows were in place, but the ceilings had yet to be panelled so bare brickwork and iron girders were still on view. They presented 'an extremely naked appearance' according to *The Times*' reporter who visited them climbing up a temporary staircase made of boards, each furnished just with plain baize-covered tables, a few chairs, a deal cupboard for committee papers, green baize skirting and coconut matting—yet they still comprised 'a magnificent suite'.[47] In fact, Barry did his utmost to court the press and encourage support for the new Houses of Parliament. This was just one example of many where journalists were given privileged access to the building to write their stories, and Barry had plans up his

sleeve for an even bigger splash for the opening of the new House of
Lords chamber.

When the debate returned to the Lords a month later they were concerned by Barry's statement that the new chamber would only be ready
if the circumstances were favourable: for 'one of the most material of
these circumstances lay in the goodwill and exertion of Mr. Barry himself'. Some peers were also galled by the news that the new committee
rooms were to be opened immediately for the use of the Commons:
'they ought not to be trifled with' and, 'there would be no more squabbles permitted between the architect and Dr. Reid' who were now at
daggers drawn over the ventilation plans. The government calmed
things down stating that 'only fifteen' of the committee rooms were for
the House of Commons, and that the other four would be made ready
for their Lordships at the same time. Brougham took aim once again,
but this time it was Reid not Barry in his sights. He had 'suffered most
severely' from Reid's systems in the temporary Lords, 'sometimes broil-
ing and sometimes freezing'. The committee had shown that 'with
proper attention' the Lords could get into their new House in the course
of a very few weeks, but only if they didn't wait 'until every nook and
cranny or rat's hole had been exposed to the ventilating process of Dr.
Reid'. The sole question they had to determine, continued Brougham,
regarded the manner of sending hot or cold air into the new House,
and that was the only thing that interfered with putting up the new fittings. They had the statement of Mr Barry that all the internal installa-
tions were ready to be fixed. The ceilings and walls were finished,
'therefore there could not be the slightest doubt that the new House
would be ready by the commencement of the next Session'.[48] The ball
was now in Reid's court.

Reid was impossible. Despite recent attempts by scholars to rehabili-
tate his scientific theories, there is no doubt that personally he was vain
and bombastic, and wholly unwilling to work cooperatively with other
experts. The want of information and documents; the vacillation, inde-

cisiveness, and unwillingness to commit his ideas to paper; and the general attitude now being shown to Barry and his assistants had become so intolerable for the architect and his office that, since the autumn of 1845, Barry had in fact been refusing to speak to Reid personally or meet him, and their only communication was in writing posted or passed between assistants.[49] An independent review of Reid's ventilation system had now been demanded to break the impasse over the best way forward. In July the reviewers, including the distinguished railway engineer, George Stephenson, and the eminent chemist, Robert Graham, came down on Barry's side. Reid had been able to provide them only with limited details of his scheme, but even those were deemed to be overcomplicated and inadvisable for introduction into the whole building. The reviewers suggested that his system was not suitable for both Houses together and should be split into two plants—one for each chamber. Furthermore, the committee rooms should be left alone to be warmed and ventilated in a much simpler manner. In a final blast against Reid, his scientific peers also concluded that even his general proposals gave them a 'strong impression' that fireproofing in the building would be compromised; that Barry had given Reid all the plans and access required to develop his system; and the 'Great Puffer' (as *The Times* called him) had not lacked for assistance in applying them to the Palace.[50]

Describing temperature fluctuations in the old Painted Chamber as between Greenland and Sumatra, the irritable Lords appealed to the Queen in the summer, praying that she would be pleased to order that the New House should be prepared for the reception of the Peers without delay. This royal address was quite in accordance with the report of the referees, they felt, who stated that the only impediment arose from a delay in the arrangements for warming and ventilating the House according to the views of Dr Reid.[51] Both Barry and Reid were grilled once more by committees of both Houses over the summer as to their respective roles in the tardy completion of the structure. In the end, the extraordinary (but by no means unusual) parliamentary outcome was that the Lords vindicated Barry and the Commons supported Reid.[52] From now on each man would be responsible for air-conditioning the Houses separate from one another, in a typically perverse decision which retained each House's independence of action, but which did nothing to reduce delay, expense, antagonism, or complication.

At the end of 1846, two years after he had returned to work on Westminster, it seemed as if Pugin had had enough. His eyes were still agonizingly painful, as was the mercury treatment dripped into them. So when, for safety reasons, Barry decided that the gas brackets for the Lords should be handed over to a specialist gas fitter—James Faraday, brother of the more famous Michael—rather than being left for Hardman to do, Pugin complained bitterly on his friend's behalf, sending up 'a tremendous letter' to London for Barry. To Hardman he wrote:

> I wish to give up altogether…I am not astonished about the house of Lords. nothing astonishes me. Mr B is a man who does not care for anybody—beyond his own interest. He would see you & me ruined with the most perfect apathy. I entered into the Parliament work against my better judgement. I have every cause to regret it. like everything for the Last 2 years it has been a misfortune. I see clearly you will *get no more* & I may go to the devil. however I shall not wait to be kicked out…I do not see that you can make a great row for there is not time to do the work & I fear if there was a great deal said that he would turn round & say very well—*get them done.*[53]

But Barry wrote back to Pugin saying he regretted he did not take his advice at the start to use someone experienced in using gas ornaments, 'but my great desire to throw all I could into your hands, and consequently into Hardman's, prevailed over my better judgement'. He really thought he was relieving Hardman of work 'he would be glad to be rid of' and had no inkling that Hardman had made arrangements to employ some gas fitters to help him and would now be out of pocket. This he regretted 'exceedingly, and I will do all in my power to make reparation to him' and to Pugin:

> When you consider that extent of my responsibilites [*sic*] and the manner in which I am constantly beset with difficulties in acting with public authorities, and endeavouring to oblige and conciliate all parties, you will not, I am sure, be surprised that I sometimes come to hasty decisions, without a full consideration of the consequences, but whatever

I may do inadvertently, I trust you will always believe that I am ever most anxious to meet your views and wishes in every respect.[54]

And so their partnership went on: Barry coaxing, soothing, and explaining from London the political and financial difficulties to his volatile friend by the seaside. In calmer moments Pugin seems to have felt morally obliged to continue, even though he was under no legal requirement to do so, and could simply have stopped. He took to pleading pathetically for permission to escape. Once the Lords fittings were done, 'then I think you might let me off. The whole work pays so badly that really I should esteem it a favour to let me give up after the heaviest part is over.'[55] Of Barry's own frame of mind as usual we hear very little or nothing. Yet that year, as well as the constant grind of parliamentary and press criticism, his beloved stepmother Sarah Barry had died, costs were now running at nearly £150,000 a year, over one thousand two hundred workmen were now employed on its construction, the original budget estimate had been exceeded, and yet the new Palace of Westminster was still only half completed.

9

A Metropolitan Asylum

1847 to 1850

'MR BARRY IS very anxious to have the great window up,' Pugin told Hardman at the end of January 1847,

> & as fast as you can do the peers lobby windows they are to be sent up & fixed. the room looks beastly without them...send up the grates dogs everything as fast as you can for they are hanging curtains and fixing stuffed seats—everything is coming out magnificently—there is a *great cry for the gates*.

He also sent a triumphant message to Barry: 'the gates are the finest job in the world...they look *brilliant*'.[1] But the following month he was 'very poorly again...I really begin to think I shall never get well...we shall see what the spring will do for me—but I am a broken man I bilieve'.[2] As snow and frost chilled London in late February, arrangements were nearing completion for the Lords chamber, and members were allowed to tour their new home, now almost fully furnished. Such was the effect of the new chamber that even Brougham, long one of most sceptical and vitriolic critics of Barry, underwent a complete conversion. It was, he thought,

> the most magnificent building that he had ever seen in any part of the world, doing the greatest possible honour to the very skilful, learned, and ingenious architect, both in the interior and the exterior of the splendid palace … and that if anything could make Gothic architecture palatable to those who had a totally different taste, it was the skill which had been exhibited by that most eminent architect Mr. Barry, in the design and construction of the new Houses of Parliament.[3]

On the last day of the Lords sitting before Easter, Earl Grey at long last rose to move the adjournment of the House to Thursday 15 April, informing it that, 'after the recess their Lordships would sit in their new House, Her Majesty being pleased to assign that portion of the new building of the Palace of Westminster to the use of their Lordships'.[4]

On the evening of Tuesday 13 April, the new lighting was tested—with perfect success. On the Wednesday morning there was intense activity in the chamber as the finishing touches were put to interiors. Women seamstresses sat on the floors finishing the upholstery of the benches. Each piece of decoration was being nervously checked by its creator—clockmakers, silversmiths, gas fitters, gilders, draftsmen, sculptors. Before noon the room was cleared and Victoria and Albert arrived, escorted by Black Rod and Mr Pulman, his sidekick, the Yeoman Usher. Making a deep bow, Barry stepped forward to show them round the chamber, with Grissell in attendance. She was hardly prepared for 'the graceful, chaste and subdued magnificence of Mr Barry's chef d'oeuvre'.[5] It was, 'unfortunately to be opened without the House of Commons, as the Lords are so impatient to get into it' she told her diary, yet:

> The building is indeed magnificent, in Gothic style, very elaborate & gorgeous. Perhaps there is a little too much brass & gold in the decorations, but the whole effect is very dignified & fine. The throne is very handsome & the proportions of the Chamber or Hall splendid. A Gallery runs round it, into which we went & there is also a Reporter's Gallery. Over this there is a very fine fresco by Dyce, representing the Baptism of Ethelbert by St. Augustine. There are still 5 more frescos to come, as well as statues in bronze of the Magna Charta Barons. The

lobby is very pretty, with tessellated pavement, & stained glass windows, as well as the Royal Ante Chamber, into which we first entered.[6]

The day after, the House of Lords sat for the first time in its new home. At half past four the sitting opened with the traditional prayers—and it was a full 15 minutes before business could start. By five in the afternoon, packed out with Members, MPs, and the sons of peers on the steps of the throne, the Strangers' and Press galleries buzzed with 'one feeling of admiration'.[7] Such was the impact on those inside that the Hansard reporter was unable to take an accurate note of proceedings. Instead, he wrote: 'Upon this occasion their Lordships held their first sitting in their New House. The attendance of Peers and of strangers was so considerable, and the noise arising from their remarks and conversation was so great, that little of what passed could be distinctly heard.'[8]

The new chamber caused a sensation, too, in the press. 'The whole glitters with colours and gilding—carving in stone, stained glass, encaustic tiles, and fine work in metal', enthused *The Builder*.[9] The Throne was a particular source of comment: 'the most striking point of beauty and splendour in an apartment overflowing with every form of elegance', gushed *The Times*.[10] And *The Illustrated London News* (to which Barry had given exclusive access beforehand to allow drawings to be made), declared the Chamber,

> without doubt, the finest specimen of Gothic civil architecture in Europe: its proportions, arrangement, and decoration, being perfect, and worthy of the great nation at whose cost it has been erected. Entering from the Peers' Lobby, the effect of the house is magnificent in the extreme; the length and loftiness of the apartment, its finely proportioned windows, with the gilded and canopied niches between them; the Royal—*truly* Royal Throne, glowing with gold and colours; the richly-carved panelling which lines the walls, with its gilded and emblazoned cover, and the balcony, of brass, of light and elegant design, rising from the canopy; the roof, most elaborately painted; its massy beams and sculptured ornaments, and pendants richly gilded; all unite in forming a scene of Royal magnificence as brilliant as it is unequalled.[11]

The Throne it thought 'the most exquisite marvel of art. The intricacy, variety, and appropriateness of its decoration are so wonderful, that

THE NEW THRONE.

The Throne, House of Lords Chamber: Pugin's masterpiece

many visits to the House must be taken before they are all detected, and every visit will excite still greater admiration at the genius displayed in the design and enrichments of the Throne and its towering Canopy.'[12] It devoted 11 pages over five issues to a detailed discussion of the interior for its avid readers, praising the work of Barry; Crace's decorations and carpet; Minton's gorgeous tiles—lions with a red ground and initials with a blue ground; and John Webb, who had been responsible for constructing the Throne. Pugin was not mentioned at all.[13]

Why Barry failed to ensure that Pugin's contribution was acknowledged has caused controversy ever since. Did he deliberately suppress his name through jealousy? Or was it that overtly mentioning a co-designer might renew the assaults on his own position (and, indirectly, Pugin's) which had characterized debates since 1844? Barry's subsequent reputation among architectural historians has never really recovered from this fatal error of judgement and uncharacteristic lack of generosity, and his or his family's destruction of personal letters and the 1835 drawings which might have given an insight into his motives have made things worse. Yet Pugin, it seems, was not at the opening because he was not much interested. In February friends had become increasingly worried about him. 'I am deeply grieved by the accounts I receive of poor Pugin', wrote one, 'I fear the worst.' His architectural work was decreasing and most of his practice was now decorative. This reduced his income severely as well as his self-esteem: other architects were now taking up Catholic commissions he would have got five years earlier. Depression, misery over his love life, mysterious physical ailments all combined to heighten his frustration at the pressure of work demanded of him by Barry. But unlike Barry he lacked the physical and mental robustness to cope. Friends encouraged him to travel to Italy in the spring, to ward off an incipient breakdown, and he had left London just before the grand opening of the Lords chamber, now recognized as his masterpiece. Crace organized an uproarious party in the Trafalgar Tavern at Greenwich where toasts to all those involved—including Pugin—were made with a bumper of claret.[14] By the day of the opening Pugin had got as far as Carcassonne.[15]

'Rome', declared Pugin to Barry, 'is the worse place in all Italy for architecture.' However by May he had recovered his spirits thanks to a tour of Tuscany and told Barry happily that he was in

a perfect mine of medieval art since I left Rome (which is a horrid place)
I have seen most glorious things. the finest stained glass in the world & some
of the finest metal work...I wonder you never told me of all this you have
been here but I fear it was at a time when you did not perceive or you was
too full of those accursed grecian Dorics—you would be as wild as I am if
you were here. why Italy is the finest country for Gothic after all in the way
of decoration...I long to hear how all went off at the Palace...what was
your diary when you was here? you ought to come now.[16]

The public acclaim showered upon the Lords chamber served only to
increase the envy and ire of the Commons. Now each time more money
was required, the Commons debates became clogged with criticism.
When it came to consider an additional £150,000 for the new Palace in
May, the decoration of the Lords was declared variously as 'gaudy',
'unfortunate', 'expensive', and 'disfigured' by the 'enormous quantity
of painting and gilding'. Mr Barry himself 'cared nothing for the public
purse; his only object was to glorify himself'. With the resignation of
Peel following the repeal of the Corn Laws in the face of his own party's
opposition, and the arrival of a Whig government in the autumn of
1846, Barry had lost one of his main defenders in the Commons. However, the batteries continued to be manned by Viscount Morpeth, MP
for the town of his title, appointed First Commissioner for Woods and
Forests in the Whig government to replace his other staunch ally, Lincoln. Morpeth pointed out that its splendour was appropriate for the
meeting place of the three estates of the realm, and that the Commons
would be fitted out much more plainly, 'such as to suit better with their
simpler and severer taste'. The vote was agreed to.[17]

At two in the afternoon on 23 July Queen Victoria opened Parliament for the first time in the new Lords chamber. It 'looked magnificent', she thought, 'quite full of people as it was. Had the satisfaction of
learning that large as the space was, my voice was perfectly well heard
at the other end of the House.'[18] She was also no doubt pleased with the
arrangements for her ermine and velvet train. In devising the design for
the new Throne, Barry had reassured her equerry that he had made
'such an increase to be given to Her Majesty's Chair in the new House
of Lords as will I have no doubt afford ample room for the Train without throwing it over the back as heretofore and still afford Her Majesty

convenient accommodation'.[19] Nevertheless, in reply to the address from the Commons she told her MPs,

> it is My anxious wish that there should not be any unnecessary delay in the completion of the Buildings for the permanent use and occupation of the Members of the House, and I will give directions accordingly.[20]

The sultry summer weather brought ventilation to the fore again. The Commons continued in its dogged support of Dr Reid in sorting out the air in their own chamber, and some members thought he should have had a public testimonial from them. Reid was preparing detailed plans for Barry to put into execution, and it was suggested that some sort of mediation between the two should be attempted. However, 'I do not think', said Morpeth, wearily, 'that any proposition to bring those distinguished individuals together would be attended with any success.'[21]

On a fine summer's day in early August Henry Cole boarded a Chelsea steamer and bumped into John Shaw-Lefevre. Since his heroic efforts on the night of the 1834 fire at Westminster, the archivist Henry Cole had risen further up the civil service ladder and was now an Assistant Keeper at the new Public Record Office. He had been seconded to help with the establishment of the new penny postage system in 1838, and had invented the Christmas card in 1843 as a method of further boosting his novel pre-paid national postal service. The irrepressible—and opinionated—Cole was by 1845 a contributor of travel articles to the *Railway Chronicle*, as well as a campaigner for a standard gauge and the separation of passenger from freight services. An ardent reformer of all things which seemed to him in need of fixing, he was also a member of the Society for the Encouragement of Arts, Manufactures, and Commerce.[22]

He had been particularly impressed by the 1844 exhibition of decorative arts for the new Palace—woodcarving, metalwork, stained glass, and flooring—which the Fine Arts Commission had put on display in the St James's Bazaar in the spring of 1844 (the same one that had made Barry despair). About the Commission itself he was less than enthusiastic: 'who would think of fighting a battle with a Council of War consisting of twenty-three commanding officers?': an opinion just as applicable to the entire construction of the Houses of Parliament.[23] It was the middle of the 'Hungry Forties', with trade and agriculture in a slump, so just as the cartoon, sculpture, and fresco competitions at Westminster earlier in the 1840s had been intended to encourage the fine and decorative arts, so the Society of Arts had from 1845 developed a series of small exhibitions to encourage better industrial design of porcelain, silverware, papiermâché, and so on. The one in 1847 had attracted over 20,000 visitors.[24]

The two men already knew one another by sight, because Shaw-Lefevre was a member of the Society of Arts as well as Permanent Secretary of the Board of Trade. They fell to talking. Out of this conversation and via a series of mutual contacts over the next two years grew the idea of a 'Great Exhibition of the Works of Industry of all Nations' in which Barry and Pugin would play major, but very different, roles.[25]

Barry had won the battle with the Lords. But now fresh battalions were gathering in the Commons to launch a new offensive from the other end of Westminster. By the winter the Commons Library was in a 'state of considerable forwardness' but MPs were now complaining that it and the residences for the Speaker, Black Rod, and other officials were not yet completed. Progress on these miniature palaces-within-the-Palace could not move forward until the whole carcass was in place, but Morpeth and the architect had 'no doubt' that the once Reid's plans for ventilating, lighting, and warming the House had been settled it would only be 15 or 18 months before everyone could move into the new chamber.[26]

For some this was not good enough. Ralph Bernal Osborne MP, who—like Hume—represented Middlesex, had over the years rumbled with discontent in debates on the rebuilding. The original estimate had been £780,000 but expenditure (he now believed) stood at £1.5 million. This well-known wag and comic turn—the House's jester, but with a filthy temper—now stood up to ridicule the situation. As guardians of the public purse, he thought the Commons were bound not to suffer the gross job of the Houses of Parliament to proceed any further. He was prepared to prove that a more profligate and gross expenditure of the public money had never taken place; and he was determined, as far as he could, to prevent the public from being any longer deluded upon the subject.

Morpeth disagreed. In his opinion, Barry's character and conduct had been 'somewhat coarsely assailed' by this latest intervention, without the benefit of being able to defend himself. Yet Osborne was appointed to the latest Commons committee on the rebuilding, partly so that Barry could appear before them to answer his accusations, and also partly to shut Osborne up in debates.[27]

On seeing Osborne's views reported in the papers, Pugin wrote to Crace, 'I was as indignant as yourself when I read the attack on Mr Barry—but there is always a beast of that kind barking at everything good—I think the government are most to blame in not defending the case better. however it is all smoke.'[28] But to Hardman, who was a closer friend, he worried 'that infernal row made by that Blackguard Osborne about the cost of the Palace at Westminster will *play the devil with our work.* that you may be sure—everything is bad. miserable & bad.'[29]

On 17 December the Commons received a petition from the suspicious Reid to see all correspondence discussing the ventilation of the Palace.[30] These were presented to the House, plus all the contracts entered into by Barry. This revealed that over the summer Reid had told the Office of Woods that the reason why Barry was delaying implementing his air-conditioning for the Commons was that

> Mr Barry has, no doubt, long made the discovery, although he has not had the candour to acknowledge it, namely, that he has failed in securing a proper foundation for the tower [of the Central Spire]; and to save him himself the mortification of acknowledging his want of skill, he seeks, by disparaging the system of ventilation, to render the building of the tower... unnecessary.[31]

In 1848 the wind of change blew through the public finances and its chill was felt through Barry's office and those of his suppliers. The country was facing an economic crisis in trade and manufacturing, so the Treasury cut the budget request for that year for the Palace by a third to £100,000. All non-essential ornaments were to be stopped. With commitments already made well ahead of the budget, Barry was unable to reduce his expenditure without stopping work altogether on some parts of the building. Craftsmen had to be laid off when the Treasury refused to cover the deficit.[32] Pugin's salary was cut in half by Barry to £100, as was that of John Thomas, the head of stonecarving. Pugin was furious. He told the long-suffering Hardman, 'everything gets worse & worse—I struck yesterday for the Westminster work & refused to do any more without I had some money. I have advanced about £200 so we shall see what this will do. wretched prospects. wretched times.'[33] 'My dear Pugin,' wrote Barry in response to this protest, 'you little know or appreciate my consideration for you and my great desire to accomplish all your wishes.' As well as the advance, he had secured another sum of £84 for Pugin for each stained glass window design instead of £68, and had arranged an immediate payment from his bankers from them. Secondly, he had also issued a certificate for his salary up to Christmas which was to be paid in a day or two. He signed off: 'Ever your sincere friend &c &c...'. Pugin still felt hard done by, and complained that the fresco painters like Dyce and Maclise had received £800 each for a few weeks' work. In fact, they had been promised £800 for a six-year contract which was quite a different thing. Pugin was deeply miserable. 'It is more than I have got all the time I have worked for the building. I feel broken hearted. I am a mere tool—a fool—& I will not work—however I have some distant prospect of cutting EVERYTHING & thats is the only thing that keeps me up.'[34] His mood dipped very low: 'it is quite disheartening to me to design these things & have them all thrown away for I really cannot tell what we will do'.[35]

The giant carcass of the building was now mostly complete, except for the upper portions of the towers and the west front of the Lords overlooking Old Palace Yard. The roof leading of St Stephen's Hall was 8 feet away from completion at the top, and the central masses of the building were being roofed in. Scaffolding and hoisting tackle to construct the upper portions of the towers were nearly completed and the fittings for the libraries, Peers' refreshment rooms, and offices nearby were so far advanced that an Easter occupation of them was in sight.

The superstructure of the Palace under construction before the roof, in 1848

The paintings in the Robing Room were underway, while wooden ceilings, wainscots, and doors across many parts of the building were being fixed. Working on the Palace were 1,399 men: 799 on site with 120 still at the quarries, 335 at Thames Bank, and 168 moving between the building and other sites.[36] The confirmed bill now stood at £1,037,505.[37]

A further attack on Barry by Osborne and Hume took place that month. They now accused him of spending public money for his own self-aggrandizement and promotion. The sums which had been voted for the building were very large, Morpeth admitted, but let them consider the object to which it had been applied and the special circumstances of the Palace. Where was there a building at all comparable to it? It covered between 8 and 9 acres of land. It was, in fact, more like a whole town than a building. How many rooms did his honourable friend think there were? Between 500 and 600, and 150 staircases; and he believed he might say that no such building could be found in Europe, except St Peter's in Rome, that took not ten years, but *two hundred* years to create. Morpeth believed that Barry had been actuated by a single desire to make the work a credit and glory to the country, and of course, derivatively, to his own reputation. The devotion of his time and talent to the subject had been most unremitting; and the many anxieties which it had brought upon him had been most harassing to his mind to support.

He was not 'disposed to deny that the mind of the architect might have been sometimes more intent on the credit of the building he was commissioned to construct, than on the credit of the Exchequer'. However, he 'was most decidedly of opinion that the building would be an honour and an ornament to the country' and,

> with respect to Mr. Barry, he must take leave to say, that as a man he knew him to be regarded by those who knew him best with feelings of the highest respect and the sincerest attachment. As an architect he united the most brilliant conceptions with the most consummate skill; and amidst all the classes of excellence for which this era had been distinguished, he believed that a prominent and most honourable place would be assigned by those who came after them to the genius of Barry.[38]

Peel, driven to distraction for nearly two decades by Hume's opposition, now rallied for yet another attack. While it was very unfortunate that the Treasury had allowed building to commence without being clear about how Barry should be paid—by lump sum or a percentage commission—'I must further observe, that I do not think the blame falls either upon the architect, or the Woods and Forests, or the Treasury, exclusively. I think the House of Commons itself must bear a very considerable portion of the blame.' 'I must say also', he glared at Hume, 'that if the result of the deliberations of the Committee in 1835 had been to present to you a building according to the beau ideal of excellence in the hon. Gentleman's estimation—namely, according to the plan of Somerset House—there would have been universal disgust.'[39] Peel made it clear he was fed up with Hume's familiar pattern of outrage: first waging a campaign to limit the architect's budget, and then raging that the end result was so disappointing due to this parsimony that he launched a second campaign to have the new building pulled down. This he had done with both the recent Treasury building and the National Gallery. Mr Barry, he said,

> was naturally solicitous that the work should be worthy of his fame, and the purposes for which it was intended; but there was no disposition whatever on his part to increase unnecessarily the expense, or on his own authority to depart from the plans originally laid down. Whatever we may now think, or however we may smart under the expense of this building, this is satisfactory.

The mild Richard Milnes, MP for Pontefract, pointed out that he was very well contented with the current Commons, 'though it was very like a railway station'. He wanted a great work of art to be created in the form of the new building and, 'this was the first time that an attempt had ever been made to complete a great public work of this magnitude within a single decade; and he was sure that the attempt must fail'. The building of St Peter's spread over a century; that of St Paul's occupied the lifetime of Sir Christopher Wren; and the Madeleine at Paris, recently finished, was commenced during the consulate of Napoleon. He objected, therefore, to forcing the completion of this work within any limited period; and he believed that the creation of a wonderful new Houses of Parliament, 'would not be realised if the architect was to be limited as to the time of its completion'. He was in the minority.

Lincoln pointed out that when members claimed that Barry was being overpaid, they should bear in mind that he had

> to supply all details—that he was called upon to exercise a general and vigilant superintendence—that the wear and tear on his brain and mental faculties was such as few architects had ever encountered—and then they would be ready to admit that it would be difficult to estimate the value of such services. They should also bear in mind that Mr. Barry, by undertaking the erection of this great public building, was unable to undertake works for private individuals—works certainly less in extent, but much more remunerative in their character. Under these circumstances, it ought not to go forth to the world that the House had been ill-treated, plundered, and deceived by Mr. Barry...when almost the only remuneration which Mr. Barry had received for ten years was that applause which he had gained, not merely from his own countrymen, but from every distinguished foreigner who had visited the building. Every foreign architect, every foreign sovereign, or scientific professor, who had examined the New Palace, concurred in declaring that it was an erection tending greatly to the honour of the nation, and reflecting unbounded credit upon the talent and taste of the architect.

At the end of hours of this debate, the subject was dropped. 'What a dreadful row that osborne is making about the Palace', thought Pugin, 'I fear it will cut short our gilding.'[40]

It was just about this time that one of the most important parts of the Palace was being completed. Variously known during its planning as the Octagonal Hall or the Central Hall, today the busy, beating heart of the building—from where all the arterial corridors on the Principal Floor spring—is known as the Central Lobby. With eight walls and four lofty archways, lit from above by arched windows and topped by a huge groin vault studded with heraldic sculpture, carved angels, and decorative bosses, 'its exquisite proportions and enrichments will not fail to cite universal admiration', predicted the *Illustrated London News*. The models for the carvings had been made by John Thomas to patterns by Pugin. Forty workmen were busy just then completing their fixing to the vault on a platform of scaffolding high above the tessellated floor, balanced on 'all kinds of rough contrivances to aid in giving them height, such as old tables, planks, tubs &c' and lit by gaslight.[41]

The Central Lobby vault under construction

Some members did recognize the immense economic benefit which the Palace had brought the country. It provided vast employment opportunities during the depression of the 1840s, and a 25 per cent duty on all materials was flowing into the Exchequer. But Osborne would not let go. In March he asked for a Royal Commission of inquiry, not simply a select committee, and asked just what sort of building it was that they had got. 'An Italian composition, with a Gothic dress', that was what: 'a thing that was so frittered away in details, that in the course of a few years it would be nothing more than a metropolitan asylum for birds' nests and soot'. The wall-paintings were miserable, he declared: Cope's rendition of the *Order of the Garter* being 'nothing more than a gigantic exhibition of legs'. And why was the new name for the building 'the new Palace at Westminster' and not the 'House of Commons'? This according to him was its historic name going back to the time of Edward the Confessor. About the House of Lords—earlier denounced by him as a 'gothic gewgaw'—at the other end of the building he conveniently forgot, and also showed a distinct ignorance of parliamentary history to boot.[42] Lord Lincoln responded, deprecating 'the practice of the House resolving itself into a dilettanti society'.

When he was feeling well, Pugin showed a good deal of sympathy for Barry's struggles and even demonstrated some modest political awareness himself. 'The Osborne row will all end in smoke', he told Hardman, 'comissioners will be appointed & we shall go on...you know there are great difficulties to contend with & great annoyances at the Houses of Parliament work but still it is quite a thing to do & I manage as *well* as I *can*.'[43] In the end Pugin was right. A new Royal Commission was appointed on 17 March 1848 to superintend the completion of the new Palace of Westminster. Both Houses were saying not only that they no longer trusted Barry's assurances on timescales, but also that they no longer trusted the government, in the form of the Office of Woods, to manage the finances effectively.[44]

Revolution was afoot elsewhere too. Monarchies toppled across Europe throughout 1848 as popular nationalist movements took hold. On 10 April a very brief entry in Hansard noted the arrival of a petition in the House of Commons, 'by Mr. Bright, and other Hon. Members, from several Places, for the Adoption of Universal Suffrage'. This was the third Chartist petition, containing nearly 2 million signatures, presented on the day of the demonstration on Kennington Common, across the river, to the alarm and consternation of the authorities. Five thousand police and seven thousand soldiers were mobilized in and around Westminster for fear of revolution. The ancient Duke of Wellington made a dawn reconnaissance of the potential battlefield. One hundred thousand special constables were recruited to keep order, including among their number the ambitious rising star William Gladstone MP, not yet 40.[45] Some hundred and fifty thousand people attended and it formed the subject of one of the most famous early photographs, but the petition's arrival at Westminster occurred in the quietest manner, transported across the Thames in cabs hired for the purpose. In the Lords the old Whig firebrand Brougham growled against the illegality of such 'monster meetings' and the Duke of Wellington considered that 'no great society has ever suffered such a grievance as this metropolis has suffered within the last few days from the error of this great meeting'.[46] It fizzled out, and Victoria remained safe on the throne—as she always had been.

Another £30,000 was voted through in August, bringing the total expenditure approved to £1,021,010. But the new Palace of Westminster had now grown so enormous that it was never quite clear how much had been agreed, or how much actually spent on it, and the new Commission was having a devil of a job working out the sums. Henry Drummond, MP for Western Surrey, rarely spoke in the House. But on this occasion he got to his feet, clearly worried about his own safety. The building could surely not both be ventilated *and* fireproofed at the same time. He was also alarmed at the rate at which the Victoria Tower was going up. It would not be safe to carry the tower up more than 30 feet a year.[47] He would have been even more alarmed to discover that, just a few days later, Barry was engaged during the night at Trafalgar Square at a successful demonstration of the gas burners to be used to light the interior of the Houses of Parliament. A branch of eight burners was introduced into a reflector at the south-east corner of the square which 'threw a most brilliant light, by which small print could be read at 40 paces.'[48]

In September Barry went on a tour of Scotland, travelling from Glasgow to Glencoe (which he loved), planning and sketching the new Dunrobin Castle, seat of his patrons the Sutherlands.[49] Pugin was also in a happy and relaxed state for once. That summer, after various false starts, he married for the third and final time. In the devoted and compliant Jane Knill he declared he had 'a first rate gothic woman at last'. So much so, in fact, that when Barry wrote to him at the end of October to break some bad news, his response was uncharacteristically pragmatic. More austerity was required, and procurement changes were afoot that would affect Pugin's favourite suppliers. 'The most rigid and searching economy is henceforth to be the order of the day', Barry told him. All production of fixtures, fittings, and furniture at the Palace was to be put out to competitive tender on the orders of the new Commissioners. 'We must therefore settle at once upon the designs for the gas coronals, table candlesticks, pole screens, easy chairs, and portable steps for the libraries and refreshment rooms' which the competitors would use to tender their costs. Pugin recognized that Barry 'cannot help himself or else I should blow up but he is in a miserable position…this is a bad job about the House of Lords…I dare say eventually there will be a reaction', he told Hardman, 'but we must expect the 7 Lean years of Pharaoh'.[50] He didn't see how he could refuse to make sketches for Barry, '*if* I get well paid for them But if I do not see a good prospect of getting money I shall certainly refuse'. He expected the 'very next thing' to be another slash to his salary at Thames Bank '& then of course I shall cut the concern'.[51]

He also foresaw that Barry was nearing the end of his tether as well. 'There will be a row soon there for Mr B means to prosecute his claims & very justly too', Pugin told Hardman.[52] And indeed, at the beginning of 1849, Barry decided that now was the time to make good his promise to the Office of Woods that he would be renewing his attempts to get an increase in his salary. The prodigious amount of work he had undertaken on the Palace was hard to imagine. 'No less than between 8,000 and 9,000 original drawings and models have been prepared for it, a large portion of which have emanated from my own hand', he declared, 'while the whole of the remainder have been made under my own immediate direction and supervision.'[53] He had, he estimated, over ten years received money equivalent to a salary of £1,500 a year, and 'have been obliged to give up more than two-thirds of a lucrative practice'. Other professionals in the law, medicine, or civil engineering could reasonably expect to earn between £12,000 and £20,000. 'It is scarcely necessary for me to add', he wrote to them, 'that such an income does not by any means recompense me for the labours, responsibilities and sacrifices which I have incurred.' He claimed a further very exact sum of £22,602, 6s. 10d., which brought his total fee from the Great Work up to the equivalent of a 5 per cent commission for the whole job.[54] The Treasury stalled.

Pugin returned from London 'in extreme disgust' at the end of March. Barry had told him that owing to all the parliamentary attacks on the building and its architect that the Office of Woods were indeed going to have to make severe cuts and—Pugin thought—his salary would probably be taken away:

I then swore that if it was I would never draw another line for the job. it is infamous. I declare for two years the whole money was swallowed up in expenses training up all those carvers. it is only lately I have got any benefit by it—it is really all I get for my services which have been very great & if it is cut off I will do no more. I am disgusted with everything— for I get shamefully treated on all sides—& wretchedly paid . . . I am quite furious—For I have Earnt every shilling of the money if they pay it to me as long as I live. great gooness what treatment. A man to slave for a few years for a miserable pittance like that, & then kicked out because that infernal rascal that double hypocrite humbug thief & imposter Cobden who has got £100000 to his own whack makes a trade of crying out against a little carving & painting.[55]

Osborne told the House he had heard it stated by an eminent architect that the building could not be finished for less than £3.5 million; Hume was puzzled by the holes in the walls newly made for windows, bricked up doors, and constructions and destructions he did not understand; and Osborne commented further that the 'miserable squabble' between Reid and Barry was not over. The change in direction as to who should be responsible for the ventilation of the committee rooms from Reid to Barry had in fact left those areas in limbo while Barry struggled to complete the Commons chamber itself: Hume was staring at the practical results of his interference. One Member suggested floss wallpaper as a means of improving the acoustics. Captain Henry Boldero, MP for Chippenham, complained that during the previous three weeks the smoke from the fireplaces had been so annoying that they had been obliged to open the windows and sit in their greatcoats and he had caught 'a severe cold'. The ventilation of the committee room he had used was bad in the extreme and the smell 'intolerable, and he could only compare it to that of bilge-water in an open sewer'.[56] By the summer the estimate for the total costs on completion rose again—to £2,045,924.[57]

IV

EARTH

1852–1860

Then shall the dust return to the earth as it was;
and the spirit shall return unto God who gave it.

Ecclesiastes 12:7

10

A Monstrous Failure

1849 to 1851

THE FEARFULNESS WITH which MPs demonstrated about their health in 1849 was not, for once, unreasonable. An Indian cholera epidemic had broken out in London, and claimed nearly fifteen thousand lives that year in the city.[1] Barry's own household was affected by the terrible scourge. At the height of the summer he removed them to Blackheath, south-east of the city, where his delicate son Edward had been at school, supposing that the air would be fresher and cleaner there. 'Thank God,' he informed Pugin that October,

> we are all well as yet, which I ascribe to us having pitched our tent on this high and dry place where we have been for more than 3 months & shall remain a few weeks longer. I am glad to find you are jolly and am longing to see your late priggings on the Continent. With kind regards to your Lady fair.[2]

The fearsome disease, produced by the bacterium *Vibrio cholerae*, was spread by excrement-infected water, and food contaminated by that water. But in 1849 it was still almost universally understood to be caused by foul and stagnant air (literally *mal-aria*). In a debate in May on ventilation in the Commons one member, commenting on the vile atmosphere, pointed out that, 'Gentlemen attending their duty there were exposed

ST. JAMES, WESTMINSTER.

The GOVERNORS and DIRECTORS of the POOR

HEREBY GIVE NOTICE,

That, with the view of affording prompt and Gratuitous assistance to Poor Persons resident in this Parish, affected with Bowel Complaints and

CHOLERA,

The following Medical Gentlemen are appointed, either of whom may be immediately applied to for Medicine and Attendance, on the occurrence of those Complaints, viz.—

Mr. FRENCH, 41, Gt. Marlborough St.
(Surgery, Brown's Court, Marshall Street.)

Mr. HOUSLEY, 28, Broad Street.

Mr. WILSON, 16, Great Ryder St.

Mr. JAMES, - 49, Princes Street.

Mr. DAVIES, 25, Brewer Street.

SUGGESTIONS AS TO FOOD, CLOTHING, &c.

Regularity in the Hours of taking Meals, which should consist of any description of wholesome Food, with the moderate use of sound Beer.

Abstinence from Spirituous Liquors.

Warm Clothing and Cleanliness of Person.

The avoidance of unnecessary exposure to Cold and Wet, and the wearing of Damp Clothes, or Wet Shoes.

Regularity in obtaining sufficient Rest and Sleep.

Cleanliness of Rooms, which should be aired by opening the Windows in the middle of each day.

By Order of the Board,

GEORGE BUZZARD,

PAROCHIAL OFFICE, *Poland Street,*
9th November, 1853.

Clerk.

☞ **It is requested that this Paper be taken care of, and placed where it can be easily referred to.**

J. SHORMAN, PRINTER, 4, BREWER STREET, GOLDEN SQUARE.

Westminster cholera poster, 1853

to considerable inconvenience, if not danger'.[3] The 'miasma' theory of cholera transmission was one which John Snow, the epidemiologist, challenged that very year in his paper *On the Mode of Communication of Cholera*. In 1854 he was able to prove that cholera was water-borne by tracing the outbreak of the disease to an infected pump in Broad Street, Soho, and removing its handle—but it was to be much longer before the 'germ' theory of disease finally replaced the miasma one.[4]

Filth at Westminster was also on Barry's mind. Workmen from the Commissioners for Westminster Sewers had broken into the drains of the new Palace at the end of 1848 to conduct an inspection without his permission. The consulting engineer, Mr Austin, reported that the basements were filled with sewage which had nowhere to escape at high tide. Reid had stirred this noisome pot further by providing Austin with plans of the cellars and his ventilation plans, and it was felt that the malignant air rising from the nightsoil beneath the Palace posed a polluting danger to all above. In a stiff rejoinder to the Commissioners for Sewers, Barry pointed out that all the drainage in the Palace had been designed and installed before the sewers built by the Commissioners in the neighbourhood whose incompetence in managing the subsequent laying of the Victoria Street and Bridge Street sewers was to blame for the accumulation of waste.[5] The new thoroughfare, Victoria Street, running from Broad Sanctuary outside Westminster Abbey westwards for nearly a mile towards Belgravia, was one of the most prominent attempts at cleansing the city at this time. Intended to 'ventilate' the ghastly Devil's Acre slum ('a maze of filth and squalor' according to Dickens), its creation between 1847 and 1851 cut a wide swathe through the teeming rookery, demolishing 200 houses and displacing 2,500 of London's most desperate poor. By 1860 the opposite end of the boulevard terminated in the new Victoria Station allowing easier access from west London to Brighton, Dover, and the Continent.[6]

The wall-paintings in the Poet's Hall, today the Upper Waiting Hall, were meanwhile underway, embellishing the staircase landing leading from the Principal Floor to the Committee Corridor above. Also underway (since 1848) were J. C. Horsley's *Milton* and C. W. Cope's *Chaucer*, and J. R. Herbert (who had painted the most well-known portrait of Pugin in 1845) had completed his *King Lear*: 'a noble work, full of power and beauty', stated *The Builder.* John Tenniel—better known for his illustrations of *Alice in Wonderland* and *Alice through the Looking Glass*—produced *A Song for St Cecilia.* In the Lords chamber, Daniel Maclise was hard at work, perched on a distant recess, to complete *The Spirit of Chivalry.* In the almost-completed Commons chamber, the plain polished oak woodwork, ungilded and uncoloured, contrasted strongly with the Lords' sparklingly profuse decorations. The Commons Lobby and library rooms were close to finishing. The piles of the cofferdam, which for over a decade had held back the Thames from lapping against the riverwall of the Palace, began to be sliced off close to the riverbed, now that the Terrace was complete.[7]

Pugin wrote to Hardman:

> I could almost believe that I lie under some evil power that drags me down. I feel convinced that as far this world is concerned I am completely a broken man—I shall never recover myself ... I see I shall not be much Longer wanted at Westminster & may go to the Devil.[8]

1850 opened badly for him. Despite his protests, it was now certain that

> the rascally commissioners have reduced my salary at westminster to £100 a year. just half—& no man has worked harder or better than I have. I have a great mind to throw up the whole thing but my spirit is so broken by poverty that I hardly know what to do & they say half a loaf is better than no bread. I am very much annoyed at it indeed but there is no remedy or justice.[9]

Journalists from *The Builder* magazine visited and 'were grieved by the air of desolation which everywhere prevailed', which would continue until the Commons itself permitted work to proceed.[10] Yet Barry, when pressed on when the Commons would be ready for them, had said that the refreshment rooms and other facilities for members were 'now so far advanced towards completion that, if a sufficient vote is taken shortly, the whole will be got ready for use by the commencement of the next Session of Parliament'.[11] Pugin's finances were still preying on his mind in March, when he wrote to Hardman:

> if I had a little more money I should altogether retire & leave the whole things to go to the devil. I cannot well get over the loss of that £100 a

year. I am sure I have Earned it for life at the works at westminster. it is too bad & I am certain it might have been prevented. I am quite sure of it—for it is like an insult to give me £2 a week for such services I perform in that job. it goes dreadfully against me—& if was no for the expense of this building [the Grange at Ramsgate] I would not stand it for a day but it swallows up such sums that I can hardly in coscience turn away any money.[12]

Pugin seems not to have drawn parallels between the rising costs of his own project at Ramsgate with Barry's at Westminster. By April 1850 he was raging at Hardman:

I am almost wild. I see I am goin to Le[e]ward as fast as possible—I will not go on as I have been—I will either give up altogether or I will not [be] the servant of a set of architects who get the jobs & leave me to do their keyholes. I cannot do it. other people get the profit & I the work & I will not do it. I will not be a draftsman for other peoples credit. my life is completely sacrificed look how I have worked for Westminster & now as good as kicked out & I cleared nothing. I believe you would have been better off if you had never had the work for you have been doing litle else but pattern making & going up and down to look at them. I am sick of the whole job and everything else . . . I am very savage tonight & cannot write more.[13]

The Queen visited on a bitterly cold afternoon in March, much admired the King Lear fresco in the Upper Waiting Hall lit by gas but thought the unfinished Commons chamber 'certainly seems small'.[14] The courts were now about to hear an action by Barry against Reid for defamation. For while Reid was free to cast aspersions on Barry's skill and veracity in the presence of select committees, where he was under the protection of Parliamentary Privilege, when he went on to repeat those assertions outside the walls of the Palace in his 1849 pamphlet *Narrative of facts as to the new Houses of Parliament*, he was subject to libel laws just like anyone else. Osborne declared that unless the 'squabbling' stopped, the Commons would never get into its new home, and he intended to bring it to the House's attention 'with the view of getting rid of both Mr Barry and

Dr Reid'.[15] In May he stood up to ask whether the House would be ready by Whitsun, and what were the nine boilers occupying one of the quadrangles for, and had Barry put in an estimate for their cost? He was levelly informed that the House would be ready in the course of the next week, but it would depend on the weather. This was greeted by guffaws of laughter. But in fact the Commons was able to test its new chamber on 10 May 1850, with temporary furnishings and without heating or ventilation, to see how they liked its arrangement, and Osborne was told sharply that the boilers were there waiting to be installed to provide just that heating for the chamber and the committee rooms he so desired.[16] Members had also just realized that the new chamber was not going to be able to accommodate them all at once. Twenty inches per political rear had been allowed in the seating, which meant that out of 658 MPs, only 462 of their bottoms could be accommodated on the benches.[17] The Chair of Committees of the Whole House had to remind them that this was not Mr Barry's fault. Based on the dimensions specified by the House for the floor of the chamber, he had suggested that a gallery behind the Speaker's Chair could be added to his design to hold 120 remaining members who would not otherwise fit. As the House had rejected this suggestion as being too inconvenient to them, he had proceeded with the plan he had originally proposed, in consequence of no objection having been taken by the House to this at that time.

Now even the government started to lose patience with the Commons. The Chancellor of the Exchequer reminded the House that *it* was 'mainly responsible for the great expenditure' which had been incurred:

It was a Committee of the two Houses of Parliament which decided upon certain plans which were to be adopted. They selected the architect, they approved of the design, and the whole framework of the building was decided, not by the Government, but by the Parliament of the day ... expense beyond [Mr Barry's original] estimate had been incurred in consequence of alterations and additions which had been suggested by various Committees and Members of Parliament, which alterations and deviations were not of course included in the original estimate.[18]

William Clay, MP for Tower Hamlets, said it had become 'very much the fashion to undervalue the design' but it would be a 'noble and magnificent work', and the legislature was answerable for decisions about the location and the building's style. To gales of laughter, Henry Drummond, eyeing Alderman Humphery (MP for Southwark), pointed out that Commissioners had only to take the fattest member they could find and multiply him by 658. As regarded the brilliant external ornaments of the new Houses, they would all be utterly thrown away but for the probability of their forming the most magnificent aviary for swallows and sparrows the world ever saw.

A battalion of guards had been marched into the House to test its capacity. Alderman Humphery worried about his suffocating in the crush there would be when members took to the voting lobbies, as at 'the black hole of Calcutta'. The new chamber was, in his view, 'a perfectly ridiculous composition, which reflected no credit on anybody who had anything to do with it'. But Sir Harry Verney MP recalled (correctly) that after the fire there had been a feeling, similar to the one echoed by Churchill nearly one hundred years later,

> that it was important for the transaction of business that the House should not be too large. If it accommodated conveniently from 150 to 250 Members, and could admit a crowded House with some sacrifice of convenience, that would be better than a very large building in which the small average number of Members attending the House would be comparatively lost.

For Osborne, instead of being an honour to the country, it 'was a disgrace to the House of Commons, and a satire on its character; and with reference to the future, it was necessary that immediate steps should be taken to bring Mr. Barry under some sort of control'. 'It was not easy', sighed the Chancellor of the Exchequer, 'to please so many masters.' The Institute of British Architects agreed. That month it awarded Charles Barry its top annual prize—a Gold Medal. Handing it over to its grateful recipient, the Institute's President Lord de Grey, who was also a commissioner for the new Palace, made the point that not only was the building at Westminster superb, but that the architect had had to overcome unprecedented political and bureaucratic obstacles: 'the means have been withheld, and difficulties unnecessarily created'.[19] This made him no friends at Westminster.

Finally, on 30 May, the Commons moved into their new chamber, with its sober woodwork and painted coffered ceiling, and began to try it out—completely without the fanfare accorded the Lords' opening. One later recalled that many did not take the testing seriously—it being a quiet time in public business—and they approached it as 'a lark'. Some felt the acoustics were a problem: 'I don't know whether you can hear down there, but we certainly cannot hear at all up here', yelled one. Hume suggested that they test it by the examination of a witness at the bar and, 'there was no person whom it would be more proper to examine than Mr. Barry himself'.[20]

On 11 June Barry was up before the latest select committee on the rebuilding to offer some suggestions as to how to accommodate more members in the House. Things did not go well. Two days later he wrote to Pugin of the outcome:

> My dear Pugin—I am in a towering rage, and in the right humour for throwing up my appointment at the New Palace of Westminster, which I expect I shall be driven to do before long. All the arrangements of the New House of Commons, including the form, size, proportions, taste, and everything else concerning it are in abeyance, and awaiting the fiat of a Committee of the House of Commons, of all tribunals the most unfit to decide. It is premature therefore to think of stained glass, or of any other decoration at present. Who would be an architect engaged on public works?

Pugin agreed. 'I am properly disgusted by the findings of these men and it is only on your account that I consent to put my foot in Thames bank or any place belonging to such a set of people. I am astonished how you can work with them. No inducement in the world could make me trans-act business with persons who can act in this manner.'[21] To Hardman the same day, he confessed, 'This glass order being recalled at Westmin-ster has made me very low. It was the only paying job I had seen for some time & I had taken immense pains in collecting all the arms & had even got the cartoons ready.' He had had to lay off all his assistants except one, and a labourer. '[I]t is blowing a dreaful gale. My poor Rose trees are scattering away—& everything breaking and bending—though the trees have three braces to each. These severe gales destroy us. it is blowing as hard as November—the weather is in accordance with the times. dispiriting and disheartening.'[22]

On that first day of that year the Queen had established a Royal Commission for The Great Exhibition, to be opened on 1 May 1851. The Commissioners, headed by Prince Albert, included the Prime Minister Lord John Russell, Sir Robert Peel, and Charles Barry. In addition, Barry joined William Cubitt and his fellow engineers, Robert Stephenson and Isambard Kingdom Brunel, in forming the building's subcommittee. With 16 months to go until it opened, the Commissioners had launched their competition for a suitable building and received 245 proposals.[23] Most were lumpen, uninspiring, or too expensive. Brunel came up with his own proposal on behalf of the committee—a vast brick building with a giant iron dome that was twice the size of St Paul's. On 22 June *The Illustrated London News* had published the design, to universal outrage. There were also concerns about Hyde Park as a venue, and the destruction of the elms which would be necessary. Inevitably the matter reached the House of Commons. As he sat next to Henry Cole in the public gallery during the debate on 4 July, and keen to distance himself from yet more criticism in that chamber, Barry told him, 'I have had nothing to do with the design and repudiate it.'[24] His mood was low. Two days previously Robert Peel had died an agonizing and prolonged death following a fall from his horse on Constitution Hill. Barry's longstanding ally was no more. Yet the same tragedy also dulled the Commons' appetite for a fight over the ugly solution for the exhibition building and the Hyde Park location went ahead.

Then at the end of July Barry's worst fears came true. The committee considering the newly completed Commons chamber recommended the alteration of the shape of the galleries and aisles to allow more seating, but most intrusive of all, following the House's sound test, the flat ceiling was to be removed, and pitched until it was half way across the windows, to make MPs audible to one another.[25] By August it was described by members as a 'pigstye', or a harem. Why, any schoolboy would be flogged for designing such a place! The future Prime Minister, Benjamin Disraeli, stepped into the debate:

> no profession had ever yet succeeded in this country till it had furnished what was called 'an example'...it really became the Government to consider the case, and they might rest assured that if once they contemplated the possibility of hanging an architect, they would put a stop to such blunders in future.[26]

The victorious members moved triumphantly back to the temporary chamber. Barry was clearly aware of Pugin's distress, both financial and emotional, as well as his own. In October he contrived to get Pugin a commission, with Hardman, to furnish stained glass for Canford Manor in Dorset. When corresponding about Westminster in October, he made sure to bolster Pugin's fragile confidence: 'I return your sketch for the light of the House of Commons which I admire exceedingly—the Beasts and Crests are glorious and the effect of the whole if properly coloured will be "*The Thing*".'[27] But, throughout the autumn, Pugin's worries about his reduced salary and the delay in receiving it preyed more and more on his mind.

By November Pugin was telling Hardman excitedly how a dealer had offered him 600 seals in a case for 10 guineas which would furnish inspiration for all the arms they could ever want for heraldic designs, especially for their glasswork. Barry had agreed to pay for getting sources for heraldry and here was a way of Pugin buying authorities for his own use via the Westminster work.[28] But his mood shifted and in December he announced to his best friend:

> I have at length *struck* for westminster & I have sent a fair proposal to Mr Barry to restore me the full salary or I will not [go] on—he has given me *3 weeks work* of details for which I shall never receive *a penny* & at half salary. that will not do. I have told calmly and deliberaly that I will unless the full salary is give me & the arrears paid up. i don't care how it turns out. I would gladly give up. the expense it entails on me is enormous in travelling alone & I will not be sacrificed any Longer in this way. It is *infamous*. I am worst treated than a felon. £100 to give up all my details & knowledge & out of this to pay all sorts of expenses.

He had told Barry,

> I fear the details will not get on very fast unless I receive advices from my
> bankers relative to <u>the</u> balance…I do not care where it comes from, if
> you like to advance it. I shall consider it as a sort of noble act. But at all
> events the pencil will not march & the ink will not flow till this is settled
> & what I have paid works and all…I must strike—it will go on to next
> year if I don't so I <u>have struck</u>.[29]

Pugin felt there was 'a compleat change' coming over him. 'I fall asleep
20 times of an evening—I can't keep up to my work at all. I feel as if I
[have] no inside like a wasp. I am afraid the best of the Work is out of
me—I had hoped to have done more', he told Hardman.[30] Barry again
tried the tactic of encouraging Pugin to think of the nobler object of
their work not the money. It failed. Pugin's anxiety about finances and
his health led to an enraged reply, partly illegible and rambling. 'Great
as you are in grand compositions', he wrote to Barry,

> it is nothing to your diplomatic Talents…if I was not so poor and mis-
> erable as I am I should have fairly shrunk again when I read your exhor-
> tation to turn my mind to nobler objects than that of making some
> return for ones labour why my dear friend I can show you the counter-
> part of that letter *three years ago* in which you held out *indistinct* prospects
> of future emolument & conclude also by expressing a hope that I would
> not allow such sublunary consideration to weigh against *more Glorious
> pursuits*. since that time—the only result has been the reduction by one
> half of the little I got before but the vision of futurity is held up & the
> same exhortation to *nobler ideas*—it is wonderful…But some of those
> days when you touch the £5 per cent on the *3 millions all in a lump* you will
> be tortured by a horrible vision of enormous lists of stencils & tiles pat-
> terns covers curtains diapers stuffs…expenses lodging bills held aloft by
> angry demons pointing to a poor gothic fellow who is fairly starved out.
> only conceive that about 12 at night particularly if you are coming alone
> through the great octagon.

He continued:

> I must get something out of somebody for I know there is no getting
> anything out of you. how well I know your smile that dreadful smile by
> which one can see at once what it means (I wish you may get it). How
> you must have smiled when you exhorted me to *nobler objects* and you
> finish up there. You had no argument beyond that to convince a man he

should not be paid you are the only man I ever knew on whom it is impossible to make an impression I therefore abandon all appeals to you as hopeless I am fairly beat at it.[31]

Next, he told Hardman he was now determined never to enter the building unless they restored his money to him.[32] 'I wonder how Mr Barry & me shall get on', he mused, 'for I have struck now.'[33] Ten days later he found out. Barry penned a firm response:

> My dear Pugin—I have no fear of visions that will only appear before me *when* I touch the 5 per cent upon the three millions in lump. You forget that *all* who are employed in the direction of the works of the Houses by *the Government* are inadequately paid, and the architect worst of all; and also that all the salaries of the Heads of Departments have been cut down, since the work has been reduced within narrower compass; so that in that respect you fare no worse than others. Talk of *your* poverty and ill-paid services. I will undertake to show you that I am in a much more pitiable state than yourself. However this may be, I wish I could make you believe that not only is it my desire, but my determination that you shall either in meal or in malt be well paid for all your services in respect of the Great Work; but pray do not ask for meal when I wish to satisfy you with malt. When we next meet, I hope we shall understand each other better, and come to a definite arrangement that will render unnecessary all further allusion to this most disagreeable subject.[34]

At half-past two in the afternoon on 28 January 1851 fire broke out on a riverside storey of the Clock Tower. History appeared to be about to repeat itself. Barry rushed to the scene with Captain Hay of the Metropolitan Police. As in 1834, Westminster Bridge became crowded with spectators and for an hour it must have passed through everyone's minds that another awful blaze was about to engulf the new Palace. The wooden scaffolding inside had somehow been kindled and between a quarter to three and half past the Tower was concealed in a cloud of dense smoke. But a fire engine on site, and seven or eight more from the London Fire Engine Establishment, put it out within about 30 minutes of arriving and the only damage in the end was a few cracked ornamental stones and scorching of the outside stonework which was quickly rubbed away. Its cause was thought by some to be overheated soot in a flue inside the Tower being used by the plumbers to melt their lead. Others suspected the carelessness of some smoking workmen.[35]

The Clock Tower itself was now two-thirds complete. Tall but unbuttressed, like the Victoria Tower, it had risen slowly on the cramped site at the northern end of the Palace from the inside out, powered by an ingenious framework of gantries on top of the walls which moved higher as the tower grew. Nothing had been tried like this before—not even in medieval cathedrals. The internal scaffolding in both the Clock Tower to the north and the Victoria Tower to the south allowed steam engines to run along rails inside to deposit building materials at each level ready for use, while the tower itself balanced on the 10-foot thick Barry Raft, the weight taken by the stone-clad brick walls with iron used only for the flooring, bell frame, roof, and in horizontal ties in the walls.

Barry's technology amazed the public. According to the *Illustrated London News*,

> There are few mechanical contrivances employed in the various works at the New Palace, Westminster, of more interest than the novel and admirable scaffold used in the erection of that enormous and magnificent pile, than Victoria Tower...seemingly nothing more than three huge cranes...from the interest with which the progress of the Houses of Parliament is watched, it is no little addition to the pleasure of seeing so glorious a range of buildings in progress, to be enabled to note the gradual development of the design freed from all incumbrances.[36]

But the design for the top-most storey containing the clock stage and bell chamber had yet to be finalized. Barry had struggled for years to find a design which satisfied his desire to see the clock stand out, and still none of his own attempts met his exacting standards. At the other end of the building, however, the Victoria Tower continued to rise to Barry's pattern. At its base was the great archway of the Sovereign's Entrance adorned with Pugin's giant Tudor roses the size of cartwheels, while the upper storeys for the storage of records contained a cantilevered iron spiral stair which ran helter-skelter up its entire length. On 4 February 1851 at

203

two in the afternoon, the Queen was excited, 'to drive straight through the new entrance, & only the railing is not yet finished'. The former archway of John Soane's Royal Entrance which Victoria had known up to this time had been demolished as well as his Scala Regia and his original top-lit classical Royal Gallery. Only the Lawcourts outside Westminster Hall remained now of his work from the 1820s. The Painted Chamber, having served its function as the temporary Lords' home for 16 years, was finally pulled down in 1851 too. Originally Henry III's bedroom in the thirteenth century, the location of early parliamentary meetings, and the room where Charles I's death warrant had been signed by Oliver Cromwell in 1649, its consignment to oblivion caused little outcry in the press. The new Palace—the 'fairy Palace' the Tsar had called it—was already working its magic. Just 15 years into the build and still without its towers, it had already obliterated memories of its predecessor.

Memories remained short among Members, not least about their own specifications and choice of Gothic for the building. 'After all the

George Scharf's drawing of the new Palace under construction around the remains of the old Palace just before they were pulled down, 1851

expenditure incurred, had they not produced a monstrous failure, not only as regarded the architecture, but convenience itself?' exploded the MP for Mallow, who went by the extraordinary name of Sir Charles Denham Orlando Jephson-Norreys. Barry had 'desecrated' Westminster Hall by the construction of 'a monstrous passage to a more monstrous staircase' and 'the country had been misled by him in the adoption of a bad style of architecture'.[37] *Domine, salvam fac Reginam nostram Victoriam primam*—'Oh Lord, make safe our Queen, Victoria the First', implored the prayer on Pugin and Minton's tiles again and again across the floor of the Royal Gallery. But God was not inclined to save the architect just yet from his tormenters.

The solution to the problem of a building for the Great Exhibition in Hyde Park had finally been found when Joseph Paxton, the Duke of Devonshire's Head Gardener and agent, went to Westminster to meet the Chairman of the Midland Railway, John Ellis MP. Paxton and his master were closely involved in the railway's development because of its impact on Derbyshire and Chatsworth in particular. The ventilation and acoustic problems in the new Palace came up in conversation, as did the risk of the same happening in Brunel's new brick Exhibition Hall. Paxton, who had designed the fabulous orchid and lily glasshouses at Chatsworth, wondered if a similar construction would solve the problem of letting air and light into the vast showroom space. Four days later he idly doodled his first design for the building on blotting paper, while at a tedious disciplinary hearing relating to a railway pointsman's conduct.[38] His friend, Robert Stephenson, was on the building committee and introduced the plan to them at the last moment. It won most of the Members over.

For Barry, the contrast with his own travails at Parliament was stark. It brought home how slowly his own work on the Palace was proceeding. He was coming round to Paxton's idea—Stephenson and Brunel were strongly for it, but William Cubitt (MP and building contractor, as well as brother of Thomas, the architect of Osborne House) was against. Barry suggested that the design should be vaulted and felt strongly enough about this to threaten to resign on the issue, in the face of Cubitt's obstinacy. In the end, Paxton took on board Barry's suggestion and made the transepts vaulted, which allowed the building to be constructed around the elm trees in the park rather than having them chopped down. The fate of the trees had exercised a number of MPs in their debates about the building, and had provided Barry with a temporary respite from the criticism of Westminster.

The Crystal Palace, as it was christened by *Punch*, was everything Westminster Palace was not and yet many of the same personnel were involved in their creation and success. It was a flat-pack marvel, made up of a handful of repeating components of glass and cast iron assembled onsite. At 1,848 feet long, 456 feet wide, and 108 feet high in the transept it covered 19 acres. That was twice the length of the 47-bay Palace of Westminster and nearly two and half times its ground plan. Like Westminster, nearly two thousand men were at work to build it in Hyde Park.[39] Yet it took just six months to construct. *Punch* joked that the new Palace at Westminster should be ditched in favour of a glass one.[40] Time was slipping by and, at 55, Barry knew it. Sixteen years of his life had now been occupied by the Houses of Parliament. Paxton and Barry were both self-made men, and just eight years apart in age; both men had grown up in the age of the stagecoach but were now using the industrial technology of the railway age to achieve their ends. Their two most iconic buildings spawned offspring for the rest of the century. The Midland Grand Hotel at St Pancras by George Gilbert Scott was a grandchild of the Palace of Westminster, while Brunel's Paddington Station was half-sister to the Crystal Palace.

On 1 May 1851 the glass wonder opened at a colourful ceremony attended by the royal family with Barry present, along with all the other Commissioners including Charles Eastlake. After some hesitation, Pugin had determined to be involved. He conceived the 'Medieval Court' for Henry Cole, a giant booth in the middle of the show, which would display the Gothic designs and manufactures of him and his collaborators at Westminster: Hardman, Minton, and Grace, plus Pugin's favourite builder, George Myers. All other displays were by country or type of manufacture, rather than a decorative theme. Barry had been asked to persuade Pugin to remove a very prominent cross above the Court, which looked set to cause an Evangelical scandal, but as it turned out its position was simply a workman's mistake and was lowered.[41] The Court was an enormous hit, and a poignant one, given the fate of the Painted Chamber that year, once one of the sights of medieval Europe. Greater fame for Pugin brought envy and vitriol along with admiration, and he had a taste of what Barry had already endured for 15 years. John Ruskin, whose ideas on Gothic were about to supersede Pugin's in the popular mind, was particularly harsh. In *The Stones of Venice*, first published in March 1851, Ruskin railed against Pugin. 'He has been brought forward and partly received, as an example of the effect of ceremonial splendour on the mind of a great architect. It is very necessary, therefore, that all... should know at once that he is not a great architect, but one of the smallest possible.' 'Let the fellow build something himself', responded Pugin, returning to the mountain of work still before him.[42]

All the remaining decorations and flooring for the Commons' corridors, the refreshment rooms, libraries, and lobbies still had to be designed and made in 1851, along with many portable items including letter racks, coat hooks, inkwells and umbrella stands. Pugin worked frantically on the patterns, emptying his library of designs while roping in his children to help him fill in the colouring schemes for the hundreds of different tiling schemes before they were sent to Minton.[43] Yet the designs he had used in the Commons chamber did not meet with universal approval. Members complained about the cost of decorating the roof of the Commons, intended to relieve its sombre wooden appearance, and Mr Barry's 'enormous propensity for gilding whatever he laid his hands on'. They complained about the two hundred 'gaudy and very glaring' coloured heraldic shields which afforded no contrast with the 'gorgeous and gingerbread gilding' of the House of Lords. And they complained 'that there were not two square inches of the wainscotting, or any part of the interior, that had not been ornamented, or rather... disfigured, by wretched fantastic carving, so that it looked more like some monastery of the tenth or twelfth century, than a representative chamber of the nineteenth'.[44] Others, however, recognized that these rich decorations added immensely to the sense of history and gravity in the world's most important debating chamber.

Outside the Crystal Palace's western entrance had stood a plaster equestrian statue of Richard the Lionheart by the Sicilian sculptor Pietro Marochetti. When the Crystal Palace was dismantled and moved to Sydenham, a group of supporters campaigned for the statue's erection in bronze 'on some conspicuous site in the metropolis'. Marochetti's patron, Prince Albert, was responsible for the decision to place it in Old Palace Yard close to the site of the former Painted Chamber, where it was installed in 1860 and has remained ever since. This was the statue that survived the Blitz in 1941, brandishing its bent sword towards the skies above Westminster, and it can still be seen there today.

At the same time that MPs were up in arms about the uncomfortableness of their new chamber and the deleterious effects it might have on their own health, it was perfectly possible for them to be debating, without any irony, the housing conditions of the metropolitan poor and 'the effects which those who are crowded into gloomy cellars and ill-*ventilated* apartments suffer in the stunted growth, the deformed limbs, the broken constitutions, and the enfeebled intellects which are the consequences of the deprivation of air and light'.[45] Meanwhile, Reid's boiler engines were proving so noisy that they drowned out members' speeches.[46] 'What was the use of having an architect at all', asked Hume, 'if he would not act on the instructions given him? He had failed entirely, in every single department in the whole building. He defied any man to find a single apartment in the building that was suited to the purpose for which it was intended.' In justice to Mr Barry, said another, he had found that on taking overseas visitors around the new Houses of Parliament, he had never had to make any apology to them, and they were 'impressed with general feelings of admiration'.[47]

The change wrought in Barry during the fight for the Palace since 1844, and by the constant barrage of vitriolic criticism, is evident in the 1851 portrait of him by John Prescott Knight. Now in the National Portrait Gallery, the painting shows Barry looking directly at the viewer from eyes now hooded by too little sleep and too much worry, but with the hint of a defiant smile on his lips. With his black silk neckerchief, gold watch chain, and velvet smoking jacket, this could be the portrait of any northern industrialist or railway entrepreneur were it not for the pair of architectural compasses he brandishes in his right hand rather than a cigar, and the fact that his elbow leans comfortably and proprietarily on a roll of plans of the Victoria Tower, which rises two-thirds complete behind him. The iconography and composition is strikingly similar to that found in the famous portrait of Sir Christopher Wren by Sir Godfrey Kneller, and it had clearly not escaped the artist that comparisons were now being made between the two architects and their most famous buildings. War-weary Barry of 1851 seems very different from the fresh-faced and eager young man portrayed by William Bradley, probably in the mid-1830s; and from the peculiarly baby-faced portrait of Barry by H. W. Pickersgill from the early 1840s, which bears little resemblance to other paintings of him, but which now hangs opposite the J. R. Herbert painting of Pugin in the Pugin Room of the Palace of Westminster where the clink of members' teacups and the buzz of political conversation rises from the floor.

In September and October of 1851 Barry fell seriously ill and retreated to Brighton to recover, while getting more and more anxious about the reopening of the House of Commons chamber in the New Year. Pugin was not particularly sympathetic, as Barry's instructions from his hotel sick-bed became vague, and he was worried that the carvings in the chamber were going to have to be removed: 'there is a horrid Row. What a world it is.'[48] Pugin had gained much public fame for his work on the Medieval Court. And he enjoyed further national recognition when he was appointed to the judging panel for the purchase of items from the Great Exhibition (these later became the foundation collection of the Victoria & Albert Museum). This belated celebrity made him increasingly aware of his position in relation to Barry. He felt unappreciated and his ideas ignored. The heraldry and glass designs for the new Commons chamber were, he thought, 'murdering' him: 'I am an ill used ill treated man. My expenses over that job are frightful ... I am now nearly forty & am handled as a boy as a clerk upon work of which I only have the key.' His growing resentment mingled with his deteriorating mental state in the autumn of 1851 and he claimed to harbour 'every suspicion & above all of certain great men. useful men to great men were usually poisoned or put in a sack when the enterprise was nearly ready.' His letters to Hardman about errors became more than irritable, they became vicious.[49] With less than three months to go before the opening, Barry pressed Pugin hard, but at the same time was becoming overwhelmed himself by the decisions of taste to be made. He told Pugin that if he did not hurry up with the designs, 'inferior things of a modern kind' would have to be brought in, to which Pugin replied that there could be 'no steam without heat and no heat without fuel and that I have no fuel to keep up steam'.[50]

The Commission set up in 1848 to manage the expenditure of building the new Houses of Parliament finally admitted defeat. Suggesting that the building was completed in its most important parts, it handed back without regret the 'great and intricate undertaking...to put an end, as early as convenient to an organisation that leads in some degree to a mixture of duties and responsibilities, by two independent bodies in the management of one concern'. The Office of Woods also collapsed under the pressure of administering the cost of the Palace's reconstruction. In October 1851 it was replaced by the Office of Works, a department under the direct control of government, in an effort by Parliament to gain some control over the decisions of the executive on matters of public buildings.[51] At the end of the year Grissell's construction contract was terminated by the new minister, to their shock. Grissell (who had dissolved his partnership with Peto in 1846) defended his costs as 'barely remunerative' due to 'this most unusual and elaborate work'. He was so angry that he refused to bid for further contracts, thus the towers of the Palace and the west front were completed by the firm of John Jay.[52] All around those involved in the Palace from early on were falling by the wayside, and it looked like Barry would be next.

Yet, he recovered, and by the middle of November Pugin felt 'the Governor' had returned to being 'so pleasant', and that all was well again at Westminster. From that time too, Barry took more care to express his gratitude to Pugin for all his work. Drawings were praised effusively and the older man confided his anxiety about 'the criticism and hyper criticism, that I find is in store for me when the House opens', which went some way to explaining his earlier behaviour.[53] Then Pugin

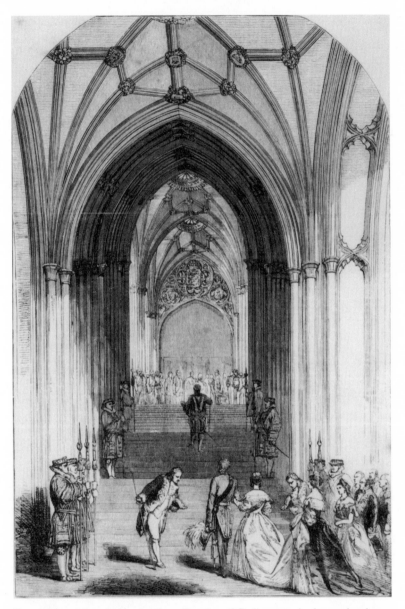

Queen Victoria's arrival at the State Opening of Parliament, via the royal staircase, Victoria Tower

himself became ill. He had a nervous fever with a pulse of 108 in early December; Barry informed Pugin's friends in London, who were shocked, and wrote to the younger man on his recovery: 'pray take care of yourself for the sake of your friends, and I may add the country at large...Again beware of tasking your energies too much'.[54] Barry had promised Pugin that, 'when the present turmoil is over, and I can get away, I will certainly pay you a visit for a day or two, when I have no doubt we shall be able to hatch together much more mischief.' The turmoil was the forthcoming State Opening, along with the opening of the reworked Commons chamber.

11

A More Cunning and Intriguing Man

1852 to 1856

Q UEEN VICTORIA SET off for the 1852 State Opening after lunch on 3 February and, 'with my usual good fortune, which indeed seldom deserts me, had a beautiful bright day'. This was the first time she was able to process the full length of Barry's ceremonial line of route. 'The old Houses are pulled down', she noted,

> & the new ones nearly completed. We drove in under the new covered entrance, which is magnificent & had a beautiful effect. Went up into the new Robing Room, a fine spacious room; & then the Procession proceeded through the Queen's Gallery, & the room, in which I formerly robed, —to the Hse of Lds, which was very full. Got through the reading of my speech well. Were back at the Palace by 3. There was an immense number of people out.

The *Illustrated London News* concurred that the Lords chamber was 'gorgeous and stately', and although the Commons roof was 'materially altered from Mr Barry's original design...it is a magnificent and imposing apartment' complemented by the 'very fine' Commons Lobby containing a post office.[1] The alterations, however, disgusted Barry and he never entered the chamber again.[2] From this part of the Palace he could at least walk away. That year he and his family also moved from the townhouse in Great George Street, where they had been for over ten years, to the semi-rural delights of Clapham, some 4 miles south of the river. The Elms, a large villa on the north side of the common, which still played host to grazing cows, was a chance for Barry and his family to breathe the air more freely away from the poisonous atmosphere of Westminster.

Hume and Osborne remained discontented men. They turned the debate on the report of the House on the Queen's Speech into yet another offensive against Barry. The gas lamps were medieval, the atmosphere in the chamber hazardous and suffocating, the stained glass figures were monstrous daubs, even Minton's beautiful encaustic tiles offered the prospect of a slip and broken bones to members.[3] Then Reid was called to the Bar of the House to give evidence in the chamber he had failed to heat or ventilate. Even Barry had never suffered this indignity. The verbose Reid was given ten minutes to make his case, and then the First Commissioner was ordered to report back five days later into whether, once and for all, there was any objection to Reid's plans being implemented.[4]

Pugin had once again been left out of the public reports of the Commons opening. 'Everything passed off yesterday *à merveille*', Barry told him,

> and the Queen herself announced to me personally that the effect of the whole was 'most beautiful'. So far so good. I am now anxious to add farther to the glories already accomplished, and farther to invoke your aid towards the attainment of that object. Would it be perfectly convenient and agreeable to you to give me bed and board if I was to be with you until Monday or Tuesday?[5]

The designs produced by Pugin in Barry's presence during those few days in February became the most emblematic of all at the new Palace of Westminster. They included the Great South Window of Westminster Hall, and the upper part of the Clock Tower. There had been bell towers in and around Westminster since the middle ages, and Pugin chose to return to one of his earliest designs—that at Scarisbrick Hall in

Design for the great south window of Westminster Hall by Pugin

215

Lancashire—as the inspiration for the clock stage of the Palace's Gothic campanile. Pugin's pen marched *Domine, salvam fac Reginam nostram Victoriam primam* once again round each of the four clock faces with their familiar Gothic numbering. The steeply pitched, tiered roofs of the Tower with their delicate finials picked out in gold leaf, recalled the Flemish cloth halls of the Middle Ages. Barry told Pugin that without him and Hardman he would not have the drive to continue himself. This may well have been true. Pugin was the only man who fully understood Barry's vision and, try as he might, could not pull himself away from helping the older man to achieve it. Sustained by glasses of hot water and brandy, a bottle of sarsparilla, warmed stockings, and heated drawers, he slipped in and out of consciousness, working furiously to finish his crowning glory for his partner. He knew he was dying. 'I never worked so hard in my life. Mr Barry—goes tomorrow. I made all the designs for finishing his bell tower & it is beautiful & *I am the whole machinery of the clock* on a new principle cheap and yet exact.'[6] The Clock Tower was indeed his epitaph.

Barry returned with the designs to London, where the Commons was due to resolve that Reid

> be authorised to complete such temporary arrangements as are imperatively necessary at present for the maintenance of a better atmosphere during the Sittings of the House; That the warming, lighting, and ventilating of the House of Commons, and its Libraries, shall be placed under one responsible authority; and That he be called upon to submit forthwith to the First Commissioner of Works, a full Report of all the measures he considers essential for the health and comfort of the House, together with an Estimate of the probable expense, and the time which he would require for the execution of the works; also, to state specially what plan he would propose for the lighting of the House.[7]

At last Barry was gaining the upper hand over Reid. The same afternoon, 11 February 1852, at Windsor Castle, Charles Barry was knighted by the Queen in an afternoon audience.[8] '*Sir charles* Barry is alright. I am very glad of it. he wrote me a very kind letter, he deserves it well', Pugin told Hardman. But three days after his investiture, Sir Charles received a telegraph which gave him 'such a shock that I shall not easily forget'. Pugin had collapsed, perhaps fatally, and all weekend Barry was in 'an agony of suspense' about him. On the Monday, he received a letter in Pugin's hand 'and was rejoiced to find that you are restored to health again...Do not I beseech of you', he wrote anxiously, 'think of anything you have offered to do for me, except so far as it may afford amusement...take things calmly and quietly for the future. You have really already done enough for the world and for your own repose here and hereafter.'[9] A week later, Pugin wrote again reassuring him, and Barry, much relieved, told him:

> My dear Pugin, I have received your joyous letter of this morning, and was rejoiced to find that you are restored to health again; I am much pressed respecting the Clock Tower and the new front in Old Palace Yard as the building is at a stand in respect of those portions of it, for working drawings. I cannot bear that you should be bothered upon the subject, particularly as several new thoughts have occurred to me respecting it &c &c., &c.[10]

But it was too late. Arriving in London on 26 February, with his son Edward, Pugin was in the grip of a complete breakdown, hallucinating, incoherent, and sometimes lashing out at those around him. Visitors came, were shocked, and left. Edward (then aged just 16) and other close friends, including Myers, were left to deal with the crisis ineffectually, helpless and distressed. Then Barry visited and, seeing the state Pugin was in, immediately sent for Dr Tweedie, an eminent figure and physician to the London Fever Hospital.[11] Tweedie was about the same age as Barry and had lived in Ely Place at the same time as him, which maybe suggests that Barry was here asking an old friend (who was also perhaps his own doctor) to help. Whatever suspicions may have attended Barry's behaviour to Pugin over the years, there seems little doubt that on this occasion he was the only person who understood what was needed *in extremis* and had the good sense and compassion to take charge. Tweedie saw to it that Pugin was placed in the private asylum, Kensington House, and there he stayed for the next months in a state of psychosis, treated by bloodletting with his violence sedated with chloroform. Eventually he was transferred by his family to Bedlam.[12]

Things were also drawing to a close for Reid, or at least his reputation in the Commons. In March, members had yet to receive any relief from

Reid's emergency ventilation works and his formal plans had yet to be published. Some members 'were conscious of a burning sensation of the most painful description around the head; others said that they felt a swelling in the temples; others that they experienced a kind of nervous fever; and some complained of a terrible sensation, resembling that which distinguishes a fit of apoplexy'. A number really felt it was a question of life or death: either suffer from freezing drafts in one corner of the chamber, or suffocate from the evil stench in another.[13] Visiting on a beautiful sunny day in June, Victoria and Albert and their four eldest children toured around, 'entering by Westminster Hall, which is magnificent & walking through the Corridors, Committee & Refreshment Rooms &c'. 'It is a splendid building', mused the Queen.[14] Summer recess brought yet vain hopes among the MPs that their heating, ventilation, and lighting would be improved before they returned in the autumn.[15]

Pugin died at home in Ramsgate on 14 September, where he had been transferred during a remission. He was 40 years old. Cause of death at the time was attributed to exhaustion ('He overdid it', said *The Builder*). Modern diagnoses, speculative but convincing, instead suggest his symptoms were a combination of hyperthyroidism and—fatally—tertiary syphilis, contracted in his teens from an unwise encounter when a scenery painter at Drury Lane.[16] The mood swings, the mania, the despair, and the mental confusion were largely attributable to that terrible and shameful secret. Barry attended Pugin's funeral a week later, along with Hardman, Crace, and others, in Pugin's own church of St Augustine's, Ramsgate, at the bottom of his garden. For Barry as for the Duke of Wellington, who had died on the same day as Pugin, there was nothing half so melancholy as a battle lost than a battle won. Among Barry's personal papers after his own death was found a copy of Pugin's obituary from *The Morning Chronicle* which he had transcribed in his own hand and stored away:

It is hardly necessary for us here to notice—well known as the fact is—how much that great national work The Palace of Westminster has all along owed to the taste and talents of Pugin ungrudgingly bestowed to help its architect in carrying out that vast and intricate edifice—Sir Charles Barry we feel convinced will be glad to reflect that future ages will annex the name of Pugin with his in speaking of that gigantic reproduction of a long forgotten style of indigenous architecture. Cut off comparatively in his youth—without a title and not R.A.—Pugin is yet a name with which the most decorated of artists need never blush to have been associated.[17]

Together, he and Pugin had created what was now being acknowledged in the wider world as the greatest building of the age, but at the greatest personal cost to them both. It was not just that the Palace ultimately killed both men. It was that Barry's name and honour took a severe blow after his own death. The vicious pamphlet war which broke out between Edward Pugin and Barry's sons in 1867 over their respective fathers' reputations was partly due to the enduring sense of grievance which the Pugin family felt towards Barry over both money and Pugin's place in history. They claimed that, following the funeral, Barry destroyed a bundle of letters from Pugin and also the competition plans which showed how much Pugin had contributed. For their part, Charles, Edward, and Alfred Barry did their best to suppress any suggestion that Pugin should have been regarded as anything other than one assistant amongst many, and that the destruction of correspondence and unexecuted plans was to be expected as normal professional practice at the time—and in any case, given the rows in Parliament over the building, Sir Charles may not have wished anything to survive which would revive the memory of those terrible times. Alfred in particular was particularly pompous and defensive about Pugin in his biography of his father. As it was, the official Warrington guides to the Palace of Westminster did not mention Pugin's involvement in the Palace until after the Second World War. Edward Pugin also claimed that Sir Charles had rudely turned down a request by a family friend to be a trustee of Pugin's estate (he died intestate but worth £10,000, so was not quite as poverty-stricken as he feared). Barry vehemently denied this when he found out about it just before he himself died.[18] But Edward Pugin may also have been embarrassed by the scenes which Barry had witnessed on those days in January and February 1852, as well as smarting from—he alleged—having been turned down for a position in Barry's office.[19] A disappointed and embittered man, he died aged 41 from an overindulgence in Turkish baths and chloral hydrate.[20] All in all, it is a sad and confusing tale on both sides, impossible now to resolve, except to say that in life, both men found in each other a closer and far more harmonious and sympathetic artistic association than their sons—and some later commentators—ever wished to believe possible.

Reid was at last dismissed as Ventilator to the Commons. The Office of Works let Barry know. 'My dear Philipps', wrote Barry on 25 October from Brighton, carefully underlining the word 'Private' twice at the top of the letter,

> Many thanks for your note, which has just been forwarded to me at this place—I cannot tell you how much I feel to be in your debt, for the part you have taken in the removal of the Incubus which has for so many years acted as a blight upon my operations at Westminster. It will add at least 10 years to my life.[21]

By February 1853 control of lighting and ventilation was under the control of the Palace's new building services engineer, Alfred Meeson, reporting directly to the First Commissioner of Works.[22] It was a sign that maintenance of the Palace had now moved from Barry's practice across to business as usual. Meeson had been his confidential assistant and right-hand man in the office since 1842. An architect and surveyor with a practice in Wakefield, he had been specifically headhunted by Barry to oversee all the structural engineering detail of the new building as it grew; and he had also played a prominent part in the erection of the Crystal Palace. Meeson was behind the design of the fireproof iron-work for the massive floors at Westminster, which were then cast at the Regent's Canal Ironworks by the ironmaster, Henry Grissell (nephew of the Palace's building contractor), who also was responsible for the manufacture of the fireproof iron roof tiles for the building. It was Meeson's expertise which ensured that the three towers of the Palace were stable, and which kept the building safe from collapse as Reid's ventilating shafts tunnelled interminably through the building. After years of diligent hard work, his reward was this post, which brought with it a residence inside the building itself. At much the same time, the entrance and stairs from Westminster Hall into St Stephen's Hall, Barry's intended Valhalla, were completed, as was the stairway from St Stephen's Porch to the outside world, offering in the form of an elegant corridor the ghostly image of the former chapel.[23]

Reid claimed compensation as a consequence of his removal. It was submitted to arbitration and two arbiters were appointed for each side with the Hon. George Denman as the umpire. They found against the House of Commons. Reid claimed £10,280 in compensation, but in the end received just £3,230, which he noisily but futilely contested. The shorthand writer's notes at the arbitration hearing were banned from being printed by the First Commissioner of Works because, aided by Reid's bluster and spleen, they amounted to some six thousand folios, and the expense would be considerable. Three years later, Reid emigrated to the United States where he lectured at the Smithsonian on his theories. He eventually became a professor of hygiene at the University of Wisconsin and a member of the federal Sanitary Commission. Appointed an inspector of military hospitals on the outbreak of the Civil War, he succumbed to a sudden infection as he was about to start his inspection tour in Washington DC and died there in April 1863.[24]

Reid's compensation was a tiny drop in the ocean of expenditure on the Palace. The sums voted by Parliament since 1835 were now £1,539,000. Hume still believed that, 'as long as Sir Charles Barry lived the new houses of Parliament would never be finished'. He was 'convinced that there would be constant alterations going on, not for any beneficial purpose, but merely to please some middle-aged taste. Why, the very locks and bolts on the doors appeared as if they belonged to the age of Tubal Cain.'[25] Vitriolic though Hume continued to be, for once he had hit the nail squarely on the head. As Barry got older, his inability to draw a line under his plans for Westminster became pathological. And as others were noticing too, Pugin's Romantic Gothic ornamentation was already starting to look dated, so quickly were tastes changing in terms of High Victorian taste. The heraldic animals on the painted glass of the chamber were mentioned in debates on ventilation. Would members 'be guilty of any breach of the rules if they broke the windows, and destroyed the extraordinary beasts which disfigured them and astonished naturalists?' The windows let in too little light for the Speaker to adequately see MPs in the shadowy benches against the walls of the chamber, and he ordered lamps to be fitted, which provoked more complaints about heat and fire hazards from Osborne.[26] It was invariably the noisiest, politically motivated members who stood up in the House to make complaints as a way of attacking the financial competence of the government or to display their own political credentials. Yet each of these lengthy debates also saw a quieter and more reasonable member stand up to wonder what all the fuss was about. On this occasion it was Richard Malins for Wallingford who said, 'he believed from his own experience a better ventilated or more comfortable room than that House could not be found anywhere'.

That summer another international figure, the Duke of Genoa, came to tour the new Palace with the Sardinian Ambassador.[27] Some 18 months later their kingdom of Piedmont-Sardinia joined the British, French, and Ottoman forces which had allied themselves against Russia in the Crimean War. Shortly after this visit Barry became seriously ill.[28] The pressures of Pugin's death and difficulties with the Pugin family, the strain of dealing with the Great Puffer for so many years, the continual grind of his struggle with the Treasury to pay him enough for his work, and the unrelenting personal and professional criticism from politicians seem finally to have undermined his robust health. It is not clear exactly what the problem was, but it was severe enough to put him out of action for some months. He may even have had some intimations of his own mortality. Barry's actions at Westminster from 1854 onwards suggest he emerged from his sick-bed with a determination to defeat all the forces still ranged against him, no matter the personal cost, and with a sense that not much time was left to him. He dived further into developing new projects at the Palace, rather than seeking to detach himself from both his lifetime's achievement and his heaviest burden. Half a league, half a league, half a league onward, into the Valley of Death he rode, openly defiant of the government and of the officials of the Office of Works. At the end of 1853 he presented a set of new plans for the removal of the Lawcourts from the front of Westminster Hall, whose roof he intended would also be raised. He had been hatching this plan to enclose New Palace Yard completely since at least 1843, filling in the northern and western sides with more buildings and creating a north-western towered gateway, larger than the Sovereign's Entrance for the public to enter the Palace. Not only would it provide more accommodation for parliamentary select committees, it could also replace the dilapidated accommodation for government departments nearby. It would, he estimated, take four and a half years to complete from July 1854, at a cost of a further £583,577.[29] 'There *may* be more cunning or intriguing men than our friend Sir Charles, but I don't happen to know such', wrote a rival, Sydney Smirke, around this time.[30]

Goldsworthy Gurney, the Cornish inventor, was now called back to help at Westminster. Members heard how he had spent just £80 removing Reid's ventilation system which had cost £240,000 and had by doing so made the House healthy, and effectually air-conditioned it.[31] He had also caused a stir in the House of Lords chamber by letting off 60 pounds of gunpowder in tiny quantities 'by flashing small portions in rapid succession...I watched the first appearance of the smoke in various parts, its apparent quantity, and noted the time it took in coming and going out.'[32]

Barry's planned but unexecuted New Palace Yard enclosure from the north

The Members' hopes were short-lived. Gurney had in fact reversed Reid's air-conditioning system, so that instead of drawing in air downwards through the turrets of the Towers, coal furnaces were installed at the base of the Victoria and Clock Towers to pull foul air upwards and vent it out through the top.[33] To help the foul air along, each turret also contained three gas jets keep it moving upwards. In a further refinement, Gurney believed that the vitiated fumes of the Palace could be burned off in a flare from the top of the Clock Tower. As a result, he got the main Victoria Street sewer connected to the Clock Tower flues, a practice which was swiftly stopped when the sewer engineer, Joseph Bazalgette, investigated when a small explosion occurred. Bazalgette discovered that methane from a fractured coal-gas pipe was only a trap-door away from the furnace Gurney had installed; only a trap-door away, in fact, from blowing the whole Clock Tower to smithereens.[34] From that point onwards, the simple expedient of keeping as many doors and windows open as possible was introduced. Sir Harry Verney MP kept a pair of worsted stockings and gaiters with him to slip on during particularly ankle-chilling debates. Gurney himself was in the building during the day, and then on call after 10 at night in case of difficulties.[35]

In the Commons, Gladstone, by now Chancellor of the Exchequer, 'could not acknowledge that any blame was due either to himself or to his predecessors for anything defective in the arrangement for the construction of the New Houses of Parliament'. 'It must be remembered that Parliament had never effectually committed the responsibility for these works to the Executive Government.' For himself, he wished it had. Furthermore, Hume,

> was incorrect in saying that Sir Charles Barry was paid for pulling down and altering his own work. A great deal of work had certainly been undone and done over again, but many of the changes that had been made in that, and especially in the other House of Parliament, had been undertaken against Sir Charles Barry's opinion, and had exposed him to much additional labour. The various alterations had trebled the amount of design work the architect had to originally forecast—an amount of toil which very few Members of that House were able to appreciate.[36]

In the Lords the Duke of Newcastle (formerly Barry's champion, Lincoln, when First Commissioner of Works), challenged the House to

> Condemn the buildings if you will,—admire them if you like; but, whatever you do, bear in mind that, from the first year up to the present day, the management and control as well as the expenditure connected with the new Houses of Parliament had been taken out of the ordinary channel, and had been assumed by Committees of the House of Commons and the House of Lords. He admitted that the expenditure upon these Houses had been very enormous, but, if it was made a question of taste, he had no hesitation in saying that, when the present generation of their Lordships had passed away, the name of Sir Charles Barry as a man of genius and as an architect would be classed with those of the greatest ornaments of our country in the kindred branches of art. He confessed he did not like to hear a man of eminence and high character like Sir Charles Barry condemned for what certainly had not been his fault, but for which their Lordships and the House of Commons were alone responsible.[37]

Then there were worries about the stonework which appeared to be starting to decay on the terrace and in the walls. In the Upper House, Lord Ellenborough predicted that the Victoria Tower, 'the very last portion of the building, and the most beautiful one', was so covered with elaborate workmanship that 'its beauty will remain only for a very short period, probably not more than two or three years after its completion'.[38] As early as 1844, the architectural sculptor, Charles Harriot Smith (one of the original stone commissioners) admitted that they had probably mistaken the identity of the stone at Southwell Minster on which they had based their choice. It was not Bolsover stone but more likely Mansfield White and that may have resulted in it not standing up to the harsh atmospheric pollution of Victorian London. The fog of coal soot and sulphurous acids, in which the new Houses of Parliament sat stewing, was quite capable of blackening and eating away at its body in just a short space of time. What also subsequently emerged was that the orientation of the natural bed of the stone blocks from Anston was not marked when despatched to London so that many of them were wrongly laid on the building's exterior.[39] This in turn affected their resistance to erosion from the elements, and allowed it to peel away in layers, a process known as delamination.

In 1855 one the most spectacular pieces of metalwork in the Palace was installed, and is still there today. This was Hardman's brass chandelier in the Central Lobby. Its two ranges of gas burners gave off 84 jets of light: 'when lit the effect is gorgeous in the extreme' gushed *The Illustrated London News*.[40] Barry's new scheme for enclosing New Palace Yard was estimated at £650,000. It would take the total cost of the Palace to £2.5 million: 'a monument to extravagance' thought one Member.[41] Even Dickens complained of it being in the second million of expenditure due to the red tape and ridiculous bureaucracy: 'the national pig is not nearly over the stile yet; and the little old woman, Britannia, hasn't got home to-night'.[42]

That autumn Sir Charles sought relaxation in an extended trip to Paris. With his wife, son Charles (who that year had produced the first of the Barrys' grandchildren), and daughter Emily he toured all the sites once so familiar to him as a young man, as well as attending the *Exposition Universelle* (a French answer to the Great Exhibition), for which he had been appointed a judge. He went to see the Chamber of Deputies at the *Assemblée Nationale*, and the Chamber of Council of State, and frequently breakfasted with his friend, the architect, C. R. Cockerell. He returned for the prize ceremony of the Paris Exposition in November and in return received the *Grande Medaille d'Honneur* from Napoleon III.[43]

Early in 1856 it became clear that the Office of Works was attempting to wrest control of the building from Barry by alternative means. With its 1,180 rooms, 100 staircases, and 2 miles of corridors (the land side of the Palace occupied the length of a full quarter mile) it required permanent management in place. Fire protection for the Palace moved from Sir Charles to the First Commissioner, Sir Benjamin Hall, to avoid a division of responsibility and to avert another crisis such as had occurred with the Clock Tower. At the same time there was clear evidence that the government was attempting to remove Barry's men from permanent posts at Westminster.[44] One of the courtyards was resurfaced with India-rubber, in an ill-advised experiment, and a wooden pavement had to be placed on top as a temporary measure. 'It was not at the suggestion of Sir Charles Barry that this experiment was tried', admitted Hall.[45]

At long last, in the summer of 1856, Barry had to admit defeat in defending his right to a fair remuneration for his work. He had been offered 3 per cent commission on the total costs of the Palace and a further 1 per cent to cover his measuring fees, as opposed to the normal 5 per cent expected by the profession. His last-ditch attempt to improve the offer failed, and on 15 July he wrote from his site office to the Treasury:

> It is with the deepest regret and disappointment that I find their Lordships have put aside my proposal to refer all matters in dispute between us to arbitration. Their Lordships must be perfectly aware that no individual in my position could with the least chance of success contend with the Government, and therefore that the power of decision virtually rests with themselves ... With respect to the completion of the works in hand, I beg to add, that as every other architect employed on public building has been, and is still being paid his full commission, nothing would induce me to continue my services upon the reduced rate of commission proposed but the strong and natural desire I have to complete a work which, by the devotion of so many years of labour and anxiety, I have endeavoured to render not unworthy of the country.[46]

It was, in the words of *The Builder*, 'the greatest injustice that has ever been the lot of architect employed for ... a government'.[47] But Barry got his revenge on Hall and the Treasury by a combination of disingenuousness, evasion, and downright lying: stating that he was unable to stop expenditure on works in line with government budget constraints, as the penalties involved in cancelling contracts and paying for materials already ordered would wipe out any savings to be had.[48] In a row reminiscent of the difficulties faced with Pugin in 1845, Barry then found that he was embroiled in an argument with his erstwhile civil engineer, James Walker, over who had been responsible for the design and construction of the river walls in the late 1830s. Walker claimed than Barry had had nothing to do with it while Barry pointed out that the contract was jointly let, jointly supervised and their commission jointly shared. This time, however, the argument was made public, and conducted unedifyingly through the letters page of *The Times* in February 1856.[49] The architect also found himself having to write to the papers frequently to rebut the publicity of various companies misusing his name in their claims that their chemical solutions were being used to seal the stonework of the Palace and prevent further damage from pollution.[50] Others were writing to the papers with their own remedies, such as the architectural facepack being used at Notre Dame in Paris: a silicate of potash injected every three hours into clay pressed against the damaged stonework over a period of four days (silicalization was reported to have been tested at Westminster without success).[51]

The northern end of the Houses of Parliament, it seemed to Lord St Leonards,

> had been left unfinished, manifestly with the intention that the clock-tower should be continued on that side of New Palace Yard. Really the Government seemed to have created eyesores for the purpose of compelling Parliament to acquiesce in their schemes. The clock-tower obviously could not be left in its present state; it should be continued and New Palace Yard should be enclosed with handsome gates to admit the carriages of Members, and suitable accommodation should be provided for both carriages and horses, instead of the present ugly coal-shed, which any one could get put up for £10, and which, if they did, they would be glad to give £20 to pull down again.[52]

All this time, work to furnish the mechanism to go at the top of the Clock Tower had been underway. It too had fallen prey to what was described in the House of Lords as 'a system of blundering, conflicting authorities, and contradictory orders', in other words, the chronic parliamentary malady.[53] As early as 1844 Barry had, in his normal fashion, approached his expert friend, the Queen's Clock-Maker, Benjamin Vulliamy, to offer up some plans for 'The Great Clock' at a cost of 100 guineas (200 if he was not subsequently given the contract to make it). In echoes of the 1835 acrimony, Vulliamy's rivals, notably Edward Dent, pressed for a competition to be judged by the Astronomer Royal, George Airy (for whom he had made clocks for the Royal Observatory at Greenwich). This had happened and the entrants to make 'a King of Clocks' in 1846, as Benjamin Hall called it, were Dent, John Whitehurst of Derby, and a very reluctant Vulliamy, who was 'excessively angry' with Airy for having pulled the rug from under his feet and whom he felt to be prejudiced in favour of Dent. All three tenders had to meet a range of highly demanding specifications for a striking turret clock as set by Airy, incorporating four giant dials with eight hands in total, which had to comply with the requirement that 'the first blow for each shall be accurate to a second of time'.[54] Dent submitted a quarter-sized cardboard model with his plans; Vulliamy referred the judges to his work at Batchwood Hall, the country seat of the Palace's construction contractor Morton Peto; while Whitehurst used his turret clock at the parish church of Bray as his reference example.[55]

By 1849 things had become mired in delay. The House ordered all correspondence on the matter to be published. Two more competitors asked to be considered. Dent threatened to withdraw when he heard a rumour that Vulliamy was set to supply the mantel and long-case clocks for the Palace interior. Vulliamy demanded his 100 guineas regardless, as he saw no prospect of completing the work before he died (he was 70). At this point the appallingly difficult character, Edmund Beckett Denison—ecclesiastical lawyer, amateur architect, professional controversialist, and horologist—hove into view.

At the Great Exhibition Dent's turret clock mechanism had been much admired, with its three-train flatbed movement, built to the

Edmund Beckett Denison

designs of Denison himself. At the end of 1851 Airy suggested bringing Denison on board as a co-adjudicator of the competition in an attempt to come to a final decision. Denison was arrogant, spiteful, and opinion-ated, but also a talented horologist. His father was also MP for the West Riding and Chairman of the Great Northern Railway (whose London terminus, King's Cross, became the home of the Denison–Dent clock after the Great Exhibition closed).[56] His favoured method of attacking his enemies was to fire fusillades of bilious correspondence at the letters pages of *The Times,* and he was so notoriously misanthropic that a con-dition of his election as President of the Horological Institute was that he would agree not to attend its dinners for fear of chewing up his pro-fessional colleagues. On building himself a house at Batch Wood, near St Albans in Hertfordshire (the gross over-restoration of the nearby cathedral was down to him), he proudly declared himself to be 'the only architect with whom I have never quarrelled'.[57] In clarifying how the design for the Great Clock should incorporate a telegraphic signal to Greenwich to assure its accuracy, Denison produced a completely new design, and Dent agreed to make it for the Office of Works at a cost of £1,800.[58] Airy had dismissed Vulliamy's offering as 'a village clock of very superior character'. Vulliamy initiated legal proceedings but died three years later. But Dent also died, in 1853, halfway through making Denison's mechanism, and the works at Somerset Wharf off the Strand in London was inherited by his alcoholic stepson, Frederick.[59] The clock was finally completed in 1854 but, as it was without bells, dials, or even a completed bell chamber and clock stage, it would have to wait for an unspecified amount of time before it was placed in its final home at the top of the Tower. For the next 18 months, the four dial openings gaped sadly across Westminster, waiting to be filled, and it was to be another five years before the mechanism was installed.

By February 1856 the Earl of Eglinton (he of the 1839 Tournament), was complaining to his fellow peers that while,

> that beautiful edifice was rapidly approaching completion...he knew not whether their Lordships had observed the dial-plate put up on one side of the tower; but it certainly appeared to him that if all the dial-plates

Work on the Clock Stage progresses

were to be furnished with the same hieroglyphics which disfigured the face of the dial-plate now put up, the public at large would not be very much the wiser as regarded the time of day, though it might give some information to those of their Lordships who had obtained some knowledge of mediæval art. He would suggest that the figures should be modernised, and made intelligible.

He had also heard a rumour that the Tower that was now nearly roofed in had been so constructed as to exclude the possibility of the clock or bells being got in. If that were so, it would certainly be a very curious oversight on the part of the architect. Barry sought to justify the Gothic numerals on the cast iron and opaque white glass dials, each 7 metres in diameter and weighing 4 tons each.

> The truth is, that the clearness of the numerals is of little importance if their position is clearly defined within some definite form that will duly correspond with the point of the hour hand. The clearness of the division of the minutes is really of the only great importance, and you will see, therefore, that an unusual prominence is given to the minute-hand for that purpose.

As to Eglinton's other concern, Barry brushed it away: 'there was no foundation for the rumour—it would be found that the clock and bells would go in perfectly well'.[60]

But Barry knew different. Airy had been referred to the unreliable Dr Reid to ascertain the size and shape of the air shaft down which the clock weights would hand, and up which the bells would be hauled on installation.[61] As with most things with which Reid was involved, obfuscation and confusion resulted. This was certainly true about the Great Bell, as *The Times* discovered:

> Of course, no one is to blame; no one ever is to blame when Government affairs get into a scrape…this systematic clock tower has built itself up, like George III's dumpling, so that there is no knowing how the apple is to get in. When Mr Disraeli hears of the £3,000 required to pull down the scaffolding and stonework he will 'give up all notion of hanging the architect'.[62]

12

The Great Work

1856 to 1860

T HE CLOCK TOWER, with its elegant dial faces and world-famous chiming bells, was a miracle of civil engineering. The hundred or so ounces of gold leaf decoration cost over £1,000, and three times the thickness of the usual gilding was applied because of the poisonous atmosphere in the skies above Westminster.[1] Down on the ground, Denison had opposed the addition of the First Commissioner of Works as a referee for the bells contract, in characteristic form:

> I beg to decline acting as a referee with a person who must be incompetent to give any useful directions on the subject of the reference...and I will be no party to any such absurdity as that of subjecting the bell founder to the control and the competent referees to the interference of an incompetent one, who is, moreover, pretty sure to act under the advice of somebody else behind the scenes.[2]

Messrs Warner & Sons of Cripplegate were duly chosen to cast the bells, but their works at Jewin Street had too small a furnace for the job of creating the 14-ton bell that Barry required for the Palace's time-keeper. Instead, the work was to be done at Warner's new foundry in the village of Norton, near Stockton on Tees. On the morning of 6 August 1856 18 tons of metal in a mix of 22 parts copper to seven of tin was loaded into two furnaces, and two hours later was released in a molten stream around the mould of the Great Bell to the cheers and applause of invited visitors. A fortnight later the mould was broken open to reveal the largest bell ever to have been made in Britain and of an unusual shape so that it could be hoisted sideways up inside the narrow shaft of the Clock Tower. Of the quarter bells, the biggest was also cast at the Norton foundry, the remaining three at Cripplegate.[3]

For the first week of September, the public paid sixpence an adult (or threepence for a child) to view it: 7.5 feet high, pitched to ring out an E natural, and weighing over 15 tons. It then travelled by rail to West Hartlepool docks to be loaded onto *Wave*, a coastal schooner plying the east coast of England. Surviving a plummet onto the deck of the flat-bottomed barge, when one of the chains hauling it over snapped, the weight of the bell started to sink the boat which had to be towed onto a sandbank by two steamers. Refloated, *Wave*, with its cargo repositioned on deck and insured for £3,000, set off in early October to London through the choppy waters of the North Sea. About five days later she arrived at Maudsley's Wharf on the Lambeth side of Westminster Bridge, no worse for a storm encountered at sea, and the bell was duly christened 'Big Ben' by *The Times*, probably in dubious honour of Sir Benjamin Hall, the most recent First Commissioner of Works. It was unloaded onto a strong wheeled truck on 21 October, and then pulled by a team of 16 dray horses across the river to New Palace Yard where Barry and others were waiting to receive it. It was at last suspended on a huge timber frame at the base of the Clock Tower for testing. On 13 November Denison led the first trial of the bell using its 7-hundred-weight clapper, forged in Houghton-le-Spring, County Durham. Ringings of the bell continued over the next months for public amusement.[4]

And then, at the end of October 1857, Big Ben cracked. Denison explained to Hall:

> Through some mistake or accident, which the founders say they cannot account for, the waist (or thin part of the bell) was made one-eighth inch thicker than I designed it. The consequence was that it required a clapper of twelve cwt. instead of seven cwt. to bring the full sound out; and although the sound-bow or striking part of the bell bore this clapper for nearly a year, it gave way at last. If the bell had cracked when it was first

tried with this clapper the founders would undoubtedly have had to recast it at their own expense, as they had engaged to make it according to my drawings, and in fact had refused (as you know) to undertake the job unless I would take the responsibility of designing all the bells.

The new bell, Denison promised, was to be delivered sound by the middle of February, 'and is not to be paid for until it has been tried by ringing with a seven cwt. clapper, nor unless it agrees with the prescribed dimensions, composition, and specific gravity. Nothing more can be done to secure its goodness and its durability.'[5] What Denison failed to tell Hall was that his prescribed mix of bell metal, which he had insisted on in spite of Warner's protests, had produced a casting more brittle than usual, and the hammer had been excessively heavy when he showed off the bell's sound to the public. Over the course of a week, Big Ben was broken up by means of a giant wrecking ball. The spectators were 'like mourners at a funeral', according to the *Illustrated London News*. The shattered pieces were then transported to George Mears' Whitechapel Bell Foundry in east London.[6] It was back to the drawing-board.

It took 20 hours for Mears' to melt the first Big Ben, and two weeks for the recast bell to cool in its pit. The cost of recasting was £572 exactly.[7] It still sounded an E, and the intact quarter bells were tuned to a B, E, F# and the G# an octave above it. At 11 in the morning on 28 May 1858, the new bell, nicknamed 'Victoria', crossed over Westminster Bridge to cheering crowds. So much so, in fact, that the police had considerable difficulty in keeping the approaches to the Palace clear, in scenes reminiscent of the surging spectators at the fire in 1834. 'Victoria' was not the only name suggested for the Great Hour Bell. One MP suggested that as its predecessor's namesake was now out of office, and replaced in the new government by Sir John Manners as First Commissioner of Works, 'he thought the new bell would be very appropriately designated as "Little John"'.[8] At one point, the *Manchester Guardian* referred to the Great Hour Bell as 'St Stephen's', but in the end, the name Big Ben rose again, inscribed with the words:

This bell, weighing 13 tons, 10 Cwt, 3 Qrs, 15 lbs was cast by George Mears of Whitechapel, for the Clock of the Houses of Parliament, under the direction of Edmund Beckett Denison, Q.C. in the Twenty

The second Big Ben entering the Clock Tower sideways

first year of the reign of Queen Victoria, and in the Year of Our Lord, MDCCCLVIII.

The bell was rolled into the base of the Clock Tower and then a hand-powered winch, wound by shifts of eight men at a time (instead of a steam-engine, which was thought to be too dangerous), was used to haul the bells up the weight shaft. Over a day and a night, Big Ben was slowly pulled up the Tower fixed sideways into a wooden cage, illuminated by gas jets to show progress up to the belfry 200 feet above.[9]

236

Far below, trouble was brewing in the river itself. In August 1857 MPs had been in contact with the local authorities of Lambeth, 'with regard to certain noxious trades carried on in that parish, and which, as was obvious to the perception of every one who put his nose out of the library windows of that House, were to a considerable extent the cause of the bad vapours which entered the House from the direction of the Thames'.[10] Hall was as truculent and difficult with the civil engineer, Joseph Bazalgette, about the expenditure and design of the desperately needed metropolitan sewerage system as he had been with Barry about the Palace.

By June the following year, with Manners at the helm of the Office of Works, the quantity of sewage discharged daily into the river amounted to 90 million gallons. Only 400 million gallons of freshwater gushed into the tidal Thames over Teddington Lock, 'so that the bulk of wholesome water which daily flowed down the river was not more than four times that of the sewage with which it mixed', and was insufficient to dilute and deodorize the filthy outfall mixed with the poisonous industrial waste expelled day and night from soap-makers, bone glue-boilers, potteries, tar manufactories, and the growing number of other industries along its banks. Goldsworthy Gurney had recently proved before a select committee that the sewage, instead of being carried down the estuary and out to sea, never to be seen again, was in large part making an unwelcome, and un-decomposed, return up-river with every flood tide.[11] It was the same all along the Thames from Teddington to the Isle of Grain where the river met the North Sea. The outfall from Barry's sewers from the Palace could not help but contribute to this toxic porridge. During those hot, sweltering summer months of 1858, the occupants of the House of Lords and House of Commons were treated to the olfactory and visual sensations of their own excrement, rotting and suspended in the Thames, gently washing to and fro past the libraries and committee rooms on the eastern front of the Palace as each tide came and went. A cartoon in *Punch* (established in 1842) depicted the diseases in the river making offerings to the fair city of London, in a parody of the murals commissioned for the Palace.

Cartloads of fish were being pulled out of the water, dead. Trips by river steamer were intolerable, with passengers obliged to drink large

PUNCH, OR THE LONDON CHARIVARI.—July 3, 1858.

DIPHTHERIA.   SCROFULA.   CHOLERA.

FATHER THAMES INTRODUCING HIS OFFSPRING TO THE FAIR CITY OF LONDON.

Satirical fresco design for the Palace of Westminster at the time of the Great Stink

doses of 'stimulating alcohol', in order to counteract the nauseating effects of the voyage. And residents of the banks walked about in fear of the cloud of *mal-aria* which they believed harboured typhus, malaria, cholera, and presaged an epidemic. On 18 June Goldsworthy Gurney told the House through Manners that

> the air entering directly the House of Peers and Commons through the proper ventilating channels is purified from the river effluvia by the spray jets. For the purification of the air coming in through the windows of the House of Lords and Commons, should either be opened, I have placed canvass moistened with a weak solution of chloride of zinc and lime. The same is being fixed at all the windows likely to be opened towards the river in the libraries and committee rooms.

When Parliament was not sitting, labourers were dispatched to shift the stinking muck on the shoreline away from Barry's terrace at low tide. But when both Houses were in session, this was not desirable. Instead, Mr Gurney had been engaged all that day in distributing throughout the Thames, in the vicinity of the Houses of Parliament, four or five boat-loads of lime, and in spreading lime over the mud banks. There was nothing more that could be done.[12] Reporting the debate, *The Times* leader stated:

> Parliament was all but compelled to legislate upon the great London nuisance by the force of sheer stench. The intense heat had driven our legislators from those portions of the buildings which overlook the river. A few members, bent upon investigating the matter to its very depth, ventured into the library, but they were instantaneously driven to retreat, each man with a handkerchief to his nose. We are heartily glad of it.[13]

Parliament did not, as is often stated, suspend its sittings because of the Great Stink. There were only murmurings about moving sittings up-river to Oxford or Henley. Certainly, the Leader of the House, Disraeli, had been driven from the Commons handkerchief to his nose, and committees, as those closest to the river, complained bitterly of the vile smell. But ensconced in the chambers in the middle of the building, a flurry of debates took place in June and July, as Members desperately sought a solution which would resolve the squabbles between the government and the Metropolitan Board of Works over the exact location of the outfalls which Bazalgette had proposed in his plan to divert London's stream of excreta by means of intercepting sewers. On 15 July Disraeli introduced the Metropolis Local Management Amendment Bill which gave the Board the necessary powers to at last site the outfalls where they were needed without interference. (Disraeli himself was not above using the river for his own satirical purposes. When asked the difference between a misfortune and a calamity he is supposed to have said that, 'if Gladstone fell into the Thames, it would be a misfortune. But if someone dragged him out again, that would be a calamity.') Holding their noses, the Members passed his bill through Parliament in just 18 days and, as a result, another spectacular piece of civil engineering for London—after the Palace and Great Exhibition hall—came into being in the form of its sanitation system and the embankments which had begun with Barry's work at Westminster. By 1877 Bazalgette's scheme had proved so successful that he was able to state that in 1858 the river had been so disgusting that 'it was suggested that Parliament would have to abandon its sittings at Westminster whereas now I have the evidence before me of flounders being frequently caught in the neighbourhood of Westminster'.[14]

Rumours now circulated among members 'that serious decay has taken place in the foundation stone of this House, causing the structure to give way in several places'. Sir John Manners reassured them that Sir Charles said they were groundless, 'and that though the stones of the building, like all stones in London subject to atmospheric influence, had suffered decomposition on the surface to some degree, yet the stability of the structure was not affected, and there was no real ground for apprehension'.[15]

Barry wrote to *The Times* on 30 June 1858 on this and regarding public worries about the giant cast-iron tiles on the roof of the Palace. 'Metal roofs were not contemplated in the original design. They were resorted to upon the adoption by the Government of Dr Reid's plans for warming, ventilating &c., by which they were required to contain, as they now do, the main smoke flues of the building, and therefore it became necessary that they should be constructed entirely of fireproof materials.' Coated with zinc paint, which did not withstand the 'smoky and impure atmosphere' of London, they consequently rusted. 'As regards their stability and weatherproof qualities, however, they are none the worse on that account', he reassured readers, and trials were ongoing as to the best anti-oxide composition which could be applied. This was true and, as it turned out, they resisted for the most part the incendiary bombs of the Second World War, and were only repaired some 160 years afterwards. As to the stonework, while there had been some decay due to metropolitan pollution, Barry admitted, 'upon the whole, it has turned out to be as good as any stone hitherto employed in London…to say, therefore, as has been recklessly asserted, that the stone is perishing in all directions, conveys a most unfair and exaggerated impression relative to its accurate condition'.

By March 1859 Big Ben had still not rung. The Commons asked Manners, 'whether the Bells are now all fixed in the Clock Tower; whether the Works of the Clock have also been placed there; when the

Clock will be in working order; and the total expense of the Clock?'
Manners read out a letter from Barry:

> I have to inform you that the bells of the great clock at the New Palace,
> at Westminster, were hoisted as soon as they were approved by the refer-
> ees appointed to judge of their tone and quality, and have been fixed
> more than three months. With respect to the clock, I am unable to say
> what progress has been made with it, or when it may be completed; but
> Mr. E. B. Denison, under whose sole superintendence the manufacture
> and supply of it is placed, will, doubtless, be able to afford the informa-
> tion which the First Commissioner of Her Majesty's Works requires
> respecting it. I am, &c. Charles Barry.

While Denison said:

> The answer to the first part of the question you have sent me is that the
> bells have been fixed in the Clock Tower; but they are now let down a
> little, to enable some pieces to be put into the frame, of the nature of
> diagonal braces to strengthen it against the shake caused by the blow of
> the great hammer...I am assured that the clock-room will be ready for
> the clock in a week, and that the bell frame will be finished very soon,
> and therefore I see no reason why the clock should not drive the hands
> and be striking in a few months.[16]

On the other side of the Central Lobby, Lord Campbell pointed out in
the Upper House, that something was definitely wrong with the Great
Clock. Members observing the four dials saw that the hands on each
pointed to different figures. They had only ever worked for half an hour
at most. In April he complained they had only moved five minutes that
month. 'He did not think this rate of progress very satisfactory.' It was
explained that the parties 'who had this business in hand' (meaning Denison and Barry) 'were very difficult to deal with' but that it would soon be
fixed. In July the cause of the problem was recognized.[17] Pugin's elaborate
design for the ornamental Gothic minute hands made them too heavy to
move round the dial, to a metal mix supervised by Denison. Barry swiftly
pointed this out and Denison accused him in the press of 'carelessness
and blundering...extravagancies and miscarriages at Westminster while
others have got the blame'.[18] The solution was to recast them in a lighter
metal to a different design. Even today, the eagle-eyed visitor passing

Westminster will notice that the minute hands of the Great Clock are straight and plain, unlike their counterparts for the hour.

That summer, 10 tons of lime were still being poured every day into the Thames in order to deodorize the river, and endless linen curtains were dipped in chloride of lime for the libraries and committee rooms.[19] Cure seemed, as ever, better than prevention. In the same fashion, the Commons continued to recycle the same topics of complaint that had been favourites for at least the previous twenty years, never tiring of their themes and never producing a satisfactory remedy to any since each Member had a different opinion, and none were prepared to take expert advice or give way for the benefit of Parliament as a whole. Round and round they went, in ever-decreasing circles: on Gothic versus Classical in public buildings (this time in Whitehall); on the causes and remedies for stone decay or otherwise; on the flaking frescoes in the Upper Waiting Hall; the peril to their fragile health in such a location; on whether the most efficient mode of ventilation 'was that which they all adopted in ventilating a bed-room—namely, opening a window'; and on acoustics alleged to be so bad that, 'in some positions hon. Members were completely debarred from knowing what was going on...It was strange that those who designed that House should have ignored the excellent buildings in America, and upon the Continent for Legislative Assemblies' where hemicycles, rather than parallel benches for government and opposition, were the norm. But most of all, they really 'wished to know whether the account with Sir Charles Barry was closed?'[20]

The Great Clock began whirring on 31 May. Big Ben first struck the hour on 11 July 1859. The quarter bells joined at the beginning of September. To whom, asked Alderman Salomans, for Greenwich, were they indebted

> for the funeral notes which every hour struck upon the ear of the House? He hoped that the First Commissioner of Works, or Mr. Denison, or Sir Charles Barry, or whoever it was that was responsible, would try to make

some alteration in the tone of the bell. It was too bad that the Members of that House and the people should be condemned from hour to hour to hear that dreadful noise, a noise which they could only expect to hear when the great bell of St. Paul's was tolled on the death of a member of the Royal Family.

Thomson Hankey, MP for Peterborough, asked whether there was 'any chance of the bell sounding more like ordinary bells? At present it inflicted great annoyance upon the public and the House.' The First Lord of the Admiralty, and MP for Droitwich, Sir John Pakington, suggested a compromise. 'Why should not an arrangement be made, that all the faces of the clock should tell the hour, and the horrible tolling should cease?'[21] On 1 October 1859 they got their way. The *Daily Telegraph* reported how 'The great bell of St Stephen's tolled his last on Saturday afternoon. Big Ben like his predecessor, is cracked and his doleful E Natural will never again be heard booming over the metropolis.'[22] Denison accused Mears of filling holes in the metal with cement and then painting over them. Mears sued for libel. Denison settled out of court.

In March 1860 the MP for Stafford, John Wise, had observed that decomposition was not confined to the plain face of the stone, but extended to the sills, bases, capitals, plinths, and the stonework above and below all these. Several of the entablatures, lions, shields, and the carving generally were beginning to be affected; and he was afraid that,

> some of the old Druids might fancy they were much older than they really were, and that King John or some other old monarch might fall from his niche, and that the only ruler in British history who had not found a place in the building [Oliver Cromwell] might suppose that room was being made for him among the Sovereigns...He had seen a great deal of scraping going on, and had observed men applying several different compositions and washes, or, as he might call them, architectural cosmetics, to different parts of the building, to which they would give very much the appearance of a Joseph's coat. Some of these washes might be effectual, but, unless they entirely destroyed the porosity of the stone, it would, in his opinion, be quite impossible to prevent its decomposition.[23]

'That he was ambitious cannot be questioned', Barry's son and biographer, Alfred Barry, admitted. But there were two kinds of ambition—'there is the desire for glory itself, which seems to be its lowest form; we find higher ambition in the desire of doing something, which is not unworthy of glory, whether it obtains it or not. I think he felt both strongly.'[24] Barry's constitution, 'originally one of remarkable strength, had been tried severely by work, and still more by anxiety and disappointment'. The 'constant depreciation' of the Palace itself by critics, and 'reflexions upon the architect' over the years had worn him down. His disposition, wrote Alfred, 'craved for sympathy and appreciation, and its sensitiveness was not dulled by age'. In 1858 he became so seriously ill with a fever, that for a time he was thought to be in danger. But that passed and, even as he approached his sixty-fifth birthday, he 'preserved in great degree the elasticity and youthfulness of his nature', a sense of fun and his customary amiability.[25]

Early in 1860 the last stone of the Victoria Tower was laid, a Gothic proto-skyscraper and, at the time, the largest stone square tower in the world, visible from all across London. Built using 1,300 tons of ironwork its summit was crowned with a 72-foot flagpole capable of supporting a flag the size of a tennis court. The Union Jack first flew on top of this, Barry's crowning glory of the Palace of Westminster, on 22 May—the day before his sixty-fifth birthday. But he was not there to see it. Hoisted to half-mast, it rose over the scene of his own funeral cortege, which stretched over the river Thames.

Barry's end had come suddenly and unexpectedly. On the afternoon of 12 May, he and his wife had visited the Crystal Palace on its new permanent site at Sydenham. After supper that evening he retired to his dressing room as usual about eleven, and there died of a massive heart attack before any medical help or family could be summoned. It was later found that he had been suffering from chronic heart failure, of which the persistent cough he had experienced for some time, and which nothing would shift, would today be recognized as a sign.[26] Lady Barry and the children originally wanted the funeral to be a quiet family ceremony, 'in accordance with the privacy and simplicity of his life'. Some suggested that he be buried in St Mary Undercroft, the lower chapel of St Stephen's, much as Wren had been buried in his masterpiece, St Paul's. This 'matchless crypt' had been undergoing a wholesale restoration, virtually in secret due to the fear of complaints about

The Victoria Tower hung with black flags on the day of Barry's funeral

expenditure, under the supervision of Barry's son Edward over the previous year. Few visitors were aware of its existence but, lighted with gas,
workmen were busily engaged restoring the carved bosses and groined
roof, and replacing the polished Purbeck marble columns defaced and
'sadly misused in centuries bygone'.[27]

Yet his fellow architects were having none of it, and petitioned the Dean
of Westminster to allow him to be buried in the nave of Westminster

Abbey, whose most recent grave was that of the Whig historian, Lord Macaulay. The day of the funeral arrived and the black carriages of the family drove from Clapham, met by those from the Institute of British Architects, and other distinguished persons, to form one long cortège towards the Abbey. At the rear walked a crowd of many of the men who had laboured on the New Palace of Westminster and Barry's other buildings. Arriving in Dean's Yard just before one in the afternoon, the horses pulled up and Sir Charles's coffin was carried through the cloisters of the Abbey to the south door of the medieval church in the shadow of which Charles Barry had lived and worked nearly all his life. Some five hundred representatives of the arts and sciences gathered behind the Dean and Chapter and then the choristers, and the official mourners—Barry's five sons—and made their solemn way into the building. The pallbearers included some who had accompanied Barry's struggles at Westminster from the beginning, including Edward Cust, Charles Eastlake, and the architect, C. R. Cockerell. The Abbey was packed and there were representatives from the Commons, the Royal Academy, the Royal Society, the Institution of Civil Engineers, the Architectural Museum, and numerous patrons and clients, who took over a quarter of an hour to file into their seats in the nave. Barry was buried to the strains of Purcell and Handel, also long-time Westminster residents, and fellow occupiers of tombs in the Abbey. The brass on his grave, adjacent to that of the railway engineer, Robert Stephenson, was made by Pugin's favoured firm of Hardman's. Beneath a large cross decorated with roses, leaves, a Portcullis, and the letter B, in an echo of the patterns he chose for the Palace from the Henry VII chapel, there is an elevation of the Victoria Tower and a ground plan of the Palace of Westminster.

Engraved around the edges of the brass were some verses from St Paul's letter to the Colossians, most probably chosen by his clergyman son, Alfred: 'Whatsoever ye do, do it heartily as to the Lord and not unto Men; for ye serve the Lord Christ.' As Alfred made very clear in his biography of his father seven years later, the remuneration squabbles distressed Barry and the family very much, with a veiled implication that the government refusal to pay a fair rate for the job was responsible for Sir Charles's untimely death from stress and overwork. The words on Barry's tomb brass therefore need to be read literally between the lines, for the full text of those verses from the New Testament, properly rendered are:

> And whatsoever ye do, do it heartily, as to the Lord, and not unto men; *Knowing that of the Lord ye shall receive the reward of the inheritance*: for ye serve the Lord Christ.[28]

'We are glad to learn', wrote the *Saturday Review*,

> that his claims as one of the worthies of the age are to be recognised by a public funeral, and a resting-place beneath the vault of Westminster Abbey...it is undeniable that Sir C. Barry has not for many years been popular with officials; but we are not inclined to think the worse of him on that account. He was through life a man of large and expansive ideas, and of resolute determination to carry out those ideas; and, as might be supposed, he was continually in collision alike with red-tape officials, and the economic bullies of supply-nights. Season after season, a raid at Sir C. Barry was a sure card for a little cheap popularity in the House of Commons.[29]

A statue, carved by J. H. Foley, who had produced those of the Parliamentarians, John Hampden and John Selden, for St Stephen's Hall, was commissioned by his best friend, John Lewis Wolfe, and had many subscribers. But placing it in St Stephen's Porch at the head of Westminster Hall was deemed to be inappropriate, so instead it was installed on the public route from the Lower Waiting Hall staircase on the public route to the committee corridor, where it remains today. Foley's statue shows Barry seated with his coat thrown open, vigorously sketching the design of the Victoria Tower on a drawing board balanced on his knee—which all agreed was an inspired rendition of the friend they had known, and of the part of the building he thought would be his memorial.[30]

Of the hundred or so subscribers to the statue, which included a group of workmen from Clapham, only one was a Member of Parliament. There was no statement or official eulogy on Sir Charles Barry's death in either House, and the only comments passed in the days that followed related to who was to take over, and what the state of the accounts were.

Epilogue

W HEN CHARLES BARRY died, the Palace was virtually complete. His third son, Edward, took over the Great Work. At that stage only some final touches were required to the lantern and roof of the Victoria Tower, while the Robing Room needed floor and fireplace, and the undercroft chapel finishing. Big Ben was still silent and one Member hoped that 'the bell would be kept quiet, at all events during the sitting of Parliament'. According to another, it 'had been a perfect nuisance to the whole Metropolis, and he hoped [it] would never be used again for striking the hours . . . all the inhabitants of that part of London in which he lived, rejoiced that the great bell had been cracked'.[1]

The painting schemes were carried on separately by the Fine Arts Commission, but with the unexpected death of Prince Albert in 1861 and with money running out, work ground to a halt on the frescoes and the Octagonal Hall. The Albert Memorial in Kensington Gardens was subsequently commissioned by Queen Victoria in honour of her husband and paid for by public subscription. On one of the corners of its frieze celebrating the arts and sciences, as in Albert's original aim for the Great Exhibition, Pugin stands out, with Barry a few steps behind him to the side. Barry's ambition that the Palace would be filled with painting cycles depicting the nation's history was only partially realized in the 1920s.

Edward Barry still ended up being drawn in to working on the Palace for a further ten years after his father, completing New Palace Yard to his own design with railings only (his father's ideas for a great enclosure being dropped in 1864) and finishing the decoration of the chapel and Central Lobby. The Great Bell was slightly turned so that its hammer would hit undamaged metal and Big Ben began striking in combination with the Great Clock in 1863. The crack remains there today. The records of Parliament that had survived, or had been created, since the fire began to fill the Victoria Tower in 1864. Among them were the reports of nearly one hundred inquiries by Parliamentary select committees into the Palace's design and construction between 1834 and 1870. Thousands upon thousands of drawings of all aspects of the building and its furnishings were produced during its creation. The final cost, as far as could be determined at Edward's unceremonious dismissal in 1870, was £2.4 million—three times over his father's original budget and two and a half decades over schedule. Some people think it has never really been completed.

Responsibility for investing in and maintaining the Palace passed from the Office of Works to its successor government departments.

The completed Palace of Westminster, viewed from the south east

Over 1.25 million people visit it each year. In 1987 UNESCO declared the Houses of Parliament, along with Westminster Abbey, a World Heritage Site in recognition of its outstanding architecture and 'its great historic and symbolic significance'. In 1992 the Palace finally came under the direct control of parliamentary authorities, but the damage had already been done by over a century of neglect and under-investment.

Today the Palace of Westminster is in a dire condition. A number of the services installed by Barry have never been renewed. Reid's ventilation shafts and basement corridors are clogged with over a century of decaying wiring and corroded pipework—obsolete and much of it undocumented. Leaks and floods are common, as is water-damage to the fabric and collections. Asbestos riddles the building, preventing investigations into structural problems and slowing down repairs. The oldest lift has not been replaced since 1893. Stonework is crumbling and can be pulled away by hand. Parts of the building do not meet modern fire regulation standards. The *Restoration and Renewal of the Palace of Westminster* report of 2012 pointed out the 'great difficulty of carrying out fundamental renovation work... while Parliament remains in continuous occupation'.[2] There is now a real risk that unless significant restoration work is undertaken—and swiftly—major, irreversible damage may be done to the Palace.

So this is not the final page of our story.

Peels and Lincolns continue to debate with Broughams and Humes over the solution for Charles Barry's Great Work, as do the public and press. The ending, dear reader, is unfolding before your very eyes, even as you close this book.

NOTES

Prologue

1 *The Times*, 12 May 1941, p. 4.
2 *Big Ben and the Elizabeth Tower: Official Guide* (London, 2012), p. 46.
3 *House of Commons* Hansard, 5th series, 393, cc. 403–73 (28 Oct. 1943). See also Gavin Stamp, '"We Shape Our Buildings and Afterwards Our Buildings Shape Us": Sir Giles Gilbert Scott and the Rebuilding of the House of Commons', in Christine Riding and Jacqueline Riding, eds, *The Houses of Parliament. History. Art. Architecture* (London, 2000), pp. 149–61.
4 HC Hansard, 393, cc. 403–4.
5 Caroline Shenton, *The Day Parliament Burned Down* (Oxford, 2012), pp. 11, 28–9.
6 HC Hansard, 393, c. 404.
7 HC Hansard, 393, cc. 404–5.
8 HC Hansard, 393, c. 406.
9 HC Hansard, 393, cc. 411–12, 421, 467, 471, 472.

Chapter 1

1 See *Shenton* for the full story.
2 *Westminster Review*, 43, Jan. 1835, p. 163.
3 TNA, WORK 2/1, pp. 188–9.
4 TNA, WORK 2/1, pp. 189–90. *Shenton*, pp. 252–3.
5 TNA, WORK 2/1, pp. 193–4.
6 J. Mordaunt Crook and M. H. Port, *The History of the King's Works, vi, 1792–1851* (London, 1973), p. 195.
7 *The Spectator*, 25 Oct. 1834, p. 1013.
8 Quoted in *KW*, p. 195.
9 Quoted in *KW*, p. 196.
10 Hansard's *Parliamentary Debates*, 3rd series (1830–91), 26, c. 64.
11 Hansard, 26, c. 470. For Hume's earlier proposals, see *Shenton*, pp. 17–21.

12 *Westminster Review,* Jan. 1835, 43, p. 167.

13 M. H. Port, ed., *The Houses of Parliament* (New Haven and London, 1976), p. 23.

14 House of Commons sessional papers, 1835 (262).

15 Edward Pearce and Deanna Pearce, eds, *The Diaries of Charles Greville* (London, 2006), p. 141.

16 Richard A. Gaunt, ed., *Unrepentant Tory. Political Selections from the Diaries of the Fourth Duke of Newcastle-under-Lyne, 1827–1838* (Woodbridge, 2006), p. 264.

17 *The Diaries of Charles Greville*, p. 141.

18 *Unrepentant Tory,* p. 275.

19 TNA, WORK 2/1, p. 235.

20 Hansard, 28, c. 771.

21 R. J. Olney, and Julia Melvin, eds, *Prime Minister's Papers Series. Wellington. II: Political Correspondence November 1834–April 1835* (London, 1986), p. 519.

22 Mark Philp, 'Godwin, William (1756–1836)', *Oxford Dictionary of National Biography* (Oxford, 2004–08); for the causes of the fire, see *Shenton,* Chapter 3.

23 Peter Jackson, *George Scharf's London. Sketches and Watercolours of a Changing City, 1820–1850* (London, 1987), pp. 11–12.

24 Alfred Barry, *The Life and Works of Sir Charles Barry, RA, FRS, &c* (London, 1867), pp. 145–6.

25 *Life*, pp. 4–5. M. H. Port, 'Barry, Sir Charles (1795–1860)', *ODNB*. A biography of Barry in the *Illustrated London News* later claimed he was educated in Leicestershire.

26 *Life*, pp. 5–6.

27 For a fuller description of the old Palace at the beginning of the nineteenth century, see *Shenton*, pp. 7–14.

28 *Life*, p. 7; Port, 'Barry, Sir Charles', *ODNB.*

29 *Life*, pp. 13–14; Port, 'Barry, Sir Charles', *ODNB.*

30 Kathleen Adkins, ed., *Personal and Historical Extracts from the Travel Diaries (1817–1820) of Sir Charles Barry 1795–1860* (London, 1986), p. 29.

31 Adkins, *Travel Diaries*, pp. 34, 38.

32 David Robertson, *Sir Charles Eastlake and the Victorian Art World* (Princeton, 1978), p. 12.

33 Robertson, *Sir Charles Eastlake*, pp. 12–16; Adkins, *Travel Diaries*, pp. 44–50.

34 Adkins, *Travel Diaries*, p. 52.

35 *Life*, p. 27.

36 *Life*, p. 28.

37 Adkins, *Travel Diaries*, pp. 58, 63.
38 Adkins, *Travel Diaries*, pp. 70–1, 73–7.
39 Adkins, *Travel Diaries*, pp. 79, 82.
40 David G. Blissett, 'John Lewis Wolfe (1798–1881)', *ODNB*; Adkins, *Travel Diaries*, p. 82.
41 Port, 'Barry, Sir Charles', *ODNB*.
42 *Port*, pp. 62–3.
43 *Port*, p. 319, note 11.

Chapter 2

1 *KW*, p. 647.
2 Jane Robins, *Rebel Queen* (London, 2007), pp. 17–18; Christopher Hibbert, 'George IV', *ODNB*.
3 Judith Schneid Lewis, 'Charlotte Augusta', *ODNB*; John Peel, 'Sir Richard Croft', *ODNB*; Hibbert, 'George IV'.
4 Hibbert, 'George IV'; Robins, *Rebel Queen*, pp. 142–3.
5 *KW*, p. 520. The interior of the Lords during the process, as altered by Soane, can be seen in George Hayter's painting *The Trial of Queen Caroline 1820* at the National Portrait Gallery, London.
6 Robins, *Rebel Queen*, p. 287.
7 *KW*, p. 647; D. Gerhold, *Westminster Hall. Nine Hundred Years of History* (London, 1999), pp. 34–5; Robins, *Rebel Queen*, p. 311.
8 Robins, *Rebel Queen*, pp. 306, 308–11.
9 HCP, 1835 (262), pp. 3–5.
10 House of Lords, Report of the Select Committee on the Permanent Accommodation of the Houses of Parliament 1835 (HL 73).
11 HCP, 1835 (262), pp. 3–5.
12 TNA, WORK 11/1/1, ff. 61–62.
13 *KW*, p. 590.
14 *Life*, pp. 242–3.
15 *Life*, p. 239.
16 *The Spectator*, 20 June 1835, p. 586.
17 Hansard, 30, c. 49; Charles Kent, 'Berkeley, (George Charles) Grantley Fitzhardinge (1800–1881)', rev. Julian Lock, *ODNB*.
18 Hansard, 29, cc. 679–80.
19 Hansard, 28, c. 778.
20 *Port*, p. 28; M. H. Port, 'Goodwin, Francis (1784–1835)', *ODNB*.
21 *KW*, pp. 590–1.

22 Rosemary Hill, *God's Architect. Pugin and the Building of Romantic Britain* (London, 2007), p. 142; *Port*, p. 59.

23 Pugin's diary, 1835–51, as transcribed in Alexandra Wedgwood, *AWN Pugin and the Pugin Family* (London, 1985), p. 32.

24 Alexandra Wedgwood, 'Pugin, Auguste Charles (1768/9–1832)', *ODNB*.

25 *Hill*, p. 75; Paul Atterbury and Clive Wainwright, eds, *Pugin. A Gothic Passion* (New Haven and London, 1994), pp. 24–5.

26 Pugin. *A Gothic Passion*, p. 173.

27 *Hill*, pp. 88–9.

28 *Hill*, p. 127.

29 *Shenton*, pp. 94–5, 101, 118.

30 Margaret Belcher, ed., *Collected Letters of A. W. N Pugin,* 5 vols (Oxford, 2001–15), i, pp. 42–3. 6 Nov. 1834.

31 *Letters*, i, p. 44. 18 Dec. 1834.

32 *Diary*, p. 33.

33 *Hill*, p. 133.

34 Margaret Belcher, *A. W. N. Pugin. An Annotated Critical Bibliography* (London and New York, 1987), p. 7; *Hill*, p. 147.

35 *Letters*, p. 54.

36 *Diary*, p. 33.

37 *Port*, p. 67.

38 *Diary*, p. 33.

39 *Life*, p. 147.

40 *Diary*, p. 33.

41 *Diary*, p. 76; *Hill*, p. 151.

42 *Port*, pp. 68–9.

43 *KW*, p. 595.

44 Quoted in *Shenton*, p. 3.

45 *Hill*, pp. 146–7.

46 *Life*, p. 147.

47 TNA, WORK 11/1/1, f. 24.

48 *Port*, p. 41.

49 *Port*, p. 34; Andrea Fredrickson, 'Parliament's Genius Loci: The Politics of Place after the 1834 Fire' in *Riding*, pp. 104–5.

50 For a detailed description of many of the proposals, see *Port*, pp. 20–52.

51 *Port*, p. 37.

52 *Life*, p. 147.

53 HCP, 1836 (66), p. 2.

54 *Shenton*, p. 9.

Chapter 3

1 Hansard, 31, cc. 235–8 (9 Feb. 1836).
2 HCP, 1836 (245), p. 2.
3 HCP, 1836 (245), p. 2.
4 HCP, 1836 (245), p. 3.
5 Hansard, 32, cc. 329–30 (15 Mar. 1836).
6 *Unrepentant Tory*, p. 294.
7 HCP, 1836 (245), pp. 11–12.
8 Hansard, 32, c. 330 (15 Mar. 1836).
9 TNA, WORK 11/1/1, f. 48, ff. 55–6; TNA, WORK 1/22, p. 13.
10 *The Times*, 25 Mar. 1836, p. 5.
11 *Morning Post*, 6 Apr. 1836.
12 Hansard, 35, cc. 865–7 (11 Apr. 1836).
13 HCP, 1836 (245), pp. 18–27.
14 Quoted in *Port*, p. 76.
15 TNA, WORK 11/1/1, f. 34.
16 TNA, WORK 11/1/1, f. 36; *Port*, p. 79.
17 *Hill*, pp. 154–5; R. Windsor Liscombe, 'Wilkins, William (1778–1839)', *ODNB*.
18 *The Times*, 11 May 1836, p. 5.
19 HCP, 1836 (245), p. 27.
20 *Port*, pp. 79, 321.
21 Hansard, 35, cc. 398–9 (21 July 1836).
22 Hansard, 35, c. 403 (21 July 1836).
23 Hansard, 35, cc. 411–12 (21 July 1836).
24 Hansard, 35, cc. 415–17 (21 July 1836).
25 *The Times*, 23 July 1836, p. 6.
26 E. W. Pugin, *Who was the Art Architect of the Houses of Parliament?* (London, 1867), pp. 23–4.
27 Pugin, *Who was the Art Architect*, p. 26.
28 Pugin, *Who was the Art Architect*, pp. 28–9.
29 Kathleen Adkins, *The Barry/Rowsell Family Saga* (Canterbury, privately printed, 1977), pp. 58–62.
30 TNA, WORK 2/1, p. 235.
31 TNA, WORK 1/22, pp. 10, 22.
32 Hansard, 35, cc. 527–31 (3 May 1836).
33 TNA, WORK 1/22, p. 124 (29 Sept. 1836).
34 TNA, WORK 1/22, pp. 38, 176, 204, 347.

35 HCP, 1835 (583); Hansard, cc. 1067–71 (10 Aug. 1835).

36 TNA, WORK 1/22, pp. 108, 115, 175.

37 Elizabeth Bonython and Anthony Burton, *The Great Exhibitor. The Life and Work of Henry Cole* (London, 2003), p. 49.

38 TNA, WORK 1/22, p. 198. The first formal correspondence between Barry and the Office of Woods relating to the building of the Houses of Parliament occurred on 13 Jan. 1837 (p. 185).

39 A. W. Skempton, ed., *A Biographical Dictionary of Civil Engineers in Great Britain and Ireland*, 3 vols (London, 2002–14), ii, p. 420.

40 *Queen Victoria's Journals* (http://www.queenvictoriasjournals.org), 18 Mar. 1837.

41 *QVJ*, 17 July 1837.

42 TNA, WORK 11/1/1, f. 23v.

43 *Life*, p. 157.

Chapter 4

1 TNA, WORK 11/1/1, f. 57.

2 Denis Smith, 'Walker, James (1781–1862)', *ODNB*.

3 This description and what follows comes from Denis Smith's chapter on the construction technology used in building the Palace in *Port*, p. 197 (diagram p. 196).

4 TNA, WORK 1/22, pp. 286, 302, 310.

5 *KW*, p. 602.

6 *The Times*, 8 Sept. 1837, p. 3.

7 TNA, WORK 1/22, p. 300, 31 July 1837.

8 Hansard, 38, c. 464 (3 May 1837); TNA, WORK 1/23, p. 32.

9 TNA, WORK 1/22, pp. 333, 349. TNA, WORK 1/23, p. 78.

10 *QVJ*, 20 Nov. 1837, 23 Dec. 1837.

11 TNA, WORK 1/22, p. 393, 14 Dec. 1837.

12 Hansard, 39, cc. 1517–20 (23 Dec. 1837).

13 TNA, WORK 1/23, pp. 9–10.

14 Hansard, 41, cc. 329–32 (1 Mar. 1838); 41, cc. 1290–1 (26 Mar. 1838).

15 TNA, WORK 1/23 pp. 37–8.

16 TNA, WORK 1/23, p. 65.

17 TNA, WORK 1/23, pp. 21, 74, 95, 229, 241.

18 *KW*, p. 601.

19 TNA, WORK 1/23, p. 11; H. C. G. Matthew, 'Darling, Grace Horsley (1815–1842)', *ODNB*; http://www.royalhumanesociety.org.uk

20 *The Times*, 10 May 1838, p. 6.

21 *The Times*, 14 Dec. 1839, p. 4.

22 TNA, WORK 1/23, p. 79.

23 *Morning Chronicle*, 17 Apr. 1838.

24 TNA, WORK 1/23, pp. 92, 93, 106, 165.

25 TNA, WORK 1/23, pp. 149, 173.

26 *Shenton*, p. 254.

27 TNA, WORK 1/23, pp. 209, 219.

28 *The Times*, 5 Dec. 1838, p. 3.

29 *The Times*, 2 Feb. 1839, p. 5.

30 *The Times*, 8 Sept. 1838.

31 TNA, WORK 1/23 p. 75.

32 *Essex Standard*, 13 Apr. 1838.

33 Hansard, 42, cc. 674–5 (30 Apr. 1838).

34 Roy Strong, *Coronation. From the 8th to the 21st Century* (London, 2005), p. 401.

35 *QVJ*, 28 June 1838.

36 Mary S. Millar, 'Montgomerie, Archibald William, (1812–1861)', *ODNB*.

37 For what follows, see Mark Girouard, *The Return to Camelot. Chivalry and the English Gentleman* (New Haven and London, 1981), pp. 94–102; Ian Anstruther, *The Knight and the Umbrella. An Account of the Eglinton Tournament 1839* (London, 1963), pp. 90–3.

38 *QVJ*, 2 Sept. 1839.

39 Girouard, *Return to Camelot*, p. 115.

40 Roscoe et al., *A Biographical Dictionary of Sculptors in Britain 1660–1851* (New Haven and London, 2009), pp. 1244–7; *Port*, pp. 241–4.

41 TNA, WORK 1/23, p. 148.

42 TNA, WORK 1/23, pp. 194, 199, 243, 293, 405 and *passim*.

43 TNA, WORK 1/23, p. 174.

44 J. A. Secord, 'Beche, Sir Henry Thomas de la (1796–1855)', *ODNB*.

45 E. I. Carlyle, 'Smith, Charles Harriot (1792–1864)', rev. M. A. Goodall, *ODNB*.

46 For the full story of Strata Smith, see Simon Winchester, *The Map that Changed the World: A Tale of Rocks, Ruin and Redemption* (new edn, London, 2002).

47 Smith's journal of this expedition is at the Oxford Museum of Natural History archive, WS/D/3 (formerly William Smith, Professional Papers Box 44/F1).

48 *The Times*, 3 Sept. 1838, p. 5.

49 Oxford Museum of Natural History, WS/D/3 (formerly William Smith, Professional Papers Box 44/F1).

Chapter 5

1 TNA, WORK 1/23, p. 276

2 *The Times*, 5 Mar. 1839, p. 6.

3 *Port*, p. 197.

4 *The Times*, 1 Apr. 1839, p. 5.

5 HCP, 1839 (574), p. 2.

6 HCP, 1839 (574), Appendix A.

7 Graham K. Lott and Christine Richardson, 'Yorkshire Stone for Build-ing the Houses of Parliament (1839–c.1852)', *Proceedings of the Yorkshire Geological Society*, 51(4) (1997), pp. 265–72.

8 HCP, 1839 (574), pp. 8–9.

9 Lott and Richardson, 'Yorkshire Stone', p. 268.

10 TNA, WORK 1/23, p. 319.

11 TNA, WORK 1/23, pp. 344, 417; *Port*, p. 197.

12 *The Times*, 10 June 1839, p. 5.

13 TNA, WORK 1/23, pp. 366–7.

14 *Port*, p. 98.

15 TNA, WORK 1/23, p. 372, 24 June 1839.

16 TNA, WORK 1/23, p. 395, 16 July 1839.

17 Lott and Richardson, 'Yorkshire Stone', p. 268; *Port*, p. 98.

18 TNA, WORK 1/23, pp. 483–4.

19 M. H. Port, 'Grissell, Thomas (1801–1874)', *ODNB*; M. H. Port, 'Peto, Sir (Samuel) Morton, first baronet (1809–1889)', *ODNB*.

20 TNA, WORK 1/23, pp. 486, 494, 574.

21 TNA, WORK 1/23, pp. 507–8, 570, Nov. 1839.

22 *Port*, p. 98.

23 *Port*, pp. 197–8.

24 *Port*, p. 198.

25 Lott and Richardson, 'Yorkshire Stone', p. 269.

26 *QVJ*, 10–11 Feb. 1840.

27 *QVJ*, 16 Aug. 1839.

28 H. Colvin, *A Biographical Dictionary of British Architects 1600–1840*, 4th edn (New Haven and London, 2008), p. 101.

29 G. B. Smith, 'Gurney, Sir Goldsworthy (1793–1875)', rev. Anita McCon-nell, *ODNB* (2004). The figure of five hundred workmen on site comes from *The Times*, 22 July 1840, p. 4.

30 *The Times*, 19 Aug. 1839, p. 3. For the Bude Light debates, see Hansard, 51, cc. 1343–6 (6 Feb. 1840); 52, cc. 1158–61 (12 Mar. 1840).

31 *The Times*, 22 July 1840, p. 4.

32 HCP, 1844 (448), p. 4.

33 *The Times*, 27 Apr. 1940.

34 Hansard, 59, c. 1014 (30 Sept. 1841).

35 Hansard, 59, c. 512 (16 Sept. 1841).

36 Today's distant descendant is the Union of Construction, Allied Trades and Technicians (UCATT).

37 Coventry, University of Warwick Modern Records Centre (MRC), MSS 78/OS/4/1/4, p. 503.

38 *Morning Chronicle*, 18 Sept. 1838.

39 Hansard, 48, cc. 222–7 (14 June 1839).

40 MRC MSS 78/OS/4/1/4, p. 367.

41 *The Times*, 15 Sept. 1841, p. 7.

42 MRC, MSS 78/OS/4/1/5.

43 *The Times*, 20 Sept. 1841, p. 6.

44 *The Times*, 25 Sept. 1841, p. 6.

45 *The Times*, 28 Sept. 1841, p. 7.

46 *The Times*, 4 Oct. 1841, p. 6.

47 MRC, MSS 78/OS/4/1/5.

48 *The Times*, 15 Oct. 1841, p. 7.

49 HCP, 1844 (448), p. 14.

Chapter 6

1 MRC, MSS 78/OS/4/1/4, pp. 411–13.

2 MRC, MSS 78/OS/4/1/4, pp. 415; *The Times*, 9 Nov. 1841, p. 5.

3 *The Times*, 3 Dec. 1841, p. 5.

4 *The Times*, 28 Dec. 1841, p. 3.

5 *The Times*, 25 Jan. 1842, p. 5.

6 *The Times*, 9 Feb. 1842, p. 5.

7 *The Times*, 16 Aug. 1842, p. 4.

8 MRC, MSS 78/OS/4/1/4, p. 443.

9 MRC, MSS 78/OS/4/1/4, p. 447.

10 *Port*, p. 105.

11 MRC, MSS 78/OS/4/1/4, pp. 455, 457.

12 MRC, MSS 78/OS/4/1/6, pp. 78–80.

13 *Port*, pp. 105–6.

14 Marjorie Stone, 'Browning, Elizabeth Barrett (1806–1861)', *ODNB*.

15 See these men's respective entries in the *ODNB*.

16 As coined by the architectural historian, Michael Port.

17 *QVJ*, 18 Apr. 1842.

18 *QVJ*, 9 May 1842.

19 *QVJ*, 12 May 1842.

20 Girouard, *The Return to Camelot*, p. 112.

21 HCP, 1841 Session 1 (423).

22 HCP, 1841 (423), p. 7.

23 HCP, 1841 (423), pp. 4–9; *Life*, p. 192.

24 Stanley Weintraub, *Albert. Uncrowned King* (London, 1997), pp. 57, 60–1.

25 HCP, 1841 (423), p. 9.

26 London, RIBA Archive, SKB 402/3.

27 *The Times*, 6 Sept. 1842, p. 6, quoting *The Observer*.

28 Lott and Richardson, 'Yorkshire Stone', pp. 268–9.

29 HCP, 1841 (423), p. 10.

30 Hansard, 66, cc. 1033–6 (21 Feb. 1843).

31 Hansard, 67, cc. 713–14 (13 Mar. 1843).

32 *The Times*, 11 Apr. 1843, p. 7.

33 Hansard, 68, cc. 743–4 (10 Apr. 1843).

34 *The Observer*, 2 June 1843, p. 7.

35 *The Times*, 8 June 1843, p. 3.

36 *QVJ*, 9 June 1843.

37 *QVJ*, 30 June 1843.

38 *The Times*, 6 Sept. 1843, p. 3; Patricia H. Allderidge, 'Dadd, Richard (1817–1886)', *ODNB*.

39 *The Times*, 10 Aug. 1843, p. 7; Robyn Asleson, 'Armitage, Edward (1817–1896)', *ODNB*; Parliamentary Archives, PRC/1. The *Battle of Meanee* is RCIN 407185 in the Royal Collection.

40 *QVJ*, 29 July 1843.

41 The silver and ivory trowel used for the first stone is today in the Parliamentary Archives, OOW/50.

42 *The Times*, 6 Sept. 1843, p. 3.

43 *The Times*, 6 Sept. 1843, p. 3; *The Times*, 3 Oct. 1843, p. 4.

Chapter 7

1 *Port*, p. 106; Hansard, 73, cc. 797–8 (11 Mar. 1844).

2 For what follows, see HCP, 1844 (269).

3 *The Times*, 22 Apr. 1844, p. 3.

4 HCP, 1844 (269), pp. 12–13.

5 HCP, 1844 (269), pp. 19–20.

6 HCP, 1844 (269), p. 26.

7 HCP, 1844 (269), p. 25.

8 HCP, 1844 (288). These had been ordered to be printed on 23 Apr., in the midst of Barry's hearings in the Lords.

9 HCP, 1844 (629); *Port*, pp. 111–13.

10 Hansard, c. 1404 (17 Dec. 1847).

11 HCP, 1844 (448), p. 8.

12 HCP, 1844 (448), p. 10.

13 HCP, 1844 (448), pp. 13–14.

14 HCP, 1844 (448), p. 21.

15 William Dalrymple, *Return of a King. The Battle for Afghanistan* (London, 2013), p. 479; *The Spectator*, 8 June 1844, p. 11.

16 *The Times*, 10 June 1844, pp. 4–5.

17 Dalrymple, *Return of a King*, pp. 480–1.

18 Diana Brooks, 'Allom, Thomas (1804–1872)', *ODNB*.

19 *The Times*, 16 Aug. 1844, p. 4; 28 Nov. 1844, p. 4.

20 RIBA, SKB 402/5, p. 6, 13 Jan. 1845.

21 Quoted in *Port*, p. 115.

22 HCP, 1844 (448), p. 38.

23 HCP, 1844 (448), p. 41.

24 HCP, 1844 (448), pp. 42, 45.

25 HCP, 1844 (448), pp. 10, 56–7.

26 *QVJ*, 28 June 1844.

27 John Turpin, 'Maclise, Daniel (*bap.* 1806, *d.* 1870)', *ODNB*; Weintraub, *Albert*, p. 170. The erotic birthday paintings exchanged between Albert and Victoria are today in the Royal Collection; *The Times*, 16 July 1844, p. 5.

28 HCP, 1844 (448), p. iii; *Port*, p. 113.

29 *Life*, p. 162.

30 *Letters*, ii, p. 208. The date of this letter—assigned by Alfred Barry to 13 June 1844—is convincingly disputed by Belcher.

31 *Hill*, pp. 304–5; Alexandra Wedgwood, 'The Throne of the House of Lords and its Setting', *Architectural History*, 27 (1984), p. 63; *Port*, p. 129.

32 Quoted in *Port*, p. 115.

33 *Port*, 'Barry, Sir Charles' *ODNB*.

34 HCP, 1841 (51), pp. 7, 16–17.

35 HCP, 1842 (536), p. 3.

36 HCP, 1844 (269), p. 26

37 HCP, 1844 (448), p. 27.

38 HCP, 1844 (448), p. 36.

39 *Letters*, ii, p. 209.

40 *The Times*, 25 Sept. 1844, p. 5.

41 *The Times*, 26 Sept. 1844, p. 7.

42 *Letters*, ii, p. 271.

43 *Hill*, pp. 322–3; *Port*, p. 131.

44 *Letters*, ii, p. 384, now Parliamentary Archives, BAR/31/1/1.

Chapter 8

1 *Port*, p. 120.

2 HCP, 1841 Session 1 (423), p. 10

3 *Port*, pp. 121, 238.

4 *The Times*, 4 Jan. 1845. p. 6.

5 *Letters*, ii, 316–17, 331.

6 *Letters*, ii, 333.

7 *Letters*, ii, 349.

8 *Letters*, ii, 333, 348, 349.

9 *Letters*, ii, 354. 3 Mar. 1845.

10 Hansard, 78, cc. 323–4 (5 Mar. 1845).

11 *The Times*, 11 Mar. 1845, p. 6.

12 *Letters*, ii, p. 376.

13 Hansard, 81, cc. 121–2.

14 *The Times*, 6 June 1845, p. 4.

15 *Letters*, ii, 394. 7 June 1845.

16 *Letters*, ii, 394; *Port*, p. 132.

17 *Letters*, ii, 397.

18 *Letters*, ii, 397.

19 Hansard, 81, cc. 203–9 (9 June 1845).

20 *QVJ*, 27 June 1845.

21 *Letters*, ii, 398.

22 *Letters*, ii, 409.

23 *Letters*, ii, 409.

24 *Letters*, ii, 409.

25 *Letters*, ii, 424–5.

26 *Letters*, ii, 425.

27 Adkins, *Travel Diaries*, p. 34.

28 Port, 'Barry, Sir Charles' *ODNB*.

29 RIBA, SKB 402/4, 402/5; *Port*, p. 135.

30 I am grateful to Francis O'Gorman for this reference.

31 *The Times*, 2 Jan. 1844.

32 *Letters*, ii, 343.

33 *Port*, p. 135.

34 *The Times*, 16 Oct. 1845, p. 5.

35 Pugin, *Who was the Art Architect*, p. 36.

36 *Letters*, iii, 14.

37 *Letters*, iii, 27.

38 *Letters*, iii, 55.

39 *Letters*, iii, 148.

40 *Letters*, iii, 134.

41 *Letters*, iii, 142, 187–8.

42 *Letters*, iii, 110, 184.

43 Parliamentary Archives, BAR 31/1/2.

44 Hansard, 85, cc. 367–71 (31 Mar. 1846); *The Times*, 1 Apr. 1846, p. 4.

45 *Illustrated London News*, 22 Feb. 1845, p. 124.

46 William McKay, 'May, Thomas Erskine, Baron Farnborough (1815–1886)', *ODNB*.

47 *The Times*, 1 May 1846, p. 6.

48 Hansard, 85, cc. 970–6 (24 Apr. 1846).

49 HCP, 1846 (719), p. 6.

50 *The Times*, 1 July 1845, p. 5.

51 Hansard, 87, cc. 1033–5 (26 June 1846).

52 *Port*, p. 116.

53 *Letters*, iii, 177.

54 *Letters*, iii, 178–9.

55 Parliamentary Archives, BAR/31/1/20.

Chapter 9

1 Parliamentary Archives, BAR/31/1/19.

2 *Letters*, iii, pp. 207, 224

3 Hansard, 90, c. 513 (26 Feb. 1847).

4 Hansard, 91, c. 615 (30 Mar. 1847).

5 *ILN*, 17 Apr. 1847, p. 247; *The Times*, 15 Apr. 1847, p. 5.

6 *QVJ*, 14 Apr. 1847.

7 *ILN*, 17 Apr. 1847, p. 247.

8 Hansard, 91, c. 810 (15 Apr. 1847).

9 *Port*, p. 139.

10 *The Times*, 15 Apr. 1847, p. 5.

11 *ILN*, 17 Apr. 1847, p. 245.

12 *ILN*, 8 May 1847, p. 293.

13 *Hill*, p. 369.

14 *Letters*, ii, p. xii.

15 *Hill*, p. 369.

16 Parliamentary Archives, BAR/31/1/15.

17 Hansard, 92, cc. 327–39 (3 May 1847).

18 *QVJ*, 23 July 1847.

19 Warwickshire Record Office, CR114A/654/1.

20 Hansard, 94, c. 691 (23 July 1847).

21 Hansard, 94, cc. 663–4 (21 July 1847).

22 Ann Cooper, 'Cole, Sir Henry (1808–1882)', *ODNB*. For Cole's exploits at the 1834 fire, see *Shenton*, pp. 55–6, 176–8, 256–7.

23 Bonython, *Great Exhibitor*, p. 90.

24 Kate Colquhoun, *A Thing in Disguise. The Visionary Life of Joseph Paxton* (London, 2004), p. 162.

25 Bonython, *Great Exhibitor*, pp. 104–5.

26 Hansard, 95, cc. 858–9 (9 Dec. 1847).

27 Hansard, 95, cc. 1332–5 (16 Dec. 1847).

28 *Letters*, iii, p. 352.

29 *Letters*, iii, p. 361.

30 Hansard, 95, c. 1345 (17 Dec. 1847).

31 HCP, 1847–8, 205, p. 7; HCP, 1847, 46-II.

32 Pugin, *Who was the Art Architect*, p. 45; *Port*, p. 142.

33 *Letters*, iii, p. 386–7.

34 *Letters*, iii, p. 389.

35 *Letters*, iii, p. 419.

36 HCP, 1847–8 (55), p. 1.

37 HCP, 1847–8 (224), pp. 1–2.

38 Hansard, 96, cc. 555–7 (14 Feb. 1848).

39 Hansard, 96, cc. 564–5.

40 *Letters*, iii, 444.

41 *ILN*, 18 Mar. 1848; T. Stevens, 'Thomas, John (1813–1862)', *ODNB*.

42 Hansard, 97, cc. 138–53 (2 Mar. 1848).

43 *Letters*, iii, 464, 466.

44 HCP, 1847–8 (219), p. 1.

45 Jerry White, *London in the 19th Century* (London, 2008), p. 367; H. C. G. Matthew, 'Gladstone, William Ewart (1809–1898)', *ODNB*.

46 Hansard, 98, cc. 70–3 (10 Apr. 1848).

47 Hansard, 101, cc. 135–6 (14 Aug. 1848).

48 *The Times*, 19 Aug. 1848, p. 4.

49 RIBA, SKB, 403/1.

50 *Letters*, iii, 614–15.

51 *Letters*, iii, 618.

52 *Letters*, iii, 687.

53 *Life*, pp. 373–4.

54 HCP, 1849 (491), pp. 1–5.

55 *Letters*, iv, 79.

56 Hansard, 102, cc. 756–8 (16 Feb. 1849); 104, cc. 155–60 (2 Apr. 1849).

57 HCP, 1849 (404), p. 3.

Chapter 10

1 White, *London in the 19th Century*, p. 50.

2 *Letters*, iv, 244.

3 Hansard, 105, c. 495 (15 May 1849).

4 P. Bingham, N. Q. Verlander, M. J. Cheal, 'John Snow, William Farr and the 1849 Outbreak of Cholera that Affected London', *Public Health*, 118 (2004), pp. 388; Stephanie J. Snow, 'Snow, John (1813–1858)', *ODNB*.

5 HCP, 1850 (482).

6 White, *London in the 19th Century*, pp. 34, 45.

7 *The Times*, 5 Nov. 1849.

8 *Letters*, iv, 338.

9 *Letters*, iv, 369.

10 *The Times*, 9 Feb. 1850, p. 8.

11 Hansard, 108, c. 271 (4 Feb. 1850).

12 *Letters*, iv, 443.

13 *Letters*, iv, 502

14 *QVJ*, 15 Mar. 1850.

15 Hansard, 110, cc. 890–1 (29 Apr. 1850).

16 Hansard, 110, cc. 1314–15 (10 May 1850).

17 HCP, 1849 (325), p. 1.

18 Hansard, 111, cc. 333–4 (24 May 1850).

19 *KW*, p. 622.

20 *Port*, p. 146; Hansard, 111, cc. 459–60. 30 May 1850.

21 Parliamentary Archives, BAR/31/1/17 (undated).

22 *Letters*, iv, 559–60.

23 Colquhoun, *A Thing in Disguise*, p. 165.

24 Bonython, *The Great Exhibitor*, p. 134.

25 HCP, 1850 (650, 650-II), pp. v–vi.

26 Hansard, 113, cc. 726–39 (2 Aug. 1850).

27 *Letters*, iv, 653, 668.

28 *Letters*, iv, 692.

29 Parliamentary Archives, BAR/31/1/8.

30 *Letters*, iv, 704.

31 Parliamentary Archives, BAR/31/1/6.

32 *Letters*, iv, 707.

33 *Letters*, iv, 708–9.

34 *Letters*, iv, 705.

35 *ILN*, 1 Feb. 1851, p. 65; *The Times*, 28 Jan. 1851, p. 5; 29 Jan. 1851, p. 4.

36 *ILN*, 2 Feb. 1850, p. 68.

37 Hansard, 111, c. 1006 (10 June 1850).

38 Colquhoun, *A Thing in Disguise*, pp. 166–7.

39 Bonython, *The Great Exhibitor*, pp. 138–9.

40 Colquhoun, *A Thing in Disguise*, pp. 175–6.

41 *Letters*, v, p. 157.

42 *Hill*, pp. 458–9.

43 *Hill*, p. 455; *Letters*, v, p. 16.

44 Hansard, 116, cc. 190–200 (14 Apr. 1851).

45 Hansard, 115, c. 1052 (4 Apr. 1851).

46 *Port*, p. 119.

47 Hansard, 118, cc. 302–7 (7 July 1851).

48 *Letters*, v, pp. 368, 388, 403, 405–6.

49 *Letters*, v, pp. 424–5.

50 *Letters*, v, pp. 431–2.

51 *KW*, pp. 235, 249.

52 *Port*, pp. 156–7.

53 *Letters*, v, pp. 432, 464, 499, 522–3, 540.

54 *Letters*, v, pp. 485, 488.

Chapter 11

1 *QVJ*, 3 Feb. 1852; *ILN*, 7 Feb. 1852, pp. 7, 121; *ILN*, 13 Mar. 1852, p. 216.

2 *Port*, p. 149.

3 Hansard, 119, cc. 162–72 (4 Feb. 1852).

4 Hansard, 119, cc. 231–4 (6 Feb. 1852).

5 *Letters*, v, p. 589.
6 *Letters*, v, p. 588.
7 Hansard, 119, c. 416 (11 Feb. 1852).
8 *QVJ*, 11 Feb. 1852.
9 *Letters*, v, p. 592.
10 *Letters*, v, p. 599.
11 *Hill*, p. 484; W. W. Webb, 'Tweedie, Alexander (1794–1884)', rev. Anita McConnell, *ODNB*.
12 *Hill*, p. 484.
13 Hansard, 119, cc. 1147–50 (16 Mar. 1852).
14 *QVJ*, 24 June 1852.
15 Hansard, 122, c. 1431 (1 July 1852).
16 *Hill*, p. 492.
17 Parliamentary Archives, BAR/31/3/24.
18 Parliamentary Archives, BAR/31/3/19.
19 Roderick O'Donnell, 'Pugin, Edward Welby (1834–1875)', *ODNB*.
20 *Hill*, p. 496.
21 Parliamentary Archives, WLS 2/215—to TW Philipps of the Office of Woods.
22 Hansard, 124, cc. 180–1 (17 Feb. 1853).
23 Biographical Dictionary of Civil Engineers in Great Britain and Ireland, ii (1830–1890), 531–2. *ILN*, 12 Feb. 1853, p. 127.
24 Hansard, 127, cc. 323–4 (13 May 1853); ODNB; Biographical Dictionary of Civil Engineers, ii, 651.
25 Hansard, 129, c. 1314 (4 Aug. 1853).
26 Hansard, 129, cc. 1315, 1318 (4 Aug. 1853).
27 *The Times*, 4 June 1853, p. 7.
28 Hansard, 133, c. 1282 (8 June 1854).
29 *Port*, pp. 162–3.
30 P. R. Harris, *A History of the British Museum Library 1753*–1973 (London, 1998), p. 183.
31 Hansard, 133, c. 1283 (8 June 1854).
32 Christopher Jones, *The Great Palace* (London, 1983), p. 125.
33 *Port*, p. 226.
34 Jones, *Great Palace*, pp. 125–6.
35 Hansard, 154, c. 1341 (15 July 1859); 139, cc. 10–11 (22 June 1855).
36 Hansard, 133, cc. 1282–3 (8 June 1854).
37 Hansard, 134, cc. 237–45 (16 June 1854).
38 Hansard, 134, c. 237 (16 June 1854).

39 *Port*, p. 214.

40 *ILN*, 17 Mar. 1855, p. 252.

41 Hansard, 137, c. 1490 (16 April 1855).

42 *Shenton*, p. 255.

43 RIBA, SKB, 403/4.

44 Hansard, 141, cc. 1142, 1690 (17 Apr. 1856).

45 Hansard, 141, c. 239 (31 Mar. 1856).

46 HCP, 1857 session 2 (108), pp. 1–2.

47 *The Builder*, 19 May 1860, p. 305.

48 *Port*, pp. 163–8.

49 *The Times*, 22 Feb. 1856, p. 10; 26 Feb., p. 12.

50 For example, *The Times*, 26 Aug. 1856, p. 9.

51 *The Times*, 9 Sept. 1856, p. 10; 4 Sept. 1856, p. 10.

52 Hansard, 142, c. 585 (23 May 1856).

53 Hansard, 140, c. 148 (4 Feb. 1856).

54 Big Ben and the Elizabeth Tower Official Guide (London, 2012), p. 22.

55 Chris McKay, *Big Ben: The Great Clock and the Bells at the Palace of Westminster* (Oxford, 2010), pp. 65–73.

56 McKay, *Big Ben*, pp. 78–9.

57 L. C. Sanders, 'Beckett, Edmund, first Baron Grimthorpe (1816–1905)', rev. Catherine Pease-Watkin, *ODNB*.

58 McKay, *Big Ben*, pp. 79–81.

59 McKay, *Big Ben*, p. 86.

60 Hansard, 140, cc. 806–8 (15 Feb. 1856); *Big Ben and the Elizabeth Tower*, p. 55.

61 McKay, *Big Ben*, pp. 78–9.

62 *The Times*, 10 Feb. 1856, p. 10.

Chapter 12

1 HCP, 1857 session 2 (213), pp. 1–2.

2 McKay, *Big Ben*, p. 93.

3 McKay, Big Ben, p. 95; Big Ben and the Elizabeth Tower, p. 36.

4 McKay, *Big Ben*, pp. 96–102.

5 Hansard, 148, cc. 456–7.

6 McKay, *Big Ben*, p. 105.

7 McKay, *Big Ben*, p. 107.

8 Hansard, 150, c. 276 (7 May 1858).

9 McKay, *Big Ben*, pp. 112–13, 120.

10 Hansard, 147, c. 1532 (13 Aug. 1857).

11 Hansard, 151, cc. 426, 429 (25 June 1858).

12 Hansard, 151, cc. 28–9, 35–6 (18 June 1858).

13 Stephen Halliday, *The Great Stink of London: Sir Joseph Bazalgette and the Cleansing of the Victorian Metropolis* (London, 2001), p. 71.

14 Halliday, *The Great Stink*, p. 103.

15 Hansard, 151, c. 1931 (22 July 1858).

16 Hansard, 152, cc. 1173–4.

17 Hansard, 153, cc. 793–4 (1858).

18 *Port*, p. 172.

19 Hansard, 154, cc. 1344, 1339.

20 Hansard, 154, cc. 1345; 155, cc. 61–2.

21 Hansard, 154, cc. 1346.

22 Big Ben and the Elizabeth Tower, p. 39.

23 Hansard, 157, cc. 230.

24 *Life*, p. 338.

25 *Life*, p. 340.

26 *Life*, pp. 340–1.

27 *ILN*, 5 Feb. 1859, p. 125.

28 Colossians, III: 23–4 (King James version).

29 Quoted in *Life*, p. 349.

30 *Life*, pp. 350–1.

Epilogue

1 Hansard, 159, c. 219; 160, c. 686.

2 *Restoration and Renewal Study of the Palace of Westminster: Pre-feasibility study and preliminary strategic business case* (London, Oct. 2012) http://www.parliament.uk/documents/lords-information-office/2013/restoration-and-renewal-study.pdf (Accessed 28 Aug. 2015), pp. 6, 17–22. Latest news at http://www.restorationandrenewal.parliament.uk

SELECT BIBLIOGRAPHY

Abbreviations

Diary Pugin's diary, 1835–51, as transcribed in Alexandra Wedgwood, *AWN Pugin and the Pugin Family* (London, 1985), pp. 32–100.

Hansard *Hansard's Parliamentary Debates*, 3rd series (1830–91), vols 1–356.

HCP House of Commons sessional papers, also known as House of Commons Parliamentary Papers (cited by year and paper number).

Hill Rosemary Hill, *God's Architect. Pugin and the Building of Romantic Britain* (London, 2007).

ILN *Illustrated London News.*

KW J. Mordaunt Crook and M. H. Port, *The History of the King's Works, vi, 1792–1851* (London, 1973).

Letters Margaret Belcher, ed., *Collected Letters of A. W. N Pugin*, ed. Margaret Belcher, 5 vols (Oxford 2001–15).

Life Alfred Barry, *The Life and Works of Sir Charles Barry, RA, FRS, &c* (London, 1867).

ODNB *Oxford Dictionary of National Biography* (Oxford, 2004–08).

Port M. H. Port, ed., *The Houses of Parliament* (New Haven and London, 1976).

QVJ *Queen Victoria's Journals* (http://www.queenvictoriasjournals.org).

Riding Christine Riding and Jacqueline Riding, eds, *The Houses of Parliament. History. Art. Architecture* (London, 2000).

Shenton Caroline Shenton, *The Day Parliament Burned Down* (Oxford, 2012).

Manuscript Sources

Modern Records Centre (MRC), Warwick University, Coventry: MSS 78/OS.

The National Archives (TNA), Kew: WORK 1, WORK 2, WORK 5, WORK 11, WORK 29.

Natural History Museum, Oxford: WS/D/3.

Parliamentary Archives, London: BAR, GRE, MOU, OOW, PRC, PUG, WLS.
Royal Institute of British Architects Library, London: BaFam; COC/2/67, 84; LC/1/1/13; LC/1/2/130; SKB/400, 402, 403.
Society of Antiquaries, London: Barry–Pugin collection.
Warwickshire Record Office, Warwick: CR114A/654/1.

Newspapers

The Builder
Illustrated London News
Morning Chronicle
Morning Herald
Morning Post
Punch
Spectator
The Times
Westminster Review

Printed Works

Adkins, Kathleen, *The Barry/Rowsell Family Saga* (Canterbury, privately printed, 1977)
Adkins, Kathleen, ed., *Personal and Historical Extracts from the Travel Diaries (1817–1820) of Sir Charles Barry 1795–1860* (London, 1986)
Anstruther, Ian, *The Knight and the Umbrella. An Account of the Eglinton Tournament 1839* (London, 1963)
Antram, Nicholas and Morrice, Richard, *Pevsner Architectural Guides. Brighton and Hove* (New Haven & London, 2008)
Atterbury, Paul and Wainwright, Clive, eds, *Pugin. A Gothic Passion* (New Haven and London, 1994)
Barlow, Paul, ' "Fire, Flatulence and Fog": The Decoration of Westminster Palace and the Aesthetics of Prudence', in Paul Barlow and Colin Trodd, eds, *Governing Cultures: Art Institutions in Victorian London* (Aldershot, 2000), pp. 69–82
Barry, Alfred, *The Life and Works of Sir Charles Barry, RA, FRS, &c* (London, 1867)
Barry, Charles, *Illustrations of the new Palace of Westminster* [with] *A History of the Palace of Westminster by H. T. Ryde* (London, 1849)
Bassin, Joan, *Architectural Competitions in Nineteenth-Century England* (Ann Arbor, 1975)

Belcher, Margaret, *A. W. N. Pugin. An Annotated Critical Bibliography* (London and New York, 1987)

Belcher, Margaret, ed., *The Collected Letters of A. W. N Pugin*, 5 vols (Oxford 2001–15)

Big Ben and the Elizabeth Tower. Houses of Parliament Official Guide (London, 2012)

Bingham, P., Verlander, N. Q., and Cheal, M. J., 'John Snow, William Farr and the 1849 Outbreak of Cholera that Affected London: A Reworking of the Data Highlights the Importance of the Water Supply', *Public Health*, 118 (2004), pp. 387–94

Boase, T. S. R., 'The Decoration of the New Palace of Westminster, 1841–1863', *Journal of the Warburg and Courtauld Institutes*, 17 (1954), pp. 319–58

Bonython, Elizabeth and Burton, Anthony, *The Great Exhibitor. The Life and Work of Henry Cole* (London, 2003)

Bradley, Simon and Pevsner, Nikolaus, *The Buildings of England. London 6: Westminster* (London, 2003)

Colquhoun, Kate, *A Thing in Disguise. The Visionary Life of Joseph Paxton* (London, 2004)

Colvin, H., *A Biographical Dictionary of British Architects 1600–1840*, 4th edn (New Haven and London, 2008)

Dalrymple, William, *Return of a King. The Battle for Afghanistan* (London, 2013)

Eastlake, C. L., *A History of the Gothic Revival* (London, 1872)

Ferrey, Benjamin, *Recollections of AWN Pugin and his Father Augustus Pugin*, ed. Clive and Jane Wainwright (London, 1978)

Gaunt, Richard A., ed., *Unrepentant Tory. Political Selections from the Diaries of the Fourth Duke of Newcastle-under-Lyne, 1827–1838* (Woodbridge, 2006)

Gerhold, D., *Westminster Hall. Nine Hundred Years of History* (London, 1999)

Girouard, Mark, *The Return to Camelot. Chivalry and the English Gentleman* (New Haven and London, 1981)

Gleich, Moritz, 'Architect and Service Architect: The Quarrel between Charles Barry and David Boswel Reid', *Interdisciplinary Science Review*, 37(4) (2012), pp. 332–44.

Halliday, Stephen, *The Great Stink of London. Sir Joseph Bazalgette and the Cleansing of the Victorian Metropolis* (Stroud, 2001).

Hill, Rosemary, *God's Architect. Pugin and the Building of Romantic Britain* (London, 2007)

Hillier, Joseph and Bell, Sarah, 'The "Genius of Place": Mitigating Stench in the New Palace of Westminster before the Great Stink', *The London Journal*, 35 (2010), pp. 22–38

272

Select Bibliography

House of Lords, *Report of the Select Committee on the Permanent Accommodation of the Houses of Parliament* 1835 (73)

Jackson, Peter, *George Scharf's London. Sketches and Watercolours of a Changing City, 1820–1850* (London, 1987)

Jones, Christopher, *The Great Palace* (London, 1983)

Kelsey, Sean, 'Housing Parliament: Dublin, Edinburgh and Westminster', *Parliamentary History* 21(1) (2002)

Levine, Joshua, *Forgotten Voices of the Blitz and the Battle for Britain: A New History in the Words of the Men and Women on Both Sides* (London, 2007)

Lott, G. K., and Richardson, C., 'Yorkshire Stone for Building the Houses of Parliament (1839–c.1852)', *Proceedings of the Yorkshire Geological Society*, 51(4) (1997), pp. 265–71

Lott, G. K., *Strategic Stone Study. A Building Stone Atlas of West & South Yorkshire* (English Heritage, March 2012)

Macaulay, James, 'The Architectural Collaboration between J. Gillespie Graham and A. W. Pugin', *Architectural History*, 27 (1984), pp. 406–20.

MacKay, Chris, *Big Ben: The Great Clock and the Bells at the Palace of Westminster* (Oxford, 2010)

Mortimer, Gavin, *The Longest Night: Voices from the London Blitz*, new edn (London, 2006)

Olney, R. J., and Melvin, Julia, eds, *Prime Minister's Papers Series. Wellington. II: Political Correspondence November 1834–April 1835* (London, 1986)

Oxford Dictionary of National Biography (Oxford, 2004)

The Palace of Westminster. Houses of Parliament Official Guide (London, 2012)

Pearce, Edward and Pearce, Deanna, eds, *The Diaries of Charles Greville* (London, 2006)

Port, M. H., ed., *The Houses of Parliament* (New Haven and London, 1976)

Pugin, E. W., *Who was the Art Architect of the Houses of Parliament?* (London, 1867)

Pugin, E. W., *Notes on the Reply of the Rev. Alfred Barry to the 'Infatuated Statements' made by E. W. Pugin on the Houses of Parliament* (London, 1868)

Quinault, Roland, 'Westminster and the Victorian Constitution', *Transactions of the Royal Historical Society*, 6th series, 2 (1992), pp. 79–104

Reid, David Boswell, *Narrative of Facts as to the New Houses of Parliament* (London, 1849)

Robertson, David, *Sir Charles Eastlake and the Victorian Art World* (Princeton, 1978)

Robins, Jane, *Rebel Queen. How the Trial of Queen Caroline Brought England to the Brink of Revolution* (London, 2007)

Rorabaugh, W. J., 'Politics and the Architectural Competition for the Houses of Parliament', *Victorian Studies*, xviii (1973), pp. 155–75

Roscoe, Ingrid, Hardy, Emma, and Sullivan, M. G., *A Biographical Dictionary of Sculptors in Britain 1660–1851* (New Haven and London, 2009)

Salmon, Frank, 'Storming the Campo Vaccino: British Architects and the Antique Buildings of Rome after Waterloo', *Architectural History*, 38 (1995), pp. 146–75

Salmon, Frank, 'British Architects, Italian Fine Arts Academies and the Foundation of the RIBA, 1816–1843', *Architectural History*, 39 (1996), pp. 77–113

Shenton, Caroline, *The Day Parliament Burned Down* (Oxford, 2012)

Shuisky, V., 'The Architectural Graphics of Charles Barry and Thomas Allom in the USSR Academy of Arts', *Arkhitectura SSSR* (May, 1987), pp. 102–5

Skempton, A. W., ed., *A Biographical Dictionary of Civil Engineers in Great Britain and Ireland*, 3 vols (London, 2002–14)

Strong, Roy, *Coronation. From the 8th to the 21st Century* (London, 2005)

Tanfield, J. *In Parliament 1939–50. The Effect of the War on the Palace of Westminster* (London, 1991)

'The Portcullis' (House of Commons Information Office Factsheet G9 General Series, Revised Aug. 2010).

Wedgwood, Alexandra, 'The Throne in the House of Lords and its Setting', *Architectural History*, 27 (1984), pp. 59–73

Wedgwood, Alexandra, *AWN Pugin and the Pugin Family* (London, 1985)

Weintraub, Stanley, *Albert. Uncrowned King* (London, 1997)

White, Jerry, *London in the 19th Century* (London, 2008)

LIST OF ILLUSTRATIONS

List of Illustrations

List of Illustrations

LIST OF COLOUR PLATES

1. Charles Barry in the 1830s. © RIBA Collections
2. The old Westminster Barry knew, as rendered by Pugin's father in the 1820s. © Parliamentary Art Collection, WOA 6373
3. J. M. Gandy's classical fantasy of the House of Lords in St James's Park with the old Palace burning in the top left corner. © RIBA Collections
4. Charles Barry in 1851. © National Portrait Gallery, London
5. A. W. N. Pugin in 1845. © Parliamentary Art Collection, WOA 2586
6. Charles Barry at the end of his life. © John Watkins/Stringer/Getty Images
7. The Fine Arts Commissioners. Barry is standing in the foreground, demonstrating a model of the Palace to Prince Albert, seated centre. © National Portrait Gallery, London
8. The House of Lords chamber in 1857. © Parliamentary Art Collection, WOA 2941
9. The House of Commons chamber in 1858 with its lowered ceiling. © Parliamentary Art Collection, WOA 2934
10. View of the Palace from Millbank, with the stone wharfs in the foreground during the mid-1850s. © Victoria & Albert Museum/ Bridgeman Images
11. Old Palace Yard under construction, showing the rails and steam engines used to haul the stone around the site. © Parliamentary Art Collection, WOA 1638
12. View of the Palace with the incomplete clock face, 1858. © Parliamentary Art Collection, WOA 1656
13. State portrait of Queen Victoria by Winterhalter with the towers of her new Palace in the background. © Parliamentary Art Collection, WOA 3145

INDEX

Index